Ms. Jeanne Brown
855 Brookline Dr., Apt. E
Sunnyvale, CA 94087-1218

THE
MAKING
OF
PLACE

THE MAKING OF PLACE

MODERN AND CONTEMPORARY GARDENS

JOHN DIXON HUNT

REAKTION BOOKS

For Joanne Pillsbury and Edward Harwood

Published by
REAKTION BOOKS LTD
UNIT 32, WATERSIDE
44–48 WHARF ROAD
LONDON N1 7UX, UK

www.reaktionbooks.co.uk

First published 2015
Copyright © John Dixon Hunt 2015

Design by Simon McFadden

Printed and bound in China
by C&C Offset Printing Co. Ltd

A catalogue record for this book is available from
the British Library

ISBN 978 1 78023 520 2

CONTENTS

PREFACE

This is a book about the various types of modern and contemporary gardens and parks to be found in the world today. What once were fairly clear typologies, carefully programmed to fit the needs of the persons for whom they were created, have mushroomed into a variety of place-making that takes up not only our residual ideas of a park and a garden, but the many variations that each of those types have spawned and the new activities that are now accommodated within them. However, this book is not a survey, or even anthology, of gardens and parks; instead, it asks how a careful discussion of some key examples can illuminate each of the thirteen types chosen here, so that we can understand the exciting and stimulating repertoire of modern and contemporary work.

The book ranges widely in search of exemplary sites – in the process, I am sure, neglecting the work of many excellent and worthwhile designers whose work should be acknowledged; their absence is not intended as a slight, but simply that the examples I have chosen (from work I do know personally as much as possible) can usefully celebrate the extraordinary wealth of place-making. Indeed, it is my hope that readers will find other examples that further illustrate or amplify my own understanding of today's flourishing landscape architecture.

I have to live with my own choice of sites and designers who work in different types of place. But it is always good to step sideways and look outside my comfort zone, and I have been directed by the superb and thoughtful reviews of work featured and discussed in both Udo Weilacher's *In Gardens* (Basel, 2005) and Hervé Brunon and Monique Mosser, *Le Jardin contemporain* (Paris, 2011); their own focus upon the primacy of gardens within landscape practice coincides with my own. I am also struck by how much contemporary designers move across the different typologies – working for private and public clients, exploring the possibilities of festival exhibitions and memorial commemorations, seeing rival opportunities in responding to a scale of different parklands and gardens; there was, too, an increasing need to redeem clapped-out, derelict and toxic land. Long-standing and conventional places called out for fresh approaches.

1 One of the courtyard gardens, designed by ARM Architects and Rush Wright Associates landscape architects from 2003, in the visitors' centre at the base of the Shrine of Remembrance (1918–1934), Melbourne, Australia.

INTRODUCTION
TYPOLOGIES AND OUR IMPROVISATIONS

'For diff'rent *Styles* with diff'rent *Subjects* sort,
As several Garbs with Country, Town, and Court'
ALEXANDER POPE

'One cannot be modern for the next generation any
more than one can remain young.'
LEWIS MUMFORD

There are three general issues to take up before exploring the various modern and contemporary types of gardens that constitute *place-making*, a useful term invoked by 'Capability' Brown in the eighteenth century long before the recent and rival coinages of landscape gardening, landscape architecture or landscape urbanism.[1] These issues are, first, the typology of gardens that we must consider today, much enlarged since the earliest days of garden-making. Then the relationship (a slippery one, not always susceptible to clear demarcations) between gardens and other kinds of landscape architecture that are bigger, like parks or memorials, yet not obviously or evidently 'gardens'; but this is where 'place-making' becomes a useful term again. Third, the exact distinctions (indeed, if any are feasible) between what is modern and what contemporary.

A typology of place-making

As Alexander Pope's lines imply, suitable outfits should be worn for different social situations. So perhaps we may also see different gardens as suitable for various sites and rites. Yet if sartorial wear has diversified in the last quarter-century (and become far less socially predictable), so have gardens and parks acquired an astonishing range and versatility. Many early writers on the arts saw their particular field as marked by distinct categories. Subjects for a painter were determined by the topic he chose to work on (mythological or historical), or the genre (portrait, landscape, still-life), and these survived well into the nineteenth century; even with landscape subjects, Roger de Piles in 1708 listed different ways or 'styles' in which painters would treat their material. A writer like Alexander Pope relied on literary genres, like pastoral, georgic, epistle, satire or (mock-) epic, within each of which his subject-matter and his handling of the literary type (including his sense of its literary ancestry) confirmed, if sometimes extended, the inherited mode of writing. Likewise, garden-makers often submitted their designs to expected norms or uses; thus for Jean-Marie Morel in the late eighteenth century, landscape architects should distinguish between different types – *pays champêtre* (gardens of grand scope), *parcs*, farms or *jardins proprement dit* (actual gardens).[2]

Another category that emerged during the eighteenth century pertained to 'character', as explained by Anthony Ashley Cooper, 3rd Earl of Shaftesbury, who opined that 'the proportionate and regular state is the truly prosperous and natural in *every subject*' (my italics), and that the natural 'types' in nature must be classified and their differences observed in place-making. We will see then a close assimilation between a type and the character(s) which each displays, and this tradition can be traced back to Platonic and Aristotelian notions of form and idea. Some other typological classifications are much looser; thus Leberecht Migge in his 1913 *Die Gartenkultur des 20. Jahrhunderts* distinguishes simply between private and public gardens in chapter Two and then, in a short section in chapter Seven, argues that the vast numbers of new garden-makers and users do require 'types';[3] but this 'mass' or 'multitude of people' will be unable to 'produce more ideas and forms' than those previously acquired. So, for Migge, all subsequent gardens have derived from the earliest, the 'utilitarian garden', and it is thus useless to think that in 'our time' other types can evolve. Migge believed that a garden type could be repeated indefinitely 'without losing an identifiable appearance'. While seductive (we all know a garden or park when we see one), this is hardly useful today when landscape architecture, along with architecture and garden designers, has evolved

with a variety of cultural elements and usages that require a more sophisticated discrimination of types. Inevitably, modernity has seen the eroding and the complication of these generic norms – J.M.W. Turner, for example, merged historical and mythological subjects with his dedication to landscapes.

An amusing list of modern garden types was compiled by Hans Ulrich Obrist under the title of 'Un Jardin peut en cacher un autre' (illus. 2); its French title echoed those signs on Continental railway crossings that warned motorists not to try and get across once one train had passed, for others might well be hidden and be close behind it. Obrist's four-page list shows how many 'gardens' can be hidden behind the general idea of a 'garden', for swift on its tail comes an 'Actual Garden' and then an 'Ad hoc Garden', and what follows are a dazzling set of invented forms, some astonishingly apt ('Cartoon Garden', 'Airport Garden'), others somewhat strained ('Cordless Garden', 'Electric Garden'). Yet each type implies a garden with some focus or maybe meaning, or one that can be identified by its material form or by its usage. Yet their names, descriptions and profiles often overlap – for dirt gardens surely occupy space in college gardens, and both cordless and electric gardens are involved in suburban ones; its author would also be hard pressed to give examples of each type that clearly and unmistakably identified its scope or focus. Hence this hoarding of garden types, however amusing, will not serve this book's more austere and focused format; yet even in the chapters that follow, there will be examples where one type

2 Page one of Hans Ulrich Obrist's 'Un Jardin peut en cacher un autre', from *Landscape Journal* (2002).

Un Jardin peut en cacher un autre[1]

Compiled by
Hans Ulrich Obrist

A Garden
Actual Garden
Ad-hoc Garden
African Garden
Agglomeration Garden
Aggregative Garden
Agora Garden
Agricultural Garden
Air Garden
Airport Garden
Airship Garden
Amazon Garden
Ambiguous Garden
American Garden
Analogous Garden
Angel Garden
Apocalyptic Garden
Apotheotic Garden
Arty Garden
Artisanal Garden
Asian Garden
Astral Garden
Atopic Garden
Autonomous Garden

Banal Garden
Bastard Garden
Baton Garden
Big Garden
Bike Garden
Bio Garden
Bioclimatic Garden
Bit Garden
Bite Garden
Blitz Garden
Blood Garden
Blow Garden
Body Garden
Boom Garden
Brain Garden
Brand Garden
Broadacre Garden
Broken Garden
Bubble Garden
Bunker Garden

Camp Garden
Camping Garden
Campus Garden
Capital Garden
Capsule Garden
Captive Garden

Car Garden
Cartoon Garden
Cell Garden
Center Garden
Centerless Garden
Children Garden
Ciné Garden
City Garden
Clandestine Garden
Climax Garden
Cloud Garden
Club Garden
Cluster Garden
Cohab Garden
Collab Garden
Collapse Garden
Collage Garden
College Garden
Collective Garden
Collision Garden
Combinational Garden
Coming Garden
Commodity Garden
Communal Garden
Concrete Garden
Coming-to-be Garden
Commercial Garden
Compact Garden
Competition Garden
Complex Garden
Complex-Dynamic Garden
Complication Garden
Conglomerate Garden
Comprehensive Garden
Constellation Garden
Contemporary Garden
Context Garden
Continent Garden
Cool Garden
Cordless Garden
Core Garden
Corporate Garden
Correspondence Garden
Corridor Garden
Cosmic Garden
Cream Garden
Creative Garden
Crime Garden
Crisscross Garden
Crowd Garden
Crumpled Garden
Cross Garden

Crossing Garden
Cruise Garden
Crying Garden
Crystal Garden
Cult Garden

Dark Garden
Data Garden
Day Garden
Decentered Garden
Declining Garden
Definite Garden
Delirious Garden
Demo Garden
Demon Garden
Derelict Garden
Desert Garden
Diaspora Garden
Diffuse Garden
Dilate Garden
Dirt Garden
Disaster Garden
Disintegral Garden
Discovery Garden
Disposal Garden
Distorted Garden
Document Garden
Dog Garden
Dogma Garden
Doll Garden
Doubt Garden
Down Garden
Dream Garden
Drop Garden
Drug Garden
Drum Garden
Dust Garden
Dust Cloud Garden
Dwelling Garden
Dynamo Garden
Dystopian Garden

E-Garden
Earth Garden
Eco Garden
Eco-Media Garden
Ecstasy Garden
Ecumenical Garden
Edge Garden
Edo Garden
Electric Garden
Elementary Garden

Landscape Journal 21:2–02 ISSN 0277-2426
© 2002 by the Board of Regents of the University of Wisconsin System

Obrist   15

could, *mutatis mutandis*, be moved to, or overlap with, another: we have dirt gardens in botanical gardens, and of course contemporary makers of place do not confine themselves to working within only one type. This overlap or transference will be explored in specific chapters below as an ineluctable aspect of modern place-making.

'Type', however, has been a consistent term in discussing architecture, and so it will be used here, though it clearly merges or overlaps with rival terms like genre or character. Yet even that term, as defined by the Frenchman Quatremère de Quincy, seems opaque: it is 'the idea of an element, which ought to serve as a rule for the model';[4] thus an idea in landscape – be it 'park' or 'memorial' – will provide, will determine ('rule' the 'model' of) what a garden can be. Yet even early garden-makers had learned to play with different formal elements in different situations, and this could modify the type that they chose to work in. And in the modern and contemporary garden, playing with forms has given rise to a multiplicity of garden models (as Obrist suggests). It clearly requires a greater variety of 'styles' and activities to 'sort' the different types of gardens that we encounter and use today.

Indeed, if we review the types of gardens from antiquity to today, there has been, certainly, a sufficient repertory of gardens to satisfy the needs of most cultures.[5] In antiquity, gardens were almost always elitist (though the necessary evidence for more plebian and vernacular types has largely been lost): one type was 'a large park-like garden', another attached a garden to a specific building and was well planted, and the third was found within a structure, like an atrium or courtyard. Most were enclosed. Yet within this cluster of garden types, there was a declension of sites and forms that stretched from religious and palatial gardens to public, private and funerary gardens; so, too, the activities associated with them seem strangely familiar – swimming, dining, receptions, privacy, hunting of various sorts, prestige and display, even collections of trees in arboreta, sacred sites or sanctuaries. In the Western Middle Ages and the Renaissance, commentary also emphasized the variety and diversity of gardens, even more so if non-European sites are included. But the social range is still limited, again for lack of sufficient documentary and archaeological evidence for vernacular sites. That material begins to be more available in the eighteenth century, or at least we have more information about modest gardens and more popular uses, if not the sites themselves. But the real increase in types of gardens comes with the nineteenth century, when we find sites for health (sanatoria), peace and survival gardens, commercial gardens (nurseries), a large increase in scientific and experimental gardens, including zoological gardens, cottage gardens and allotments, the bourgeois or suburban domestic garden, and above all the public park. What occurs also in the modern period is a significant disjunction of links between gardens and buildings, which they had hitherto largely enjoyed.[6]

Thirteen garden types

The types of gardens and parks that follow here have been selected to respond to this modern diversity of forms and functions. Thirteen (a baker's dozen) have been chosen. There could be more, but even with this selection there are some interesting if also some necessary overlaps: a botanical garden and/or arboretum can be a public park and also display sculpture; an institutional campus may also serve as a sculpture garden or be visited by the general public as if it were a park. But the hope is that the book adequately ranges across a sufficient scope of recent landscape architecture and that there are no obvious lacunae. Not only are similar design elements invoked when the uses and activities expected of them are different (tennis courts may be found in both private gardens and public parks); nor is it obvious or predictable who makes what kind of gardens and parks and for what reasons, cultural and social. Professional landscapists are involved in a whole range of community and large-scale parks; though many do design for private gardens, the profession sees itself as properly and more publically committed to public work. But garden designers, consultants and landscapers (not professionally trained and licensed) also make gardens, and – as will be discussed below – the private world of gardens can inform or percolate into the public sphere.

The book starts, where all garden makers begin, with personal gardens (illus. 3). Yet chapter One on 'Domestic and Gardeners' Gardens' today responds to a huge and bewildering variety of

place-making, for with the spread of garden centres, garden magazines and TV programmes, everyone can have and make a garden.[7] This needs to be distinguished from the equally lively and more radical world of community gardens, allotments and 'guerilla gardening' (for which see chapter Four). Some gardeners' gardens may, these days, be by professionals, but their role is essentially to provide designed space for the client-inhabitant; others are self-designed by what Bernard Lassus called *habitants-paysagistes*.[8] However, given that so many professional landscape architects engage not only on private sites (despite their somewhat

3 David Jones, *The Suburban Order*, 1926, painting.

ambiguous attitude towards 'elitist' gardening) but on public and civic projects, the following chapter Two focuses on what are called 'Masters' Gardens'. This is a coinage borrowed from the 2011 Xi'an International Horticultural Exposition in China, when a series of firms were invited to design nine sites. The Masters' gardens were then juxtaposed to nine 'University' gardens, each designed by an academic teaching department. The Chinese distinction is not clear, for 'masters' often teach in universities, but the emphasis on 'mastership' points clearly to the work of some distinguished, professional landscape architects. And the term is suitably current, for a symposium at the Indianapolis Museum of Art in September 2013 presented eight talks on 'Masters of Modern Landscape Design', all (with one exception) white males and all dead.

This range of activity in gardens by gardeners draws into its field other different activities, like garden festivals, and also sits perhaps uneasily alongside vernacular or radical gardening. So a chapter on horticultural or festival gardens, usually on fixed sites and established for limited time, comes next – an interesting type of site, much in fashion in the last dozen years, that has elicited an exciting (as well as some absurd) proposals for place-making. These shows have attracted students of landscape as well as established professionals. Their influence on more communal and institutional work is uncertain, yet this inventive and avant-gardist work can play a role in work outside festivals. If festival gardens exist at the somewhat elitist and certainly temporary end of the garden spectrum, then vernacular, community and radical gardening, also a prominent modern type that has elicited new commentaries, comes in chapter Four. Though vernacular and usually productive gardens have always existed, there has been – as capitalism has grown – some need to find spaces that the homeless will take over as their own, or where those without opportunities for their own gardens have collaborated in making and sustaining community ones – these may be 'ordained' from above by municipalities or charities, or emerge spontaneously out of local energies.

From there the book moves into two chapters on parks: large ones, and small – pocket, linear and even vertical parks. Large parks, to be discussed more fully below, are to be distinguished, certainly, from gardens; but the world of garden-making has expanded into parklands that still invoke gardenist assumptions and elements. Small parks are more obviously garden-like, but into this type we need to absorb a wholly new attention to small-scale interventions into largely urban conditions, like linear parks and garden trails. Something of an extension of parkland (public and quasi-private) has informed institutional campuses: on the one hand, landscapes around big factories or headquarters, often drawing their inspiration from private estates and public parklands, are clearly designed to give a benign and pastoral context for the industrial and business activities there; but on the other, there are institutions, like museums, colleges and universities, which draw their models from both older types (like cloisters) and current garden design; sometimes these 'campuses' are scattered through urban spaces and are signalled by insertions of garden pockets and courtyards. These campuses make, then, another type.

A cluster of other different types where gardens are usually central to the given site involve memorials, of which there seems to be a sudden explosion in a sadly horrific world, but where gardens may lend some peace and thoughtfulness to the events commemorated. And while botanical gardens have been in existence for centuries, some exciting new ones have appeared in the last twenty years, while fresh perspectives on an established theme have been offered by seeing botanical gardens as serving new urban opportunities. Similarly, sculpture gardens, which equally enjoy a long history, have a new lease of life with the increase of monumental modern iron- and steel-works, items that have now to be situated outside museums, or in gardens designed specifically to accommodate them.

The final three items in this baker's dozen are all quite explicitly contemporary events and respond to new conditions. The recovery and reformulation of derelict infrastructures, toxic wastelands and abandoned waterfronts have attracted the attention of many landscape architects, who have devised a range of new garden spaces and features for them. So, too, have attempts been made to reinvent older forms, often outside the cultural zone where they originated: Chinese and Japanese gardens outside China and Japan, as 'English' gardens were imitated in India during the British Raj. This chapter on reinvention has also to consider the revival or 'conservation' of gardens and garden types: many

early gardens, grown messy or too expensive to maintain in the form in which they were originally designed, have elicited the attention (usually, but not always, of their owners) to make a new place in an old space. For many visitors, the refurbishment of these older gardens may seem to provide an 'authentic' experience, but in the process of preservation or conservation, they betray, sometimes quite deliberately, a modernist flavour and tonality; they are thus more contemporary than old, and we need to register this subtle modernization of garden spaces. And then, finally, in a modern age ever committed to the making of new places, there have been many visionary proposals that did not make it beyond the paper (or the computer screen) on which they are drawn. So a world of gardens on paper also needs to be celebrated, including some that are merely imaginary, and some that for various reasons have been unsuccessful, whether because entries did not win in a design competition, or even that winning entries failed to find the necessary finances, or succumbed to a change of government.

One last word on the topic of types: there will not be, cannot be, any attempt to chart a conspectus of each different garden type. A checklist or gazetteer, let alone lists, is not my concern. I may doubtless offend designers or owners who think *their* work is crucial to the discussion; maybe it could be, and could still be invoked by readers wishing to make their own surveys. Rather, I want to ask of each type what contributions have been made to it in the modern world, what traditions have nevertheless been observed and perhaps reformulated, and what can now constitute the possibilities and excitements of that specific type.

Gardens into parks

So far I have generally used the term 'garden', as opposed to cluttering the text with a list of alternatives. But many would argue that, say, New York's Central Park or the recent Portello Park in Milan are not gardens. Many so-called 'landscape gardens' in the eighteenth century were not, nor did they look like, gardens *proprement dits*. The garden is, though, a useful and ubiquitous term, more flexible than 'park'. But more importantly, while the garden since the Middle Ages at least has sometimes 'grown' into the park, the park has not dwindled into the garden, though they often would incorporate gardens within their larger landscape. Even professional landscape architects, who today seek prominence in the public world of design, find that gardens were the prime stimulus or model, and they celebrate the garden as the source of their work: Peter Latz has argued that 'amateur movements [in garden-making] play an important role in garden culture', while Bernard Lassus, at a conference in Sicily in 1981, championed the role of the garden in landscape work by asking why 'the garden, the hypothesis on what, from yesterday and today, will be perpetuated in the sensory approach of tomorrow and in its new ways touch and move people – why is not such a garden before all else philosophical?'

As will be seen in most of the chapters that follow, there is a philosophical basis in gardens from which all other types seem to evolve. To that extent, Migge's argument for the utilitarian garden as the basis of other types is useful. This is not to say that flowers and horticultural expertise will necessarily characterize a large park or a memorial garden, but that some of a garden's essential characteristics will be found there. Perhaps the most important characteristic is that both gardens and parks are in some way or other enclosed, or that they imply a distinct and strong sense of threshold: namely, they occupy a different territory than those from which their visitors have come. This liminal moment can be marked by gates, openings, different material conditions (including plants or sculpture) and a repertory of designed items that are not found outside either gardens or parks – paths, seats, items placed to entertain or amuse, opportunities for solitary or communal activity.

You know a garden or garden-like space when you see one or enter into it: these stepping stones (illus. 4) alongside a stream and waterfall, the trelliswork beside the path, and even the dappled shade that careful planting ensures, suggest a strong gardenist ambience, even if they are in fact only a part of a larger park. They were created by William Beckford for his estate at Sintra, outside Lisbon in Portugal, and this park was subsequently expanded by Sir Richard Cook. It is actually many things – a park that contains individual gardens and waterfalls (like this one), but also fountains, collections of different plants

4 A 'garden' moment in William Beckford's estate at Sintra, Portugal.

(ferns, scented flowers, roses), an arboretum and an exotic mansion.

In theoretical terms, a 'garden' is a category that we all recognize, even if examples point to places as different as a classical Italian garden like the Villa Lante or to the 'jardin en mouvement' that Gilles Clément established in the Parc André Citroën in 1992 ('an irregular mass of herbaceous plants and perennials, similar to what we might see in fields'[9]). Categories are important since they structure our responses to the sensible world. But they are also hierarchical, and thus enjoy what has been called a 'typicality gradient', by which we notice that Hyde Park enjoys a different place on that particular 'gradient' of types than, say, Kew Gardens, Stourhead or Central Park. We see the family resemblance, but are equally alert to their different 'personalities' or characters. And we also recognize that 'the most typical exemplars of a category (the prototypes) are *also* [writes Bernard St-Denis] those that are the least typical of or that have the least resemblance to the competing categories.' It is, in the end, a matter of negotiation between the different elements that we identify in various types of gardens and what they exemplify; that will be a crucial element in the discussions of succeeding chapters. So, too, are the categories of the modern and the contemporary, which are constantly 'renewed' by our experience of the world and how long we have been in it.

Modern and contemporary and the project of modernity

A distinction between modern and modernism is also tricky. Ezra Pound, a good modernist, wrote that 'all ages are contemporaneous'. Stanley Hart White, writing on the issue of 'What is Modern?' in the early 1930s, after citing Picasso on that issue, claims that 'There is no need of making an excuse for modern art. It is thousands of years old.'[10] While provocative – indeed there has always been 'modern' art, the remark does not easily help to focus on the differences between what is modern and what contemporary in a garden today. Contemporary means contemporary with someone or some event: so it is elastic and depends on what event or whose age is in question – the range of 'contemporary' for a person in their seventies is likely to be assessed differently than for those in their thirties or teens, though a seventy-year-old may espouse recent ideas. The English gardener Penelope Hobhouse acknowledges that the 'reasons for gardening change as you grow older'.[11]

The argument that modernity began in the late eighteenth century has been advanced by Yve-Alain Bois.[12] Marshall Berman also thought that 'to be fully modern is to be anti-modern' and traced his 'modernity' back to Goethe's *Faust*, Baudelaire or St Petersburg under Nicholas I, and to Haussmann's Paris, Robert Moses and New York.[13] For both writers, especially Berman, it is the *experience* of modernity that is crucial. 'Modernism' may be thought of 'as a struggle [writes Berman] to make ourselves at home in a constantly changing world, and we realize that no mode of modernism can ever be definitive'. So like the contemporary, modernity is also elastic, and we invoke modernism when we perceive that 'struggle', or otherwise when we look to something that seems particularly modern and we need to account for it.

But gardens do not always behave similarly to other arts, and for obvious reasons, some of which Bois addresses. Plants, to start with, have no particularly modern forms, though they may be new hybrids, or their natural forms may suddenly be perceived as 'architectural'.[14] And gardens have the ambiguous distinction of being seen as atavistic, harking back to ideas of the garden both mythical and historical. Clearly buildings also refer or glance backward to earlier types that Nikolaus Pevsner explored in *A History of Building Types* (1976); Marc-Antoine Laugier's *An Essay on Architecture* (1753) appealed to the primitive hut as the model for all modern architecture. But the modern garden enjoys an unusual dialogue between its past and its current manifestations: gardens are maintained in the present by new supplies and resources of plants and by the means through which they are maintained, for garden tools have remained astonishingly unchanged for hundreds of years. This perhaps explains the knack, as some would claim, of making modernity look ageless. Modernism is not hostile to change, and it welcomes self-criticism and self-renewal; yet when a poet like Ezra Pound cries out for 'it' to be 'new', he is himself only too aware that the 'it' has been there before.

Each of the following chapters will be focused on a cluster of typical examples: some will be iconic modern examples, in which we might trace new manifestations of the type, while for others it will be an exemplary contemporary garden that will focus on how we understand its own 'style' as well as its reliance and modification of earlier materials and uses. The modern examples are selected largely as significant precursors of contemporary work, for 'gardens have almost always foretold in advance the relationships between . . . society and nature.'[15] What is modern may not only draw on, rework and revalue the past, but offer templates for subsequent work that we find 'contemporary'. In short, while we can recognize distinctions between the modern and the contemporary, they are not always clear-cut either in usage or substance.

It sometimes seems that Western culture over-privileges the sequences of historical time, with the 'next' always outdoing the 'last', or being presumed to do so; yet when one or another contemporary art projects a new idea or form, it must often be said that 'nothing dates like the future'. In contrast, Chinese garden-making, with a long 3,000-year history, never got itself locked into set forms and static elements and always accepted the metamorphosis and adaption of its garden tradition; except of course when it collided with a specific, communist ideology that necessitated a celebration of the contemporary, dissociated from any past; but even that is now changing in the twenty-first century.

When Pope invoked the word 'style', he connected it to how a particular mode of dress would be used in different social situations. Yet 'style' has become something of a bugbear in architectural criticism; it seems an awkward term, too often used when talking of a particular period or designer in ways that detract from its cultural content. To say something has a 'modernist or modern style' without explaining what elements of modernity sustain it is ludicrous. Gardenists in the twentieth century often invoke or insist on 'the common touch of the contemporary spirit' (Peter Shepheard) or invoke the 'contemporary scene', or decry 'formal' styles borrowed from the past by appealing to 'naturalistic gardening' (as if that were not just another 'style'). But landscape (as well as buildings) cannot be labelled with this or that style, since the label gets in the way of seeing why it is actually attached to some specific design and how contemporary society has sustained it. David Leatherbarrow wants to resist the term 'style', for a landscape (as a building) needs to address issues of 'site, enclosure, and materials' as a complex and intertwined whole;[16] that may then usefully help to identify a given style with a more elaborate description and explanation. And that means observing how the 'permanence of any "architectural" [landscape] topic results from its essential *correspondence* with a recurring and fundamental human condition'. These local conditions may change, but they will recur, and their recurrence necessitates that we re-examine contemporary examples by envisaging how the site is enclosed, how it responds to current demands and expectations, and how they utilize available materials. All that necessarily involves an adequate

and exciting 'correspondence' between new experience and long-standing practice.

Modernism has become a rather tedious issue over the last 50 years, more focused on problematizing the notion than elucidating its presence in different arts, and it is not a theme with which I need to tangle. But it does, inevitably, concern landscape design, not least because in that field modernism has proved far more difficult to identify and because modern architects and landscape architects really *want* to be modern, but tend to confuse the media (buildings are not landscapes) and, for the latter, focus their agenda narrowly on form rather than on its effects or reception. One example may serve: Marc Treib has been an energetic promoter of the modern (and indeed the postmodern), notably in his 'Axioms for a Modern Landscape Architecture'.[17] These axioms concern a denial of historical styles, a concern for space not 'pattern', a focus on 'people', the destruction of the axis, plants used for themselves as individual items and for their sculptural effect, and the integration of house and garden. Yet not all of these surely apply only to modern(ist) garden work: people have always been central, and gardens and houses have a tradition of being closely connected until the advent of the truly modern park. And while some critics like to disparage historical styles, their actual use in modern work is not so simple or so easily rejected.

Many of those axioms are familiar from Christopher Tunnard's *Gardens in the Modern Landscape,* where he announced what he had learned from an exploration of European modernism in the 1930s.[18] Tunnard certainly celebrated people in his images; his designs, as drawn by Gordon Cullen (one featured on his original book jacket: illus. 5), all show people in them; he was drawn to how people lived and what spaces and forms would satisfy their contemporary needs,[19] and he was much concerned with community design; he worked to make a conjunction of house and garden amenable to social living, which his photographs and designs clearly reveal, but he also sought to relate the garden's spaces to the larger cultural landscape. He inherited and used the notion of architectural plants, yet J. C. Loudon's Gardenesque planting had also privileged the plant as a form in itself, though Tunnard himself was scornful of much nineteenth-century design. Tunnard's schemes also suggest that he could devise his own ideas of 'pattern' within a garden's spaces, although he was clearly aware that space has its own imperative. But in other respects he was both eager to promote 'historical styles' from eighteenth-century English landscaping and from Japan – and, though he did rely on the invocation of 'style' in his writing, he nevertheless quoted Le Corbusier that 'the styles are a lie'. He reassured the readers of the 1948 edition that 'a new garden technique . . . need not necessarily reject the traditional elements of the garden plan' (p. 67). He was more adventurous and enquiring about the material forms of garden items and explored their historical precedents in a search for modern equivalents. He certainly praised 'asymmetrical planting'.

For Tunnard, modernism in landscape architecture began with the burst of garden-making in

5 Dust-jacket of Tunnard's first edition of *Gardens in the Modern Landscape* (1938).

the 1930s, especially (though not exclusively) in France and Belgium. It was a period of great innovation and artistic zeal, which inevitably lost its energy during the Second World War and thereafter never recovered the vision and imagination that fuelled designers like the brothers Paul and André Vera, J.C.N. Forestier (eager to show their modernist design through the medium of their graphic representations), Pierre-Emile Legrain, Gabriel Guevrekian and Robert Mallet-Stevens.[20] Many of these modernists worked for garden owners who relished the opportunity to match their tastes in modern architecture, interior decoration, sculpture or painting with the gardens beyond their windows. Tunnard learned much when he visited Paris for a congress arranged by the Société Française des Architectes de Jardins, which occurred at the same time as the Exposition Internationale des Arts et Techniques dans la Vie Moderne, an exhibition that was visited by the American landscape architect Fletcher Steele. Yet in the aftermath of the Second World War modernism fragmented, and the collective enthusiasm of the 1930s was channelled differently by nations who determined their own modes of response to the early imperatives. And the issue of the contemporary as much as modernism is also subject to place and geography as much as to time and chronology.

Thus there are many modernisms, more varied and more interesting when they are considered within their relevant cultural context: Ernst Cramer in Switzerland, or later Pietro Porcinai in Italy, Carl Theodor Sørensen in Denmark, a 'triumvirate' of Brenda Colvin, Sylvia Crowe and Geoffrey Jellicoe in England, or in the USA the trio of Garrett Eckbo, Dan Kiley and James Rose, along with Thomas Church and Lawrence Halprin.[21] Climate, as much as local custom, determined what Peter Shepheard called the 'contemporary scene' – swimming pools in California and Italy, but not (at least for Colvin) in England. Garden traditions in England were stronger than elsewhere, and the work of Gertrude Jekyll or William Robinson continued to hold its spell into modernism (though Tunnard's colleague Frank Clark, who collaborated with him on several planting designs, found

Gertrude Jekyll's reliance on Impressionist planting dated). France still clung to some of the old seventeenth-century ways – axes, symmetry, formalism. The modern work of Porcinai found its own route from Renaissance garden-making by intervening 'in the spatial and material relationships' of hedges, emphasizing terraces, pergolas, circular seats and exedra platforms. The United States was more eclectic, looking both to Europe (Italy as much as France) and to Japan, as Tunnard had noticed. In short, modernism could be less austere than its theorists allowed, more exciting and less programmatic in specific designs. Tunnard realized that modernity was complex, and he struggled with what it could mean for gardens in a modern landscape.

In the chapters that follow nothing will attempt to take the reader back to that 'watershed' of modernity that Yve-Alain Bois places around 1800 or to the examples – St Petersburg, Goethe or the Paris of Baudelaire and Haussmann – that Marshall Berman explores; though it is tempting to ask what exactly is *not* modern about Central Park, given the history of many more recent modern parklands. While these thirteen essays will not go that far back, it is good to recall that the many gardens and parks created and visited today have long histories. The first clearly public parklands (not simply aristocratic ones opened occasionally for general visitation) were created in Munich in 1789 and for the People's Park in Birkenhead in the 1840s; botanical gardens and sculpture gardens go back at least to sixteenth-century Italy, but were exponentially enlarged as

plants were gathered around the world in the eighteenth and nineteenth centuries for display back
home, and large-scale sculptures needed new sites.
Many other places, such as beer gardens and
amusement parks like Vauxhall Gardens, continue to develop and those types are still with us.[22]
But that has not prevented the creation of new
modern ones, most of which clearly show their
modernity, not least for being aware of the precedents and eager to make something new of them.[23]
Perhaps we can rely once more on Stanley Hart
White and argue that all art is modern 'at the time
of its execution, otherwise it is merely imitation'.
But even imitations tend to bear the stamp of
their moment of origin.

The following discussions have a certain objec-
tive that is not easily achieved. They need to
describe the different types and their versatility
within that type; but descriptions by themselves
are not sufficient. Certainly, each type must be
presented in the manner that Wallace Stevens
called 'simple seeing, without reflection'; images
may help here. But there is the need to *reflect* as
well: to understand the significance, the meaning and above all the usefulness of types not only
in a contemporary world of gardens and landscape architecture but in different cultures. A type
has, as it were, a firm centre, an acknowledgement of what the type can do at its best and most
unequivocal. But no type is complete without an
equal acknowledgement of the eccentricities that
flourish within and on its margins, and these
extremes can suggest the larger potential of any
given type.

6 A front garden in San Diego, California, welcoming visitors to 'Eden'.

ONE

DOMESTIC AND GARDENERS' GARDENS

'The twentieth century was the golden age of gardens and horticulture for the greatest numbers of people ever'

DENNIS MCGLADE AND LAURIE OLIN[1]

This type of garden is, like the novel, huge, baggy and variegated.[2] It is a commonplace that Eden (illus. 6) was the first garden, and that God was its first garden-maker and owner. The site possessed a multitude of plants and animals, no garden maintenance seemed necessary, a fountain watered it effortlessly and fed adjacent rivers; it was apparently wholly sustainable, unenclosed, yet the original inhabitants found the place unexceptional, because it was the only place they knew. And it wasn't at all personal to them. Whether you consider that Eden is mythological, metaphorical or historical, it was only when Adam and Eve were banished from it that the *idea* of a garden was born. Thrust from Eden into a world where people needed to tend the land to survive, the original garden was to become the model of a lost perfection. Over doubtless many centuries, the idea of a garden emerged by comparing that long-lost paradise with other territories

– agricultural land, mountains and forests, or wildernesses which nobody wanted to inhabit or enter voluntarily. The garden, then, was to be distinguished from other places.

The idea of the garden and its practice established themselves as sites where agricultural skills and horticultural expertise became the foundation for more and more elaborate creations, worlds of aesthetic pleasure, satisfaction and prestige, and a range of social activity which Eden's first inhabitants could not envisage, like raising children. Gardens became places of assembly, of entertainment, of theatre, but also (necessary now in a crowded and busy world) of retreat and contemplation. All of these various reasons and excuses for a garden sustain today's world of place-making, and the gardeners who create and tend them can draw on an astonishing agenda of devices and desires. The unimaginable profusion of plants in that first garden became, for many, the prime motive for gardening: cultivating wild flowers, collecting them in botanical gardens from faraway places, or more recently searching them from garden centres and nurseries, to the extent that Dennis McGlade and Laurie Olin can rightly

25

say that the horticultural plenitude of gardens and their plants was to become a distinctive feature of modern gardens for more than just the elite and the powerful.

There are two kinds of gardeners' gardens: those that are created by their owners, and those for which owners seek expert help. The former rely on a multitude of ideas and elicit an astonishing variety of possibilities, which veer from exciting and eccentric to ordinary and from pretentious to low-key, but always (one must assume) to the satisfaction of the owner or for others to see and (presumably) admire. There is something about owner-created or owner-inspired gardens: 'I think most people feel that what anyone does on their own land is up to them so long as it affects no one else.'[3] But affecting others is surely part of the game, and many look enviously upon their neighbours' gardens. It is not for nothing that the UK has the 'Yellow Book', in which hundreds of gardens are listed and opened to the public for a few days each year and where owners cherish and cultivate their gardens to the perfection that opening day requires (this is a bourgeois version of those Elizabethan nobility and gentry who would hold back their flowers and fruits for the days on which the Queen was due to be fêted). The American Garden Conservancy also sponsors similar private openings, and an announcement for one in Philadelphia during May 2013 boasted the longevity of gardening owners, the often small scale of their gardens, skill with 'color preferences', woody plants, specimen trees, a thousand daffodils, flowers to encourage birds and butterflies,

and children's playhouses. In order to keep up with the folk on the other side of the garden wall or fence there is useful information on the internet from such organizations as the London College of Garden Design, the Garden Industry Manufacturer's Association and the Horticultural Trades Association or the Federation of Garden & Leisure Manufacturers (equivalents outside the UK provide the same services). People in Britain spend huge sums during their lifetimes on everything from tools and electric machinery to sheds, greenhouses and garden furniture.

There is also a mass of advice in gardening journals, posh newspaper articles and glossy books with titles like *The Perfect Country Garden*, *Garden Magic* or *Dream Gardens of England* that flatter us with the latest design or PR jargon and dazzle us with glossy images. These photographs rarely show any occupants (I suppose people would mess up the perfection of the garden setting); they are always static (though the photographer cannot help *that*) and reveal little of how the site has been responded to, where it is, or how it is used (full-time residence, holiday home, weekend retreat). Gardens created by professionals for their owners may often lack individuality. While it is extremely hard to gainsay any particular place-making, there is little capacity in the available literature and imagery to adjudicate taste.

Anne Cauquelin's *Petit Traité de jardin ordinaire* (2003) provides a grammar and lexicon for 'ordinary' gardens and lists the necessary activities to sustain them and the 'accessories' that enhance them. Nothing here is very surprising:

enclosure, light and shade, *allées,* paths, climate or time, narratives, the relation of inside to outside; nor is the listing of the 'accessories': flowers, social parasols and sunshades, even animals. All garden-makers, she argues, must have 'determined, thought and conceived' their place; everything is *placed* (though some might think *mis*placed). And every nation, and indeed different parts of a country, have their own mode of establishing a garden – the English hail 'The Front Garden' in an 'acclaimed BBC TV programme', while Americans emphasize the yard.[4] Yet it is this armada of amateur gardeners, says Peter Latz, that plays 'an important role in garden culture . . . they like to experiment and relate to new themes (self-supply, health)'.[5]

Gardens must have been originally what individuals contrived for their own needs and perhaps refreshment; that these were almost certainly focused on producing things to eat does not necessarily mean they did not give pleasure to their creators (vegetable gardens these days, in Greece, for example, and probably elsewhere, position flowers at the end of each row of produce). The urge to extend such gardens into something we could call 'pleasure' or 'aesthetic' gardens is visible first in images of medieval gardens, like the miller's walled garden and orchard in René d'Anjou's *Mortification de vaine plaisance* from around 1470.[6] Then in the Renaissance this was codified in sixteenth-century humanist writing that celebrated how 'the industry of peasants has been such that nature incorporated with art is made an artificer, and the connatural of art; and from both of them

is made a third nature, which I would not know how to name.'[7] Despite that writer's hesitation, he is clearly writing about what we would call gardens. Such gardens that are more than agriculture still survive, give or take the influence of climate, soil, economic contexts and the social status of the individual gardener. They all negotiate that strange 'incorporation' of nature and art or culture, and may still produce sites about which we, or even the maker, are uncertain as to what they are best called or how described.

Modern gardens have sought to be very modern. Some of the early efforts, as discussed in the Introduction, tried hard to be different and new. And 'newness' has been always a consuming passion for some gardeners and continues to be so. While the forms and structural elements of gardens – beds, pergolas, pools, terracing, borders, decoration – seem to be invariable, much thought has gone into how these can be manipulated, and both planting and garden decoration have tried hard to make something new. In 2013 Tim Richardson produced a book on the 'new' English garden, and we have books that 'reinvent' the garden, like *New Classic Gardens* from the Royal Horticultural Society (a nice title, appealing to both the brand new and the reliability of tradition).

One event suggests this need to rethink both garden-making and its challenges. The Parabola garden at Hadspen in Somerset was at least 200 years old, and Penelope Hobhouse transformed it into an ornamental garden, specializing in hostas; it was taken over by Nori and Sandra Pope in 1989,

7 A proposal for the oval garden at Hadspen, Somerset, by Foreign Office Architects, 2006.

who completely replanted it, enlarging the hosta collection. When they retired in 2005, Niall Hobhouse launched a competition to reformulate it, asking for 'a decisive reconfiguration of the ground itself . . . [a] brief to provide a platform that can in the future support any type, style, scale or density of planting (or 'gardening')'; the new gardener was to be imagined 'as the theatre director'. The winning design by Foreign Office Architects (illus. 7) met with a barrage of criticism and only modest applause. Meanwhile, the site had been cleared, and in the aftermath of the inconclusive debate it was decided to offer

individual plots to different gardeners who could put forward interesting proposals. These were chronicled in *The Plot*, the Parabola Garden News Sheet, where we could see in the modest dimension of these areas how 'newness' emerges. The whole 'affair', which it was indeed, suggested how conservative gardenists can be. Meanwhile Penelope Hobhouse herself had moved on to make the places she is justly famed for and on which she has widely published.[8]

What follows are some perspectives on the new, which involve both materials and, more conspicuously, strongly individual visions of the world *outside* the garden itself. Those who seek expertise either from professional (that is, licensed) landscape architects or from garden designers and jobbing landscapers will probably espouse traditional forms and materials, but satisfaction derives from the mutual agreement between client and designer, and the extent to which they contrive a place that is at once coherent and imaginative and makes something new and even unexpected on the site. There is also the rarer example of professional designers, expert in horticulture and invention, making gardens for themselves: Roberto Burle Marx's Santo Antonio da Bica (his home, his office, his laboratory – see chapter Two), or Lawrence Halprin, whose design of a dance deck for his wife had a profound effect on the choreography of other people's private gardens as well as how he conceived of public spaces and people's use of them.[9] With or without that extra help that a professional can bring, a huge majority of people in the world establish and cultivate their own gardens, heeding the injunction of Voltaire's Candide.

For a professionally designed garden, we may look to the work of Mary Barensfeld, a recently licensed landscape architect, who created a small garden on a steep hillside in Berkeley, California (illus. 8, 9). It provides two terraces of wooden boards, one by the house alongside a granite patio and a sliver of water, and another, smaller one at the top with views over San Francisco Bay. The success of the garden is both that it gladly accepts its hillside, and that its modest dimensions (1,150 sq. ft) are enlivened not simply by a collection of plants – Japanese maples, creeping jenny over the concrete walls, lemon ground thyme as ground cover – but by the deliberate play of geometry up the hillside. The board-formed concrete walls, which also do service as a staircase, pick up the texture of the wooden decks, and the sharp, irregular angles of the terracing seem to increase the garden's scope; screens of perforated Corten steel cast shadows from the adjacent bamboo grove and effectively shield this garden from its neighbours. There is (unsurprisingly in California) a strong Japanese feel to the garden that Barensfeld acknowledges; but the geometry is also reminiscent of Gabriel Guévrékian's cubist Jardin d'Hyères in Provence, and the perforated steel slices in Bernard Lassus' COLAS HQ in Paris.[10] But the small garden is attentive to (and indeed celebrates) its site, relishes its very select materials, while at the same time honouring its clients and how they and their children will use it.

A few clients know exactly want they need, expecting the expert to make sense of their requirements and provide technical recommendations that align with their wishes; yet the designer has to listen carefully and then push their wishes to 'the next level' and give the clients something more than they expected. There are gardeners who don't know what they want and look to the professional for suggestions, with which, if judged well as to the clients' funding, the site itself and its later use and maintenance, they'll go along. Sometimes the professional will be able to propose a design that is striking and the client accepts; but many people need to see and use the 'real thing' before they understand what they've got themselves into. In an ideal world the finished garden should be a surprise to both client and designer. This undercuts, though, the whole idea of making a garden, which (some gardeners would say) is more interesting than the result, more process than product.[11]

There is little scope for generalizing further about gardeners' gardens. Each may have a strong personality, none seems comparable with others, each speaks to the visitor (when they are admitted) in terms that can be enlightening, mystifying and challenging and that need – and what garden does not ask for this? – time and patience to absorb. Some of the examples that follow have been hailed in Tim Richardson's latest book, *The New English Garden*; yet their innovation (as Richardson admits) is hard to pin down, and his opening remarks could refer to all gardens, new and old. What he tends to evade is that all gardens are endemically atavistic and the past looms or infiltrates the 'new'

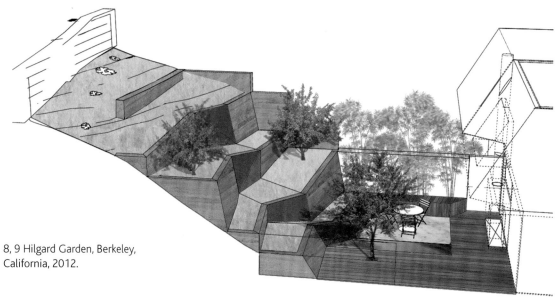

8, 9 Hilgard Garden, Berkeley,
California, 2012.

differently in each case; what Alasdair Forbes, the maker of Plaz Metaxu, calls, after Braque, its 'compenetration'.

'Newness' is indeed an elusive concept: Brenda Colvin in *Modern Gardens* (1953) appealed to 'the common touch of the contemporary spirit'. Richardson takes our own 'contemporary scene' to be mainly what he terms 'the end of a floriferous road which has been developing since the late Victorian period'. So he, rightly, lauds 'new horticulture', 'led by Piet Oudolf' in the Netherlands, and the role of gardeners in the 'new' English garden that he chronicles. None of his chosen sites neglects this strong horticultural element, but he nevertheless has to take notice of designs that foreground other things as well as plantsmanship, like symbolism, autobiography, 'modernism', historicism, abstraction and traditional forms, simply to be able to say that 'there is no danger of English gardening becoming stereotyped or stuck in the rut.' However different are the arts – as architecture, painting and sculpture necessarily are – one still looks in each 'newness' for coherence and imagination; these, too, take different forms.

One French designer, Gilles Clément, has a different perspective on the 'new gardening'. His 'Garden of Movement' is perhaps a misleading phrase, but it alludes to his celebration of how plants move and self-propagate and how humans must adjust to their movements, not ours.[12] He records his dismay, when visiting Sissinghurst, that a plant that had trespassed onto a path was removed from where it was not wanted! He is most famous for the eponymous section of Parc André Citroën in Paris, but that 'garden of movement' (illus. 10) has not prospered in a public park, nor have his gardens below the walkway to the west of the Grande Arche at La Défense in the same city, doubtless because both places are too frequented: too many human rather than plant movements perhaps. So his major claim for fame is his own garden at La Creuse, where gardening in its valley and upper meadow 'consists in constant interpretation of the dynamics of work. The object is not to maintain a pre-set image or aesthetic, but to consider a sculptural and biological balance, open to the greatest possible diversity, to wonder and impermanence.' That work is indeed wonderful, but it doesn't seem a mode of gardening that could be readily and widely adopted; yet his rhetoric is powerful and ultimately visionary, as his inaugural lecture at the Collège de France makes clear.

Another unusual departure from horticultural priorities, forced now by the site on which it was made, came with the garden of Derek Jarman at Prospect Cottage, begun in 1986 on the inhospitable shingle near the nuclear power station on the Kent coast. Sir Roy Strong finds it a clarion call for those who 'are ready for startling changes to what constitutes a garden'.[13] It was both a profound gesture against the threats of the modern world, nuclear disasters and AIDS, a triumphant declaration of Jarman's own artistry, and a reproof of the usual Sussex gardens of 'Close' and 'Crescent', that 'would give Gertrude Jekyll a heart attack' with their 'desert of fuchsias' and omnipresent lawns ('I am so glad there are no

10 The Garden of Movement, Parc André Citroën, Paris, late 1986–98; photograph 2014.

lawns in Dungeness . . . lawns, it seems to me, are against nature . . . the enemy of a good garden' (pp. 105, 107). Created on the largest shingle formation in the world, Jarman accepted the beach as *his* place, with no trees, no protecting fence, using the debris thrown up on the beach to decorate his garden, welcoming the rabbits and moths, the plants like gorse elder, blackthorn and *Crambe maritime* that can survive, even if deformed by beta-ray contamination from the power station, and cultivating the giant sea kale, viper's bugloss and valerian. It is, as Michael Charlesworth says, 'a space of an aesthetics', where found objects, allusions to lay lines and the stone circle at Avebury (which Jarman filmed in 1973) blend with his interest in wild plants and material from nurseries, the upright posts and poles that militate against the flatness of the site (illus. 11), the geometrical and circular organization of large stones (which he called 'henges', reminiscent of Stonehenge) and his acknowledgement of other mythic gestures, writing of 'my dragon-toothed garden' (p. 47), an allusion to Cadmus sowing dragon's teeth to protect Thebes. Prospect Cottage garden, coherent and imaginative, has become a memorial to his own life and artistry, protected against an otherwise embattled world, a garden at once of therapy and of pharmacopoeia (p. 12), a paradise or 'green place' (p. 40) of a different sort than we usually want. A few words from John Donne on the wall of the Cottage are the only inscription: 'Busie old foole, unruly Sunne . . .' taunts or teases the sun that lovers know 'no season . . . nor clyme, / Nor houres, dayes, moneths, which are the rags of time' and proposes that the lovers' bed is the centre of the world, since 'the world's contracted thus.'

Alasdair Forbes has made his garden of Plaz Metaxu in mid-Devon since 1992. The name means 'The Place that is Between', a mixture of a neologism (not the Welsh *plas*) and Greek, and signals, first, its position in a valley between two hills and, second, a 'betweeness' ''twixt real space and what Forbes calls an 'Orphic spatiality'. The garden is beautiful, carefully maintained, intriguing at every turn and (though difficult) a photographer's paradise. Photographers have indeed captured its beauties – Neil Hepworth in a privately published book with an introduction by Forbes, Emily T. Cooperman (whose images are used here) and Andrew Lawson, whose many images sustain Tim Richardson's chapter on Plaz

11 The garden at Prospect Cottage, Kent, created by Derek Jarman, from 1986.
Dungeness nuclear power station is in the background.

Metaxu.[14] But this is where photography – despite its acute focus – lets the garden down. The valley is clearly a strong visual presence (illus. 12), its forms are recognizable and even conventional – hedges, paths, enclosures, groves (*Alsos* is the Greek for a sacred grove), the hillside slopes, and many stones, some with, some without, inscriptions; but their disposition inevitably asks how their forms mediate significance. For Plaz Metaxu is, to start with, the fruit of a designer's imagination; but, in the last instance, it is also a garden of reception. It has, as Forbes writes, 'expressive potential'. The site is lovingly and carefully *designed* (and is, incidentally, ongoing), so the visitor's role is to respond to the careful contrivance that he or she finds, to listen for what it expresses. Then comes the more difficult part – another betweenity of the physical site and its meanings.

In his short introduction to Hepworth's anthology of images, Forbes tells how Orpheus ('a mythical poet') descended into the Underworld to find his dead wife, failed, and, returning to earth, lived in the two worlds of everyday and a 'world of imaginations' (this 'need not be Hades'). Forbes's garden exists equally between those two realms, and the visitor also has to negotiate between them. It is interesting that Hepworth provides only three photographs where inscriptions

12 The valley at Plaz Metaxu, Devon, from 1992; photograph 2013.

can be made out, whereas Lawson captures more examples, though they can still be enigmatic. For Plaz Metaxu exists in a limbo between word and image, dependent on how we relate language to its spaces and its insertions: part of that is, aptly, a guessing game, a kind of four-dimensional crossword puzzle, for which Forbes's clues are given personally to his visitors, in chapters of an unpublished book on the garden, and in Forbes's comments embedded in Richardson's chapter and captions; these 'clues' depend, above all, on how he identifies specific locations in the garden. He gives Greek names to the whole territory – at one point he writes that 'the fields were beginning to acquire names', as if they enjoyed and required a self-nomination. But it is he who designates them. The names are taken from a polytheistic Greek pantheon: Hermes, Artemis, Pothos, Ithaka, Imbros, Eos, Eleusis, Demeter, Pan, Ariadne, Hesperos, Dionysos, Orexis. These dedications are not revealed on site, though provided on a plan of the garden and in a list explaining names, inscriptions and references, and they are intended to reveal or suggest the meaning and identity of each location. Forbes himself says these names are not 'symbolic', by which (I suspect) he means non-didactic. But they are perhaps 'symbolist' – a means of suggesting larger ideas and associations if we submit ourselves to them, not always rationally, in the manner of the French Symbolists. Richardson says it is an 'unabashedly "intellectual" garden', but Forbes himself prefers to say 'a garden is inseparable from its legends. It needs, as well as walking, reading.'[15]

A good deal of reading sustains the making of this place: James Hillman's psychological readings set out in his anthology *A Blue Fire* are not well known, but are much relied on by Forbes; better known are the many works of Carl Kerényi, another informative presence here, providing interpretations of Greek gods and heroes. Yet how does one connect the walking with the reading? This is a classic case of what I discussed in both *The Afterlife of Gardens* and *Historical Ground* – the gap that lies *between* (sic) the designer's vision and how it is 'received' by visitors. In line with my understanding that the history of some ground can be invented (that is, does not have to belong historically to the place), this fits well with Plaz Metaxu, since only the landform, the topography, has a history and the rest is 'feigned',[16] which is yet another between-ness.

The signs of its new history are everywhere, if obscure (illus. 13), yet they are equally premised on old Greek myths, Jungian perspectives and the work of modern psychology: nine upright stones (maybe here we can guess the Nine Muses), twin megaliths representing man and boy, a 60-metre figure of Pan carved into the north-facing slope, a pilcrow (¶) that signals a new 'paragraph' or bend in a pathway. The idea of a caesura, like the pilcrow, is suggested by the stream and lakes through the valley that separate the facing hillsides, and is invoked also at the edge of a haha. Some inscriptions gesture clearly, if you take the references, to Paul Celan, Lorca, Rilke, Hölderlin, Emily Dickinson, or Wallace Stevens's 'The Emperor of Ice-cream'. Two inscriptions, finely carved on slate

13 Plaz Metaxu: the *Alsos* – Greek for '(sacred) grove' – with quotations from Wallace Stevens's 'Final Soliloquy of the Interior Paramour'.

by Nicholas Sloan, read: 'To the running water speak: I am', and 'Say to the constant earth: I am flowing'. We can at once seize the poetry of their insights – water is flowing, but *we* are *here*; earth is firm, yet humans are mobile or fickle. If further, we know they are quotations from Rilke's 'Silent friend of many distances' in *Sonnets to Orpheus*, then their silence can lessen the distance between us and the inscriptions. Otherwise, they are instances of prosopopoeia, or the device by which something or somebody in the landscape speaks to the visitor who may or may not understand ('Take off thy shoes, for the ground whereon you tread is holy ground', for instance, and it is curious that the entry to the garden is marked by two stones that show the mark of a bare foot and of a boot). Two inscriptions on tree plaques, also from Stevens, split open one of his lines, as we walk down a grove: first we read 'Let be be', then 'finale of seem'; on which Richardson comments that the 'play' between 'be' and 'seem' goes through 'myriad conjugations in the garden', as indeed does the notion of introits and finales.

This is an astonishing garden, which only walking, as well undoubtedly as reading, can truly capture. There are three routes or nodes to it, and we need to accept their different routes palimpsestically, layered in our mind, rather than responding to any one empirical encounter; and the nodes of the garden are contrasted clearly at various points with the agricultural territory out of which the garden is carved. It is also a garden that resists easy understanding – we get the experience, but too often miss the meaning (in T. S. Eliot's phrase) – and that surely should be a gift in a world of instant comprehension, Internet access to references and the *Reader's Digest*'s quick facts. Meanings will certainly grow here, if you have time and patience to bother with both Greek legends and a Jungian relish of their meanings. Exclusive (rather than inclusive) readings are unhelpful. We need to be capable of 'poetic courage', unafraid of pauses, echoes, intervals or caesurae, even envious of imaginative space within this material place.

Yet it will remain, betwixt and between what we can glean from it and what Forbes brings to its creation and naming, a place of mystery. I for one prefer mystery to platitude and the obvious. One example from this extraordinary garden will serve to reveal its poetic basis of mind (illus. 14): the gaping hole of a terracotta pot lying in the Hermes courtyard behind the house can be (if we know that Hermes was the messenger of the gods, and much else) a mouth that speaks to us, like the

14 The Hermes courtyard at Plaz Metaxu, Devon.

voice of the Delphic Sybil; but what it says is for the visitor to guess. Forbes can tell us in his own careful way about the 'hermetic oracle in the centre of the "Labyrinth of the Broken Heart"' that is made by the paving stones in the shape of a broken heart or, maybe, question mark and ear, and by the brushed gravel on which we must not tread. That gnomic utterance is itself partly summoned by the visual item as well as dissociated from it, should visitors wish to understand what they see differently. As Stevens wrote, in 'An Ordinary Evening in New Haven',

> Reality is the beginning not the end,
> Naked Alpha, not the hierophant Omega,
> Of dense investiture, with luminous vassals.

We must start with the real, which of course is densely invested with many significances at Plaz Metaxu. It is also 'naked' and not in the first place clothed with sacred mysteries. Yet as 'vassals' we are beholden to the site and to its creator, and our humble attention to it is a necessary service.

When I ventured to suggest to Forbes that Plaz Metaxu was similar to Ian Hamilton Finlay's Little Sparta, he noted that the 'method and motivation are different', not least because of Finlay's 'polemic attitude'; he also argued that Finlay's dedication to a ferocious Apollo privileges a 'monotheistic ideology'. Little Sparta is what Finlay called 'a tangible image of goodness and sanity far from the now-fashionable poetry of anguish and self'; it is thoughtful, imaginative, coherent and leaves visitors with a plenitude of ideas; its inscriptions also

speak more directly to visitors than Plaz Metaxu allows. Richardson says Forbes is 'avowedly non-didactic', but Finlay isn't didactic either. He may well seem to admonish his visitors, for gardens are (he says) attacks not retreats; he parades his instinct for revolutions, his distrust of secularization and an avowal of piety, and his work is more public than Forbes's and delights in its neoclassical temper, where Latin, not Greek, is the preferred language. It is, at once, a very private garden and highly communicative: its play with garden forms, references and above all inscriptions have been glossed and explained by various commentators, which give Little Sparta its much more public face; that the garden also emerged from Finlay's early work with concrete poetry makes the place address visitors succinctly and yet permits them to relish and extend its expressive potential.[17]

Finlay's public stance was muted by his own highly personal perspective on the world. But in another Scottish garden, a different public position, this time premised on modern science, is used to sustain an equally astonishing making of place: the Garden of Cosmic Speculation, designed by Charles Jencks and his late wife, Maggie Keswick. Science is certainly more public than the ideas that Finlay invokes, but it is (at least for me) a struggle to do enough 'reading' to make sense of what I find there. Jencks himself has provided a rich and informative book on the garden in which he explains how the place emerges from, and in its turn exhibits, a cluster of cosmic ideas or speculations.[18] Many things are as self-explanatory as they are fun and amusing: a 'Jumping

15 Black Hole Terrace, Garden of Cosmic Speculation, 1996–7.

Bridge' where fractals tilt against each other, a 'Black Hole' in the form of a terrace or picnic place (illus. 15), the 'Universe Cascade' that in steep steps from the pond up to the house dramatizes an evolution of the universe from quarks and plasma to sex, consciousness and ecology; there are equations across the top of the greenhouse ('MASS EQUALS ENERGY'), and the wonderful iron gates that demonstrate 'Soliton' waves that travel through other media and yet keep their identity. We have, on the one hand, a conspectus of accept-able garden forms and ornaments like gates, an octagonal folly, ponds; on the other, an unfamil-iar repertory of complexity, 'waves, twists and Folds', DNA symbols, Möbius strips, the octagon called 'Nonsense', curlicues and grass mounds with sharp edges. The mysteries and also the equa-tions of science enter and inhabit the physical site: both 'compenetration', Braque's term used by Forbes, and 'stereoscopic', from Paul Ricoeur, must accept the prose and the poetry of place, and their necessary if sometimes obscure conjunction.

16 Paolo Bürgi, a secluded seat for a private client in the Ticino, Italy.

Finlay's public attitudes, even if elusive, and Forbes's private meditations are both emphatic self-portraits; Jencks's appeal to modern physics is, on the one hand, impersonal, but on the other, a poetic and even esoteric way of constructing a place like a garden. They require our careful attention. Gardens have often, explicitly or by implication, been autobiographical. The younger

Pliny clipped his box hedges at one of his villas with the names of his gardener and himself. By contrast, in the district where I live in Philadelphia, a front garden covered with black plastic, through which an urn emerges graced with a dead plant, or a nearby garden that instead of sunflowers sports a plastic stalk crowned by a car hubcap, seems an affront to those of us who aspire to horticultural efficacy; but these, too, tell us something about the gardener. A tiny balcony designed by Paolo Bürgi in the Ticino jets over a gulley with sounds of water below (illus. 16); the solitude of its single seat is the owner's privileged seclusion among the trees.

An unabashedly autobiographical garden was created by Sir Roy Strong and Julia Trevelyan Oman from the 1970s.[19] It celebrates their lives together, and their various professional lives: Julia Oman's work as a theatre designer, Strong's work at the Victoria and Albert Museum and many publications on Elizabethan and Jacobean art, Elizabeth I, Inigo Jones, gardens and the artists who painted them. Drawing on both their lives, The Laskett is a theatrical garden: hers, because she envisages how it would be performed and be a stage for performance (personal and public); his, because it is sustained by a scholarly concern for the past and yet animated by his wit and eye for the modern. A monument to Shakespeare, in honour of Strong's 1980 award of the Hamburg Foundation's Shakespeare Prize, gazes down the Elizabethan Tudor Avenue to be answered by a commemoration of Elizabeth II's Golden Jubilee at the far end; this is a cast of one of William Kent's urns (another garden and theatre designer) designed for Alexander Pope's Twickenham garden, but here now is painted in blue and yellow to mark the contemporary vogue for Pop art (illus. 17).

The garden is essentially characterized by what Castiglione called *sprezzatura*, translated in 1561 by Sir Thomas Hoby, striving for an English equiva-

17 The Laskett Gardens, Herefordshire: Diamond Jubilee Urn, from 1973.

lent, as 'recklessnesse': a courtier's elan, his confidence, his special sense of place and behaviour, his eye for elegance and, perhaps, his disdain for anything less than perfection. Whether you are conducted through the garden by Strong himself or now by the portable sound guide for visitors (with his voice), his personal iconography is grounded in a keen sense of scale and space: he has constantly monitored how the garden grows, where trees need to be thinned or removed, where hedges are to be lowered or moved. The relatively small garden (4 acres) has several strong axes or

19 The noria in the Jardin de la Noria, Provence, late 1990s.

vistas that conceal or sometimes invite entries into intimate and less regular enclosures (illus. 18).

A plan of the gardens drawn by Jonathan Myles-Lea, with marginal miniatures of fourteen garden features (modelled on the engraving format perfected by Jacques Rigaud in the eighteenth century), is given to all visitors: it lists, dates and explains briefly each item and its planting, and the events and friends in Strong's and Julia Oman's

18 View between sections at The Laskett; the Cecil Beaton sundial is halfway down the *allée* of the Pierpoint Morgan Rose Garden.

lives that give the garden its meaning and significance – from their cats to a production at Glyndebourne, or lectures at the Pierpont Morgan Library, from Cecil Beaton (his own sundial, see illus. 18) to monumental items from Westminster Abbey or All Souls College, Oxford. The plan is clear as any bird's-eye view, but the first experience of it, even when conducted by Strong himself, is more labyrinthine and the dialogue between regular format and apparent nonchalance is enticing. Yet it is, whether accompanied or not, a very personal place, not simply because it celebrates its creators but, as photographs in *Remaking the Garden* show, because of how personable a garden it is, filled with its creators, their animals, gardeners, builders, tree surgeons and painters, all of whom seem to delight in the sheer exhilaration of its making. Never let anyone say this is an unpeopled garden!

Yet not all gardens tell us so directly and intimately of the owner. There is a certain relaxation in visiting some gardens, rich in coherence and imagination, that ask little of one except to be there and to look. Such is Le Jardin de la Noria, created in the late 1990s by two professional landscape architects, Eric Ossart and Arnaud Maurières, near St Quentin la Poterie, Provence, for Jean and Martine Deparis. It forms part of a larger *mas* or former farm that contains, beside the main house, with its double arcades, and some smaller buildings (one a former pigeon-house beside the enclosed garden), an ornamental garden, a *potager*, a *prairie* of fruit trees, a grove of fir trees, a swimming pool and the garden that gives its name to the site. The noria (illus. 19) is an ancient device for drawing water, often depicted in Arabic documents and still in use around the Mediterranean. This one is mounted on a stone platform, and draws water in leather buckets from the cistern below. This is then conveyed into the orchard. This part of Provence is blessed with quantities of water, so much so that the *potager* is decorated with a row of watering cans (illus. 20). Adjacent to the noria is a long, narrow basin with an open pavilion at its head, lined with terracotta vases, that suggests a miniaturized version of the Generalife in Granada. The inspiration for this garden comes from its designers' enthusiasm for the Islamic garden culture of the Mediterranean basin, on which they have produced a very eloquent book,[20] but it is also marked by a refusal of copyism and a strong attention to locality – the ensemble of the former *mas*, the distinctively modern vases (the nearby town is named after potteries), the austere and brightly coloured seats and benches, with a relish for water and strong scents in the hot sun.

20 Watering cans in the Jardin de la Noria, Provence.

21 Lawrence Halprin, Sea Ranch, Sonoma County, California, 1960s.

TWO

MASTERS' GARDENS

I have taken the term 'masters' from several sources: from the eponymous character in Henrik Ibsen's play *The Master Builder* (1892); from a cluster of so-called 'master' designers who were invited to exhibit their gardens at a horticultural exhibit in China in 2011;[1] and from a symposium in September 2013 at the Indianapolis Museum on 'Masters of Modern Landscape Design', organized by the Library of American Landscape History. Each of the speakers there was in the process of writing a monograph on one of the masters, a list that consisted (speakers in brackets) of Dan Kiley (Jane Amidon), James Rose (Dean Cardasis), Ruth Shellhorn – the only woman designer featured – (Kelly Comras), Lawrence Halprin (Kenneth Helphand), Robert Royston (J. C. Miller and Reuben Rainey), Garrett Eckbo (David Streatfield), Thomas Church (Marc Treib) and A. E. Bye (Thaisa Way), all of whom worked publicly as well as designing for themselves. That event was focused entirely on Americans (understandable given the Library's role, but somewhat embarrassing in a global world), and they were all dead – thus safely absolving the organizers from identifying the ambitious young, who, in *The Master Builder*, were knocking at the door of the great professional and threatening his pre-eminence.

The modern master gardeners discussed in this chapter have contributed to a wide range of different types: Kathryn Gustafson, for instance, has designed for corporate headquarters, small parks, memorials, infrastructures, botanical gardens and private gardens; Paolo Bürgi for private gardens, mountaintops and funicular stations, and institutional parklands; another Swiss, Günther Vogt, for parks, squares, gardens, country estates, campuses, harbours and fortifications, cemeteries, courtyards, promenades and interiors, and London's Parliament Square.[2] Among those 'masters' celebrated at Indianapolis, Halprin and Kiley had also worked across a diversity of types – public plazas, private estates (both small and large, like Halprin's Sea Ranch, illus. 21), museums and urban corridors. As such, their work will often feature more suitably in some of the following chapters.

Here, the focus is on what modern mastery or 'mastership' is displayed by acknowledged designers as well as by some individual landmark designs; specifically, on three ideas that clearly animate them all. First, a considered, but not copyist, dialogue with the past to thereby enhance their own contemporary work; for they seek, to use Paul Ricoeur's formulation, 'how to become modern and return to the sources, how to revive an old dominant civilization and take part in a universal civilization'.[3] Second, while many designers work internationally, responding to urban sites and large-scale infrastructure, the best work seeks to ground their work in a studied attention to locality. Finally, the role, already mooted, of gardens in larger design projects, as when Garrett Eckbo argued that 'garden design is the grassroots of landscape design . . . Private garden work is really the only way to find out about relations between people and environment.' This triad of ideas, which of course impinge on other garden types, seems of especial significance to some of the masters in the field of garden and landscape design. It is, of course, invidious to single out masters, and I am not in the business of choosing a soccer team; so an emphasis on sites rather than personalities is called for, on places where ideas are in play.

A few masters that need to be acknowledged for their modern contributions to the field, though they are dead, must include designers like Geoffrey Jellicoe, Halprin, Kiley, Dieter Kienast and Pietro Porcinai, simply because in various ways they continue to lead our thinking. We might here invoke W. H. Auden's idea that a good poet – read 'master gardener' – is 'like some valley cheese, local, but prized elsewhere'. Auden himself cherished and celebrated northern English geologies, in poems like 'In Praise of Limestone'; but he used the metaphor of limestone to compare it with

other geologies and with human behaviour at large. Master gardeners will have achieved a reputation beyond their 'valley', but they have matured locally before eventually exporting their skills and vision 'elsewhere'. They have roots, sometimes literally – in California, say, for Eckbo and Halprin, in Tuscany for Porcinai, Switzerland for Kienast, Brazil for Roberto Burle Marx, or Adriaan Geuze in the Netherlands. But many extend their base and find in other localities, not their own, a sense of the special qualities, honed at home, that sustain new designs. In a global world, influence can spread easily; but many local 'cheeses' still need time to be appreciated and understood elsewhere. We like to think that key designers have a wide influence, and even say that their local expertise 'can be translated to any country'.[4] But much can be lost in that translation.

The career of Sir Geoffrey Jellicoe, born in 1900 and spanning the twentieth century (he died in 1996), illuminates all three ideas.[5] He was drawn both to historical design (a book in 1925 on Renaissance gardens with J. C. Shepherd) and to modernist architecture (his wonderful grouping of buildings, including a pool, fountain and restaurant that, as an architect, he designed at Cheddar Gorge in 1934 – one of my first insights as a teenager into contemporary work). His range is considerable: from private gardens (his own most prominently),[6] reworking or revising early gardens like St Paul's Walden Bury, Hertfordshire, or Sutton Place in Surrey, to motorways and industrial sites, urban design, the Kennedy Memorial at Runnymede, a department-store roof garden for Harvey's of

Guildford, civic parks for Modena and Brescia in Italy, a sequence of Historical Gardens in Atlanta, Georgia, and perhaps his most elaborate and (as yet incomplete) series of Moody Gardens in Galveston, Texas. He was agile, flexible and unconstrained by any one 'style' so that Spens called his a 'timeless' modernism (p. 33). Like Tunnard, who relished English eighteenth-century picturesque, Japanese gardens and briefly consorted with European modernists in France in the 1930s, Jellicoe espoused many earlier traditions, invoking formal strategies that had a long pedigree, such as axial walks and vistas, yet all of which he viewed through the lens of minimalist abstraction. That he moved effortlessly, or so it seemed, between old and new (he much admired Burle Marx, had a good 'ear' for the modern, and projected a Florentine Ponte Vecchio over the Thames with a six-lane highway with shops and hotels), can be attributed, first, to his ability to preserve his Englishness within a wider modernism and, then, to his reliance on a richly conceived as well as on a broadly applied understanding of Jungian ideas.

That he delighted in metaphor, allegory and analogy did not obscure the sheer professionalism of his designs: the granite sets that form the path at the Kennedy Memorial (1965, illus. 22) may be 'a representation of the multitudes who will pass along its way', but it also ensures that visitors mark their arrival there and its historical threshold by what they walk on; looking back from the monumental and inscribed stone over the Thames meadowland connects Kennedy's America not only with English land but the reson-

ances and historical symbolism of Runnymede itself. The huge white urns that mark the Magritte Walk at Sutton Place and the subtle unfolding of different path surfaces are physical, formal elements (illus. 23); but they invite, by their surreal disproportions and irregularities, a psychological reading. His interest in connecting our conscious appraisal of gardens (the 'tangible') with a subconscious understanding grew out of his unease (surely, overly modest) that some of his designs were 'technically orthodox, but stillborn'; or again that when he worked at Sutton Place that long-established landscape afforded an 'intimation' of something more profound, a 'great allegory of man's place on the planet' that inserted 'itself without my conscious knowledge and consent'. When in 1984 he finally came to design the sequence of different cultural gardens at Galveston, he saw that 'all powerful ideas in history go back to archetypes'; so he sought to translate into 'visible reality' a unity of existence.[7] It was primarily and originally a botanical concept, mediated by his reading of Lucretius and Epicurean philosophy (just as he had invoked Virgil and Ovid for parks in Modena and Brescia respectively). It morphed, for commercial reasons, into a sequence of historical gardens ('technically amusing' was his disappointed sense of this declension) that were set out in a sequence of cultural forms, English, French, Italian, medieval, Islamic, ancient Roman and Persian, which drew on his knowledge of many cultures and on the book that he published in 1987 with his wife, Susan, *The Landscape of Man* (revised in 1995, and still, in my view, with no

23 Geoffrey Jellicoe, the Magritte Walk at Sutton Place, Surrey, 1980s.

22 left: Geoffrey Jellicoe (and sculptor and letter-cutter Alan Collins), The John F. Kennedy Memorial, Runnymede, Surrey, 1965.

equal among other subsequent encyclopaedic endeavours).

The sheer range and elegance of Jellicoe's oeuvre, whatever one's assessment of his Jungian perspectives, is hard to match. The United States and South America have produced something like that scope in the work of Lawrence Halprin and Roberto Burle Marx. For Halprin, gardens of innovative simplicity and cultural relevance, urban adventures and plazas (illus. 24), the FDR Memorial, writings on cities and freeways, a strong interest in pedagogical workshops to explore and understand community design. Like all great landscape architects, Halprin shares with Jellicoe (though very differently in its results) a subtext that sustains and informs his tangible work – the love of drawing, his wide travels in many countries, a relish for exploring the natural world and translating it into forms and inspiration for urban spaces, a love of theatre and dance (the choreography of urban walking), and the desire to *change* places and people in North America and in Israel, which his posthumous memoir recounts and illustrates.[8]

24 Lawrence Halprin, Denver's Skyline Park (before partial dismemberment), 1974.

Roberto Burle Marx was emphatically situated in South America, a local 'cheese' maybe, but relished and now slowly appreciated outside Brazil. Gilles Clément wrote about Burle Marx that he successfully combined the artist who draws and the gardener who works with living plants. It was skill in using his deep knowledge of South America's plants, gathered on ventures into the continent's forests and mountains and established in an astonishing collection of them in his own garden (illus. 25, 26), especially agaves, bromeliads, palms and helioconias (one named after him).[9] He extended his skill in garden-making into larger and public projects, mediated in part by his understanding of modern painting that had inspired him on an early trip to Europe. Such famous designs as the promenade along Copacabana Beach, the rooftop gardens for the Ministry of Education and Health in Rio de Janeiro (1936–8) or for the Safra Bank in São Paulo (1982) involved the curvy and geometric forms that had their origin in painting, as if he had invented a modernist parterre on a rooftop 300 years after ground-level French design. But beyond his stylistic and Western modernism, his painterly influence, his marvellous eye for plants and his 'tropical' imagination, we need also to understand how much he transformed the modern park. A look at his 1961 plan for the Parque del Este in Caracas (see illus. 27), one of his most important public parks, declares how much the modern park, in its material and ideology, has been changed by his imagination: on the base line of picturesque meanderings and botanical garden

organization, he dances variations on intimate patios, waterfalls and aquatic gardens, zoos for monkeys and crocodiles, and places for human occupation.[10] We may not, cannot and should not copy his designs; but he has up-ended our sense of parkscape, finding a place there for locality, geometry, fantasy and the arbitrary dislocation of forms. His influence has been immense, if not always as poetic and secure as his own.[11]

Another innovative imagination, though firmly premised on his native Tuscany, is that of Pietro Porcinai.[12] He accepted the Italian Renaissance idea of gardens commanding large territories from their hillsides, which in Tuscany was almost ubiquitous; he chose to extend that perspective into an 'immense garden', a modern landscape of villas and vestiges of former agriculture, but then to insert within them an apparatus of contemporary life – new villa structures and terrace decoration, modern chairs and benches, swimming pools (not a huge step from Renaissance water tanks, but often thrillingly poised on the edge of a void), lawns (*prati*), tennis courts and even accommodation for motor cars. An inveterate (and largely British) nostalgia for 'old' Tuscan gardens is subtly mediated in Porcinai by his new and indigenous understanding of older garden compartments: thin hedges are enlarged into low, expansive, horizontal forms, between which are walkways. Forms are larger, more dramatic, but also far less fussy; an infection, perhaps, of public park-making, but keenly located in a distinctive place and largely for private use. That he also suggests ways in which older Italian properties can be given new and

25, 26 The garden of Roberto Burle Marx, Sitio Santo Antonio da Bica, a former coffee plantation acquired by Burle Marx in 1949.

27 Roberto Burle Marx, plan of Parque del Este, Caracas, *c.* 1961.

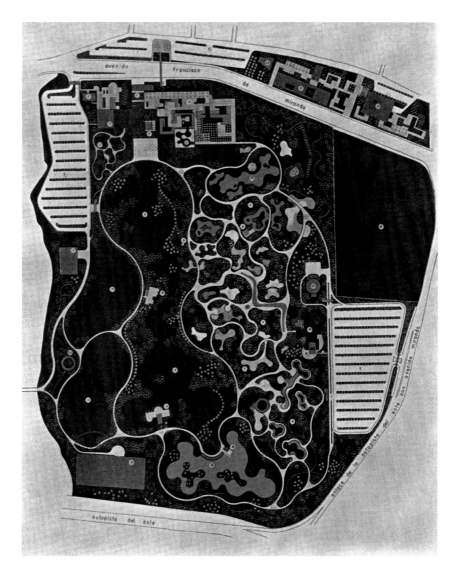

contemporary forms relates him also to how conservation might be pursued without fears of 'authenticity' (see chapter Twelve).

So far this has been an all-too-brief review of essential masters, but some individual master *designs* need to be acknowledged for their highlighting of the same triad of ideas – on gardens, on debts to the past, on locality. On the role of the garden in the larger reaches of landscape architectural thinking and, as this generally is involved in all of the examples, the search in the past for new designs, it is useful to look to Kiley's Miller House in particular, Laurie Olin's work for the Washington Monument in Washington, DC, Gustafson's gardens in Chicago and at Terrasson in France, and much work by Martha Schwartz;

on locality, work by Bernard Lassus and Paolo Bürgi, Vogt and the Portuguese designers PROAP. While the different threads of these major ideas or concepts may be separated, they weave often seamlessly through them.

Kiley has worked across a range of types – museums (at Kansas and Oakland, California), public plazas (Fountain Place, Dallas), airports (Dulles), infrastructures (Chicago Filtration Plant) – so some of these sites also appear in subsequent chapters. One of his iconic designs was for the Miller House, Columbus, Indiana, a remarkable modern essay in private garden design. The house was a 1950s modernist one by Eero Saarinen and commands a space that is both austere and old-fashioned, with an axis of hornbeams parallel with the garden facade of the building, that was focused at one end of the alley on a modern sculpture by Henry Moore (sadly now sold), like the one we see in Tunnard's frontispiece to *Gardens in the Modern Landscape*. Beyond the permeable double 'wall' of hornbeams is an empty meadow lined with trees, seemingly random on one side, on the other grouped in horseshoe clusters; they join in a woodland at the bottom of the meadow. Through the woodland runs a river that is allowed to flood, and therefore penetrates the wood during times of flooding. It is a modern masterpiece – attentive to site, to materials and to their forms of enclosure; patently 'natural', yet also totally contrived. Kiley's fondness elsewhere for tangible forms – lines, grids, circles, *allées*, sculpture and pools – marks his honouring of old, mainly French, late seventeenth-century forms; but the spirit with which he

manipulates them is modern and often minimalist; though in designing his own house and studio in Vermont, he was much more in the spirit of its very rural setting.

Among informed, but shrewd, ransackers of older garden forms to be used in ways at once witty, austere or downright unapologetic have been Martha Schwartz and Kathryn Gustafson. The latter moves easily between the very self-conscious Lurie Garden, just one part (5 acres) of the 24-acre Millennium Park in Chicago, to the collection of her gardens, Les Jardins de l'Imaginaire, in the Perigord region of France, where an anthology of old garden features is given life in a new and public setting; these are not only easily 'readable', but the different gardens are labelled with the type that they portray.[13]

The Lurie Garden plays with its relations to the lake and the history of the city, illustrating Chicago's motto, 'Urbs in Horto' (City in a Garden); the site itself is exciting and unusual in its bold formal play of hedges and open spaces, dark and light areas ('plates' they are called), with planting by Piet Oudolf. Both the ground and vertical shapes are striking: the high hedge supported on metal frames (the Shoulder Hedge references Chicago as the 'City of the Big Shoulders' in the words of Carl Sandburg) protects the garden at north and west, through which alleys cross the light plate into the dark, crossing a curved pathway and water feature that cuts through the site. The design is, both in plan and on site, a deliberate reworking

28 Kathryn Gustafson, Lurie Garden, Chicago, 2000–2004.

of traditional garden forms, with the diagonal pathway or 'Seam' a strange haha through its midst (illus. 28); yet it doesn't entirely live up to the very metaphorical understanding of the designers – the west hedge 'tells' the story of Apollo and Daphne (she who became a laurel tree); the strong contrast between the plates – the dark signals the city's old shoreline, the light promising 'the future in an exhilarating landscape' – is not a narrative that reads on site until you find the text online.

Schwartz, for her part, often isolates dominant features, decorating objects from garden centres, using bright colours that draw out otherwise more traditional and unnoticed garden forms, exaggerating conventional and unconventional elements and materials, playing with lines and grids, referencing collage and (it seems) modern quilt-making, and using odd materials (slatted wooden boxes

form walls around seating areas, plastic discs as trees). It is clear that she is referencing gardens, but their arbitrariness and sometimes distortion are part of the surprise: the mounds of grass at Jacob Javits Plaza, New York City, among the curving green benches and purple pavers (now replaced), or the same device of grassy knolls and tree trunks, now explained as a local reference to Minnesota loggers and local geography, outside the court house in Minneapolis.

While the invocation of early garden devices is not incumbent on modern designers, or indeed much avowed by critics, it springs or seeps into their work. When Laurie Olin was called on to defend the Washington Monument from possible terrorist attack, he chanced upon the idea of the haha, that eighteenth-century ditch connecting

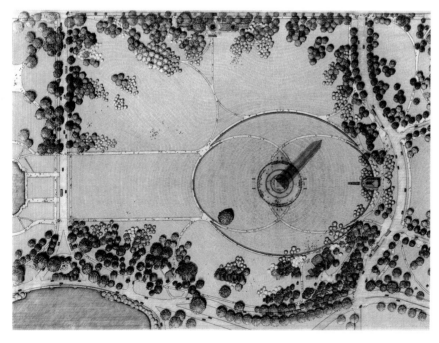

29 Laurie Olin, design for a haha at the Washington Monument, 2001.

the garden seamlessly with the landscape beyond; but in this case, it was a safety zone that vehicles could not breach, an obstacle for terrorists, a subtle threshold as you approach the monument, but invisible once visitors stood on the mount itself (illus. 29). In a similar fashion, James Corner explained the effect of the final stage of the High Line in New York by saying that the surroundings visitors see when walking along it are 'borrowed scenery', a reference both to a Chinese notion of design and to the English need to 'call in the country'.[14] Bernard Lassus used belvederes in perforated steel on the rest area outside Nîmes in the shape of, and also enclosing a miniature

version of, the city's famous Roman Tour Magne; he also projected a 'Nimetta', a brick replica of the town plan of Nîmes in the manner that the gardens of the Villa D'Este used to represent ancient Rome (a 'Rometta'). These are devices or gestures that look 'in both [geographical and historical] directions'.[15] Another modern take on the belvedere was used by Georges Descombes for the Chänzeli on the Swiss Path around Lake Uri (illus. 30): large, but with an open structure, it drew in the forest behind and the lake below, allowed a conventional opportunity to take in a beautiful view (*belvedere*) without imposing any 'kitsch' or undue 'picturesque' insertions into a

30 Georges Descombes, the Chänzeli on the Swiss Path, Lake Uri, Switzerland, 1987–91.

scenery that might otherwise have solicited such conventional responses. Follies, too, had been an architectural feature of eighteenth- and nineteenth-century designs, but Bürgi used only the trees in a park in a psychiatric hospital to create a sequence of engaging, and growing, arboreal follies along a wandering pathway through an otherwise unremarkable landscape.[16]

For all their international reach, landscape architects have learnt to respond to where and how their designs will sit. Sometimes the site itself enforces this; sometimes the designer works to make the insertion both amenable to the place and yet able to enhance it. For landscape infrastructures, the Portuguese designers PROAP have found inspiration in both local and traditional materials for cultural centres, housing projects, exhibition sites, waste-water treatment plants, vineyards, undervalued parks and large urban master plans, like the historic Ribeira das Naus in Lisbon (illus. 31). Elements that would previously be found in gardens are repurposed: vestiges of a naval port and its previous activity become a small green space at the edge of the city, with lines of trees, bosques and fossils of the former wharves slanted into the river. A careful sense of the arbitrary in the choice and situation of materials is what its principal, João Nunes, calls 'poetic'.[17] A similar infusion comes in the works by Vogt Landscape Architects, with the transference of specifically garden ideas on private properties or temporary festival sites into campuses, factories, urban sites: the infusion of smells and sounds, and their interchange from one city street to another, from Zurich and Tokyo, allows for the effects of a garden without there being one.[18]

Since the start of the twentieth century there have been landscape architects, properly so-called.[19] They are formally trained and licensed and so qualified to work in all types of landscape, public as well as private. And most of them were motivated by being seen as contributing to the public sphere, on a par with architects. In this they are like other artisans and craftsmen who have traditionally formed guilds to protect their interests and advertise their skills, and that is what happened in the United States in 1901 with the formation of the American Society of Landscape Architects (ASLA); the United Kingdom followed suit in 1919 with the Landscape Institute, granted a Royal Charter in 1997.[20]

In 1931 Henry Hubbard wrote in the journal of the ASLA that landscape work should be pushed beyond the local and 'emphatically not confined within the boundaries of the garden or the private estate'.[21] His call has been answered far and wide. Professional landscape architects have expanded the scope of their work to include large landscapes: while Tunnard and Eckbo both published their first books on gardens in 1938 and 1950 respectively, they then expanded their scope, with *American Skyline* (1955) and *The City of Man* (1970) and, for Eckbo, *Urban Landscape Design* (1964). A less well-known American figure, Warren Manning, moved from designing private estates and gardens, which he described in *Landscape Gardening* (1893), to the making of cities (*Science and Art of Modern City Making*, 1901) and to

31 PROAP, computer rendering of the design for the Ribeira das Naus, Lisbon, 2008–14.

broader planning endeavours involving entire nations or continents (*Broad Scale Planning in the United States*, 1934).[22] And yet, by the end of the twentieth century, if not the making of gardens at least the idea of gardens came once again to inform landscape architecture. Even the considerable increase in infrastructural design leans towards allowing gardens to inform or even shape projects, like TGV stations in France (Michel Desvigne) or autoroutes, freeways and especially their rest areas (Lassus), airports (Kiley at Dulles), filtration plants (Kiley again) and power stations (Brenda Colvin).[23] Thresholds, a familiar event as we enter and move through early gardens and, later, estate parks, are now invoked to introduce visitors to cities where modern modes of transportation tend to blur the old exciting anticipation of arrival. But beyond the invocation of garden ideas in larger landscape projects, this fascination with gardenist forms and

uses has drawn many professions into exhibiting at garden festivals and exhibitions, which is the focus of the next chapter.

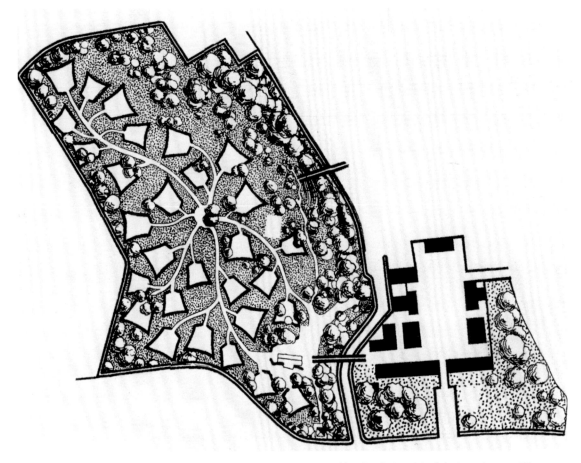

32 The design for the 3-acre gardens at Chaumont-sur-Loire, proposed by the distinguished designer Jacques Wirtz, and implemented by Michel Boulcourt. 'The design was inspired by a tulip tree branch with leaves' (Jones, p. 11).

THREE

GARDEN FESTIVALS AND EXHIBITION GARDENS

Garden festivals emerged from larger events in the late nineteenth century where nations displayed their prestige and wares at international exhibitions.[1] Those events generally took place in parks and in addition might feature special gardens, either mounted by an exhibiting nation, or used to enhance the site, which is what Frederick Law Olmsted did for the World's Columbian Exposition in Chicago in 1893. Garden designs were a major feature at the 1925 Paris Exposition des Arts Décoratifs et Industriels Modernes (see Introduction). But more recent festivals that focus on gardens have been of two kinds. First, taking on a damaged or derelict land, an exhibition then develops it with a view eventually, after the site is dismantled, to create new urban projects – as with the 1951 Hannover *Bundesgartenshau*. These German post-war exhibitions spurred the National Garden Festivals in Great Britain, beginning with that at Liverpool in 1984 and ending with one in Ebbw Vale in 1992; these left in their wake housing projects and parklands, a Science Centre at Glasgow, but also abandoned remains on some disbanded sites. The other kind of festival or exhibition is more familiar: the Chelsea Flower Show,

the Métis Gardens in Canada, the Journées des Plantes de Courson, or those at Chamont-sur-Loire, both in France.[2]

Nonetheless, gardens continue to feature as part of both international expositions and biennales. João Gomes Da Silva created his five 'Unseen Gardens' for the 1998 Expo along the banks of the Tagus at Lisbon: 'unseen', in that they represented five former Portuguese colonies (Brazil, Goa, Macau and so on) by creating for each colony a typical garden layout, planting, and distinctive constructions. These survive, but in a sadly unmaintained state (illus. 33, 34).

At the 2008 Venice Biennale, Kathryn Gustafson and Neil Porter created a temporary garden in a disused sector of the Arsenal. It celebrated a past, a present and a future for the city: the past consisted of a cabinet or storeroom of plants and animals that Venetians had once collected from their wide-ranging empire; the present, of a vegetable garden, made in the spirit of many lost Venetian plots (plants were grown in advance elsewhere and installed as a fully grown and functioning garden, illus. 35); and a future of an empty, green oval lawn, an 'uncluttered nature', with – for

33, 34 João Gomes Da Silva, 'Unseen Gardens', Lisbon: aerial view of five gardens with a detail of one of Portugal's former colonial gardens, photograph 2013.

manner of interdisciplinary teams in support of their proposals'; this interdisciplinarity resumes the well-established experience of gardens that have always been created by a mixture of talents and competences, both from before and since the establishment of landscape architecture as a profession. Third, they are essentially designed to promote an *idea* of the garden – maybe more of a garden fragment, yet 'ample material to question' what a garden is. One design at Métis in Quebec by Hal Ingberg, 'A Preference for Facts' (pp. 164–5), argues that, 'factually speaking', for a clearing in the forest 'my garden is not a garden'.

Furthermore, the 'growing' time in these gardens, any sense of process, is largely absent. Hence they seem, more often than not, fragments of gardens that would need to be situated in a 'complete' or larger landscape where time and a local context give a better sense of what they can do. Such a larger landscape is in fact around them at Métis, or in garden festivals held in urban areas. The Métis Garden Festival was established alongside an older garden, a legacy from Elsie Reford, in an area where families from Montreal and Quebec came for the summer and established gardens (menfolk came up by train at weekends). So these temporary gardens exist in dialogue, sometimes provocative, ironic or celebratory, with larger and well-established gardens around them on the shores of the St Lawrence River.[4]

These exhibits obviously use the space designated by the organizers, or artists draw lots for the available sections (illus. 32). They may relate their design to the larger landscape itself, but *genius loci*

the opening at least – a visionary cloudscape of floating muslin *à la* Tiepolo.

All festival or exhibition gardens enjoy at least three elements that are not normal in other gardens.[3] They are temporary, though some are maintained over a few years beyond the year of their first exhibition (the Lisbon ones longer, which probably explains their decay). They also tend to gather together a mix of participants – landscape architects, environment designers, graphic artists, biologists and architects who 'have formed all is not a strong emphasis – the spirit of place is largely the spirit of its own project. And these can indeed be spirited, for these small sites tend necessarily to focus on one garden idea that ensures that they maximize their effects[5] – an emphasis on humour or colour, both of which are unusual in what we might call masters' gardens, and wit can dismay or 'affront' the visitor who doesn't expect them in a garden.[6] The gardens often rely also on materials that are different – asphalt, plastic, steel, a variety of non-organic materials and leftover materials from other sites, chainlink fencing or black drainage piping; even elements you can readily find in a garden – poles, fencing, screens – but clustered and overwhelming in a smaller space, a mass of blue and orange sticks as an alternative version of some herbaceous border (pp. 34–5, 106–9). In short, everything you'd ever wanted, or possibly *not*, in a place of your own: 'Not in My Backyard', by espace drar in 2000 (pp. 136–8) made visitors aware, perhaps satirically, that in their backyard even panels of turf on top of exposed wire mesh were not implausible.[7]

Another vehicle in these exhibits can be allegory, metaphor, allusion, that we may find in other gardens but here are more insistent, as exhibitors want to get their 'idea' over unmistakably. Edmund Husserl wrote that 'the object never coincides with the meaning',[8] and many garden objects, or gardens as objects, are designed to promote their agendas irrespective of their vehicle. All garden exhibits have their manifestos,

35 Kathryn Gustafson and Neil Porter, the vegetable garden in 'Towards Paradise', Venice Biennale, 2003.

36 David Meyer and Ramsey Silberberg, 'Limelight', Westonbirt International Festival of Gardens, 2003.

some subtle, some 'in your face' like the 'Asphalt Manifesto' (p. 162). In too many the meaning is overly simple, a good one-off joke, the kind that suits a garden seen once or twice, but not one for every day: we can make fun of the notion of a level playing field, when 'Italian Fragment' (pp. 144–5) puts a kind of goalpost at one end of a football area and a slightly raised slope at the other beneath, under which are contained water-bottles, useful at halftime – a kind of *un*levelled playing field. The titles themselves direct us in many cases, usually in irony, to their meaning; texts that accom-

pany each exhibit also enlarge their significance, even by punning on French terms (this is Quebec after all). They are all desperately *meaningful*, for that is the point of festival gardens; yet there is something of relief in some *sotto voce* significance. The design by David Meyer and Ramsey Silberberg for the Westonbirt International Festival of Gardens in England is both minimal and strangely strong: entitled 'Limelight' (illus. 36), a chestnut tree, already growing there, was surrounded with an amphitheatre of gravel and grass banks ('an earthen medallion') on the slope of which visitors could lie and watch the performance. Lost in the woods the tree would be unnoticed; here in the 'limelight' it is allowed to speak for itself.

At Métis the design of 'Modulations' (pp. 54–5, 112–15) by Philippe Coignet and David Sereno was a stainless-steel framework that sheltered and mirrored the forest ferns around it, and the sun playing on the silver ribbons shows the modulations of light as well as of fern fronds. A similar dialogue between our perceptions and practice of viewing 'nature' comes in 'Living Room', by Bernard St-Denis, collaborating with Peter Fianu: reached through a long wooden tunnel that has the uncanny sense of being an elongated TV tube, we enter a room of grass walls and a chequerboard lawn on which, from a pair of bright yellow Adirondack chairs (or on another occasion a blue plastic settee), we can watch a TV screen inserted in one of the grass walls. The notion that in one's living room it is easier to watch a nature programme on the television than respond to nature itself is of course endorsed by the artificial 'nature' around one.

Some gardens at Métis look inwards. *Chambres Vertes / Garden Rooms* was the first book on Métis, and its title suggests privacy, solitude, inhabitation, or maybe some close-up garden work, hence a variety of huts and shelters, greenhouses and deliberate enclosures. Some designs simply said 'You Are Here', by Chris Matthews and Taco Iwashima, or 'Etre là un peu . . .' by Bernard Lassus. But the nearby St Lawrence River is a strong presence and beckons in strange ways. One garden in 2000 by Marie-Christine Landry aligned artemisia and junipers in rows in a forest clearing, where in each row three plants were low, three high, three low – an SOS signal for her Jardin des Appels (that is, Signal Garden), apt enough for navigation on the St Lawrence. Other exhibits turned more directly towards the river, like Diane Balmori's 'Making Circles in the Water' (illus. 37), or Maria Debije Counts's 'Petites fenêtres'. A view out from the latter's enclosure reveals the river through an open doorway or window, and this shape is echoed in the coloured plots of left-over materials within the garden itself, as if the doorway was throwing its shadows across the ground (illus. 38).

Some designers make use of picturesque devices as a form of focus: the doorway cut in Maria Counts's hedge, or the circles of Balmori, like lens shutters of cameras. Ken Smith's 'A Ditch with a View' actually invokes the multiple-framed openings of windows (illus. 39), a leitmotif that seems to go back to Tunnard and Paul Nash in their modern 'dreams' of landscape seen through such an open screen.[9] Flowerbeds are lowered into the ground and we look through a framework of gravel to see the 'picture' below. Some gardens incorporate, either literally or via representation, the riverine landscape (tidal flats, salt marshes), or (responding to the thrall of land art) colonize a tiny island in the St Lawrence, where two pillars of salt, slowly disintegrating amid the debris of a cormorant's nesting ground, could be glimpsed through binoculars (pp. 30–31). One of the most deliberate attempts to represent that river landscape came in 'Jardin territoire' by Pierre Thibault. At first

37 Diana Balmori,
'Making Circles in the
Water', Métis Festival,
2011.

39 Ken Smith photographing his own 'A Ditch with a View', 2011.

sight, a narrow, shallow canal with stones and fish-
es, a surrounding area that grows wheat within
the forest clearing, and a stone hut or grotto into
which one descends to find more pebbles and
stones: local materials, and local metaphors for
river and salt marsh. For some other mysterious
intrusions in the landscape, verbal glosses augment how we might perceive their allusions and
symbolism (pp. 22–3, 122–5); but these are less
exciting than the mysteriousness of the site itself.
Several exhibits offered definitions of 'garden', as
in the commentary for Pierre Thibault's 'A Place
to be Invented'; but verbal statements, interesting in themselves, were hardly necessary to grasp

38 Maria Debije Counts, 'Petites fenêtres',
Métis Festival, 2008.

how any one of them was both fragment and
whole, 'garden and landscape' (p. 122).

While 'gardeners are innately conservative', as
the Métis director, Alexander Reford, notes, he
also adds that it requires some 'act of daring' to
go past the conventional notion that gardens are
simply about plants and less about design.[10] Yet
in the restricted spaces of exhibition plots, design
is necessarily predominate; nor is a *lack* of daring
very apparent! The most 'daring' of moves was to
make sense of what other designers might dismiss
as arbitrary:[11] flowerbeds are skewed or buried
below ground, asphalt can be accepted as groundcover, random inserts of anything become the norm;
so the representation of a vernacular garden, beside
a railway line, is here on a par with all the rest. And

many exhibits were, nonetheless, wonderfully *about* plants, presenting them in ways that were unusual – in pots stacked on the grass as if 'they had been delivered off a ship' (p. 41), or simply by insisting that 'a garden [be] made with plants by a designer concerned with knowing and revealing complexity', accompanied by a garden of square panels that alternated water with meconopsis plants reflected in them (pp. 120–21).[12] The symbolism of that design (blue flowers signalling hope and reconciliation) is a quotation from Raymond Queneau's *Les Fleurs bleues,* and meconopsis being a 'signature flower' at Métis, are all convened to extend the meaning of this garden.

Reford also argues that the Métis Festival places itself within the 'evolving practice of landscape architecture' (p. 8) with a focus on climate change, recycling, forest management and genetically modified plants.[13] Several gardens were laboratories, literally, or satirically: so Paul Cooper's 'The Eden Laboratory' (pp. 82–3) uses plexiglass boxes to declare how humans have lengthened seasonal growth or how coloured lights affect plants – 'A virtual torture chamber for plants'; in the 'Core Sample' garden plants were in narrow glass test tubes (pp. 26–7, 146–7), and genetic experiments were displayed in the confrontational and unexpected 'In Vitro' exhibit by NIP Paysage (pp. 70–71, 152–5).

These festivals are great fun, sufficient to justify themselves. But they are also sustained by the argument that in them we reinvent the garden and that these exciting laboratories or experiments can be transferred to more permanent work out-side the festivals. Maybe they are, more properly, a mode of expression that cannot be transposed, like a writer of sonnets avoiding, for once, the long narrative poem. That so many distinguished landscape architects now participate in these festivals – the lists of participants in the volume *Hybrids* make that very clear – suggests rather that garden festivals are releases from the demands of clients and community pressures; the transference is therefore more a question of transferring professional work *into* festival sites. And in those condensed spaces, abstract ideas can dominate, which would be dissipated, even if available, in a public parkland.

Peter Latz is properly enthralled by the process of time in all of his public work, but inserts that theme less obliquely in his 'Mist Garden' for Chaumont-sur-Loire, where he can help visitors relish and visualize these effects (illus. 40): mists rise between dark stone slabs (quarried locally, placed in a circle, but returned to the site when the garden was dismantled), and the play of the mist in the sunshine constantly changes how we see the garden, its slabs and the ferns planted around them – a theatre of effects. A simple design is actually endlessly reformulated by the misting and its condensation on the stone and on the plants, which gives it a depth that would be far less focused and feasible in a large public space.

The 2011 Xi'an International Horticultural Exposition at Shanghai used the term 'master gardeners' to describe the professional firms who exhibited in nine of the gardens; these included Martha Schwartz, West 8, Gross.Max, SLA and

40 Mist Garden,
Chaumont-sur-Loire,
1997–8.

EMBT. Yet these were juxtaposed to another nine so-called 'University' gardens, variously represented by Toronto and Columbia universities, the University of California at Berkeley and the Architectural Association in London, among others; an awkward distinction, because many leading professionals teach or lecture in these schools, and to imply that teachers were not 'masters' or that 'masters' did not teach (Schwartz does so at Harvard, for example) is to muddy the waters unnecessarily. The Masters' Gardens were 10,000 sq. ft, flat, trapezoidal in plan and blocked off by stands of bamboo from their neighbours; while the University ones varied from 7,500 to 13,000 sq. ft, were placed on a slope down to an artificial lake, took different but largely oblong shapes, and

were visible from adjacent gardens.[14] The site was a former clay quarry and mine, remodelled as a 'simulacrum' of the ancient Guangyun Lake; thus it was both a response to a derelict industrial site and a reinvention of a former landscape, as well as contriving a festival on abandoned land.

The exhibits explored a variety of ideas – some were representations of other Chinese provinces or other countries, but eighteen gardens were focused on one theme, sometimes very simplistic: a garden of mazes, one of bridges leaping over bamboo thickets, gardens of passages or of quadrangles, a mud garden, a hole in the ground, a botanist's garden, a scent garden, a sky garden, gardens dedicated to time, ecology, wind, nets and a Garden of the Forking Paths. If gardens usually

41 'The Labyrinth and the Mountain', Xi'an International Horticultural Exposition, Shanghai, 2011.

have spaces through which visitors may find their own way, and with routes that may change on subsequent visits, these gardens were programmed with entrances and exits. The enclosed gardens tended to promote introspection, simply because visitors couldn't look outside through the bamboo screen; apparently, visitors preferred them to the University gardens, where adjacent lots were visible.

The 'Big Dig' (by Topotek 1) was a hole in the ground, from which sounds of other cities and landscapes emerged – yet it somehow lacked the poetry of Bernard Lassus' project for the Jardin de L'Anterieur or the unbuilt 'Bottomless Well' in France, where stones plumbed an immeasurable depth and were never heard to strike the bottom.[15] There were some narrative hints – the stacked roof tiles in Gross.Max's 'Botanist's Garden', 'battered at an angle reminiscent', writes Kallmann, 'of the ancient city walls encasing Xi'an', or the paper canaries in bird cages suspended in 'The Labyrinth and the Mountain' in the former mine, where canaries would have been used to alert miners to destructive gases (illus. 41). Two of the best gardens worked to engage their visitors. In 'The Net Garden' people responded to the unsteadiness of walking on 'paths of flexible expanded mesh of various gauges'; though balustrades were imposed (contrary to the designers' wishes), some skill was nonetheless used to concentrate on the immediate movements of visitors' feet. And in the 'Scent Garden' visitors found that aromas from the grove of small conifers were dispersed by turbines, while in the Aromatic Pavilion bottled

fragrances were displayed. Scents and smells are always present in gardens and parks, but it takes some deliberate mechanism and visual clues to make their presence palpable (illus. 42).

Some of these exhibits offered representations of distant and larger cultural landscapes: one invoked hilltop gardens from Argentina, another (by Mosbach Paysagistes) tried, via a map on the ground, to represent all of China. This global reach was one of the themes that Louise Jones took up in her *Reinventing the Garden* (2003) when discussing a similar festival in France, at Chaumont-sur-Loire.[16] That gardens have to be reinvented may be obvious – if everybody wants to keep up with the Joneses, or the Jekylls, something fresh and unusual is called for. But it is always a challenge, as gardens have always tended to be more atavistic than other art forms, and in practice or mythology they look back to resonant examples from the past. Bringing into festivals glimpses of landscapes and gardens from far away is thus a manoeuvre in space as well as in time; yet this, too, has a long tradition in place-making, from ancient Chinese rulers who recreated faraway parts of their empire to eighteenth-century European *fabriques* that called on a conspectus of alien and foreign forms to enliven their own locality or to invent some references to other cultures. A range of plants, often in need of reclimatization and even renaming, also marks a festival's global reach.

Cultural gestures at Chaumont invoked a multitude of international forms, materials, elements like terraced walls from around the Mediterranean, or skills like the pollarding of trees. Many sought to use their site to invoke an 'authenticity' of foreign places. This fabricated *genius loci* was somewhat awkward, as the festival site itself was perhaps more authentic as an exhibition space than some of the individual gardens were of places that they represented. It is certainly useful to remind people of how locality leads to and shapes identity, but identity was far harder to accept when the theatricality of the designs was so dominant, and suggested rather a film set than the 'real thing'. Some local plants, too, could not be translated to the alkaline soil of the Loire, like heather for a Scottish design.

As with Métis, other elements at Chaumont were metaphorical or representational of foreign items and in need of explication. An Imperial Chinese *potager* (p. 21) seemed to have a Western wellhead at its centre, and it needed to be glossed as being 'organized according to Taoist symbolism'; yet that clarification didn't really take us far without competence in Taoism. Almost all the sites required some sort of commentary either by the designer or by notices on display. Some irony was often invoked and was useful, though the wit, while visually available, could be heavy-handed: 'Tartan Potager' by Frazer McNaughton (pp. 22–3) had fun with the tartan patterns of cabbages (red-veined chard and sage), but the attempt to construct a bothy (a traditional Scottish shelter for use by travellers in remote areas) was unconvincing as a shelter, though the term itself was more telling when the same design was recreated back in Edinburgh. Its steel platform for the bothy and the arch filled with ironic items contributed by famous writers (beer cans and discs of bagpipe music alongside Elvis Presley) made its invocation more ironic than authentic. Can authenticity be ironic? If so, the authenticity is rather that of the designer than of what is represented. And it must be said that the French are often more adept with irony and more witty than others at festivals elsewhere.

Surprisingly, while festival gardens are modern inventions, their use of sculpture, aromas, texture, narratives and symbolism and, of course, planting have been with place-making for centuries. But what Anne Cauquelin identifies as contemporary is the unusual intrusion of art objects into a garden world that is otherwise largely atavistic (she has written other books on contemporary art).[17] The frequent use of what elsewhere would be arbitrary or eccentric gives festival gardens a provocative edge, what Ian Hamilton Finlay (though he manages it differently) calls 'attacks' rather than 'retreats'. Great gardens have always provoked or even startled visitors by moving into prominence what hitherto or elsewhere had not been central to their vocabulary and significance or to our expectations.

42 The Scent Garden, Xi'an International Horticultural Exposition, Shanghai, 2011.

43 Adrian Allinson, *The Auxiliary Fire Service (AFS) Dig for Victory in St James Square* (Piccadilly), 1942, oil on canvas.

FOUR

VERNACULAR GARDENS

At the other extreme from masters' gardens and festival exhibitions are vernacular gardens, which are always contemporary. They occur whenever there is a need for them, depending on local, demographic and cultural conditions. A love of gardens has blossomed in the strangest, as well as more usual, situations, in part because nineteenth-century urban crowding and then modern high-rise apartments buildings have eliminated the chance for many to have ground-level plots; so gardens have flourished on balconies and roofs, alongside railway sidings, even at bus stops, in community gardens and by the sometimes illegal takeover of abandoned lots for gardening. In the early twentieth century, competitions awarded prizes for the richest and busiest gardens – an ancient idea, to judge from Sir Thomas More's *Utopia*, where citizens would have vied for the best displays; but garden centres and innumerable radio and TV programmes (*Gardeners' Question Time* was one of the earliest and most famous in the UK) can now provide ideas and materials – a more democratic and reachable opportunity than the annual Chelsea Flower Show.[1]

The term 'vernacular' derives etymologically from the Latin *verna*, what the OED defines as 'a home-born slave' on some Roman master's estate, but also as 'native or peculiar to a particular country or locality'.[2] The term has morphed, in part by responding to an architectural interest in traditional building and to discussions of 'common' or 'ordinary' landscapes, like J. B. Jackson's *Discovering the Vernacular Landscape* (1984). But as so many other arts have turned, like historical studies, to exploring the vernacular – Tudor ballads or broadsides, jazz, oral history, enquiries into village culture like Emmanuel Le Roy Ladurie's *Montaillou* (1975) and other studies pioneered by *Annales* historians – landscape architecture, too, needs to expand its reach beyond the elite or high-end garden design.[3] It is interesting that, while English and French have words for 'vernacular', German has no exact word for it, and even the English word encompasses many different sorts of activity lurking under that term.

Thus the vernacular 'type' includes the allotment garden, or what has been termed 'the working man's green space'.[4] In wartime, the allotment movement was taken up by a whole society to produce needed food (illus. 43) – in the United States it was the 'Victory Garden' – and, once again in wartime, gardens found occupation for prisoners of war and those interned in concentration camps (in the United States, Japanese interned during the war found solace in making their own gardens). There are also community gardens, for those with no opportunity to garden in a city; these may have been promoted by municipalities, or by a genuinely radical movement from those in need of space in which to 'hang out' and probably to assert a strong local ethnicity.[5] Finally, there are those disadvantaged and homeless folk (though some may be so by choice) who find an empty lot to occupy where they can live and make a garden, often temporary. Vernacular gardeners also involve those who choose, in defiance of bourgeois taste and conventional garden decor, to furnish their own properties with a wondrous anthology of visual, and usually narrative, imagery.[6]

What characterizes this 'type' in general is a combination of need and desire, of opportunism and disregard of 'proper' social behaviour and aesthetic taste, though allotments and some community gardens aspire to more propriety. Allotments will look much the same wherever are they are, even though local and cultural differences will direct what plants to grow; but decorations for display suggest that the global reach of ornaments is strong (dwarfs have tended gardens ever since Disney produced his film of Snow White, and there have always been gnomes). Allotments of African Americans along suburban railroad lines in Philadelphia, or on vegetable plots alongside railway lines in the UK, have different priorities and different customs, but there is always a hut or shelter (sometimes a disused railway carriage, and even an aircraft fuselage), with chairs for resting and sharing garden lore with neighbours (as well, one imagines, as gossip) and places to store the garden tools.

The allotment has a strong hold in Europe, and a sudden and expanded increase of them in wartime has not much diminished thereafter, so it is still an important element of garden culture. The British society of allotment holders sends out Internet messages, images ('selfies') of happy gardeners and other practical information and reports. The Office International des Fédération des Jardins Ouvriers (International Association of Workers' Gardens) was founded in October 1926, and maintains an office in Luxembourg, now as the Office International du Coin de Terre et des Jardins Familiaux. Its change of title from *worker* to *family*, its choice of *coin* (corner or plot) implying locality, what the French also term *de la sociale*, suggests the spread demographically and democratically of the organization, which has over three million members.[7]

Cities and even suburbs cannot always accommodate adequate garden spaces; but many folk seek community gardens and allotments because that is where they feel that they can grow vegetables and flowers or find 'nature' and even the 'countryside'. When once, on the isle of Patmos, I went to seek help at a plumber's house in the town, I was told by his wife that he was away in the country: I was able to find him in his garden outside town, half a kilometre away. Bernard Lassus was surprised, when asked to design a recreation area alongside a river, that the fishermen who went there were oblivious to the traffic noise nearby – they had found a piece of 'nature' and simply ignored its distractions.

Anyone who has travelled through Europe, but especially in the Randstad along the north coast of the Netherlands, or visited outskirts of urban complexes throughout Germany, will register how much communal allotments flourish there. In Germany the Third Reich promoted allotment days from 1933, and a federation of allotment holders was formed after the war, one in the east, one in the west, and is now (after the fall of the Wall in 1989) a complicated bureaucratic process; building plans for development, for example, that include allotments can ensure that these allotments are permanently established.

Allotments are generally open enclaves where each gardener can do what the family wishes, and are surely scrutinized by curious neighbours in search of both ideas and criticism. A more secluded and wonderfully different design for community gardens was made in 1952 by the Danish landscape architect Carl Theodor Sørensen, who provided a cluster of 40 elliptical gardens, 25 x 15 metres, where each enclosure ensured some privacy (illus. 44). But most other communities have

44 Carl Theodor Sørensen, community garden, Denmark, 1952.

continued to deploy the usual format where fences declare ownership (or rental privilege) as well as rivalry between adjacent gardens.

A friend of mine who works in Haarlem's centre can leave her pleasant flat in a converted school and cycle several miles to a large cluster of small garden allotments outside the city. Her garden is dedicated largely to flowers (she has always decorated her apartments with them); there is a garden path, a circular lawn embraced with a box hedge, a pergola and the usual pavilion at the rear (illus. 45). All these allotments are laid out with 'roads', 'street' numbers and even letterboxes for receiving post (illus. 46), and a store where garden supplies can be purchased. There are 186 gardens in all, and the association, founded in 1933, is run by a committee of volunteers; the annual fees are very reasonable. There is a big demand for sites; none of the gardens that I saw were ill-kempt (if any were, they would have been requisitioned and passed to others on the waiting list).

These spaces vary in size, but my friend's is 9 metres wide and 38 metres long. What occupies these spaces is enormously varied in both usage

45 Anneke's garden in the community garden near Haarlem, photograph 2013.

and decoration. My friend's neighbour is Turkish and all he does is entertain his male friends for barbecues and otherwise does no gardening at all. Other neighbours grow flowers and vegetables in profusion, fill their gardens with a range of 'eccentric' items (the familiar windmill – it is Holland, after all), gnomes, birdboxes, painted animals, a Smurf lady and artificial birds, like storks and owls, and almost all establish small houses (the Dutch penchant for lace curtains in their windows is much in evidence) with porches or verandas and all the accoutrements of summer living, though some are

simply storage for garden tools and chairs. Also included are smaller 'Wendy houses' for children.

The decoration of these Dutch gardens was extremely diverse, but it relies largely on materials either salvaged or bought from a *tuincentrum* or garden centre. The fashion in which garden owners decorate their gardens can be inventive in ways that require of a critic more than some patronizing admiration of their eccentricities. Bernard Lassus, for a book published in 1977, called this group of garden-makers that he explored throughout France *habitants-paysagistes* (that is,

46 Letterbox in a lane of the community garden, near Haarlem.

47 Monsieur Charles Pecqueur's garden, Ruitz, France, 1970s: the race of the tortoise and hare at the finishing line.

those who landscape where they live). Their invention beggars belief; that such work was so prevalent at that time suggests the vitality of local imagination prior to the advent of the ubiquitous garden centre.[8]

They tell stories, like the hare and the tortoise running their race down the side of Monsieur Pecqueur's garden (illus. 47), who, when mayor of his commune of Ruitz in the Pas de Calais, started to decorate the traffic circle (roundabout) until a change of administration prevented its completion. Strange beasts confront each other on the tops of walls, or saunter on private lawns, though often visible from the street. Aircraft zoom and propellers whirl. Everything is painted to make it all new and different – doors and walls, car tyres for planters, bead curtains at doorways, trellis work (a kind of Scottish tartan effect); mechanical fragments (cogwheels) or culinary objects (mixing bowls) discover new forms in the kaleidoscope of colours (illus. 48). Massed flowers make herbaceous borders look austere and dowdy; walls and hedges turn embroidered parterres vertical. *Horror vacui* trumps modernist minimalism. Shells and porcelain fragments make mosaic decorations. Figures from girlie magazines are inserted into groups of mannequins dressed as respectable bourgeois. A full-size Sinbad the sailor, leaning on his tin of spinach in a front window, gazes through his telescope at a *paquebot*, and this telescope (even though Sinbad is looking through it from the right end) authorizes the miniaturization of the ship 'seen at a distance' immediately before him in the front garden.

One particular creation, again by the Pecqueur, narrates the story of Snow White (*Blanche Neige*) in paint and cement reliefs under the pent roof down the wall of the rear garden. Passing alongside the wall, we follow Snow White's story into the forest, tended and later lamented by dwarfs, hunted by an evil forester, rescued by an elegant cavalier, until we find her – in another life, so to speak – seated on a wellhead, beside a deer, with her back to the painted forest we have just come through. She gazes across the fields to the slag heaps of coal mines, the residue of the forests that provided the coal: Monsieur Pecqueur himself was a miner, until he was invalided out. Snow White's

eyes are made of coal. That Pecqueur was himself, besides a miner and mayor for eighteen years, an actor, had written a play in three acts in which he performed himself, designed the scenery and was part of a barnstorming company, suggests how readily he could insert the dramatic ways of the theatre into his garden, where story, impersonation and transformation thrive. But it also, along with many of the other works by the *habitants-paysagistes*, taught Lassus a series of concepts that has, in fact, sustained much of his later design work, notably what (as a painter by training) he calls *mécanismes plastiques*.

These involve the dialogue between different materials (broken glass to represent waves of the sea), the effects and surprises of *trompe-l'oeil*, miniaturization and play with scale and fragments, exchanges between facade and yard or garden

48 Image from Bernard Lassus' portfolio of gardens by *habitants-paysagistes*.

enclosure, the role of vegetation in gardens (real and fake), the reutilization of found or discarded objects, and the need for and skill in (re-)interpretation by *habitants-paysagistes* themselves. No less is the challenge for commenting on their imaginations to read and understand the coded vocabulary, whether the representation (actual and imaginary) of local agriculture for those who have lost it to new housing and industrialization, or the role of beauty in bringing the past into a new future of inhabitation. Above all is the total immersion and joy of a person tied to the landscape where he lives (illus. 49). That enough of Lassus' *paysagistes* were miners suggests a fresh perception of the land above them when they emerged daily from below ground or eventually retired.

For a sampling of other *habitants-paysagistes* or DIY garden designers and especially those not afraid of crazy ideas, the book on *Eccentric Gardens* (1990) is instructive, though not all of its examples seem as eccentric as its author (Jane Owen) and photographer (Eric Crichton) assume. Many of their eccentricities are one-off jokes: the red British pillar box or telephone booth in the garden posing as wine cooler and drink cabinet respectively; a pair of hands grasping the air before sinking beneath the pond; a bottle pouring wine into a huge garden urn, the liquid in the form of a thin plastic shaft; brightly and unusually coloured objects worthy of a bric-a-brac store – 'shopping for garden decoration', says Owen, 'can be so much more fun than a trip to the local garden centre'. Eccentricities are not always innovative, so plastic or fibreglass ducks, lemons or lobsters; but a whole row of fake cows and a thoughtful if puzzled farmer figure gazing over a neighbour's wall (illus. 50)

49 Image from Lassus' portfolio of gardens by *habitants-paysagistes*.

50 Eric Crichton, farmer and cows, from Jane Owen and Eric Crichton, *Eccentric Gardens* (1990).

are more witty than what they endlessly contemplate. Yet truly eccentric gardens don't usually pretend to be eccentric, but make places that strike one as being, while unusual or surreal, nevertheless attentive to more thoughtful and sustained ideas (the one that is said to be 'created in three weeks' doesn't give much chance of thoughtful creativity). Indeed, some of the best items in this 'eccentric' British anthology are mazes, reminiscences of Italian gardens, orangeries, wyverns guarding a swimming pool, life-size gravestone figures, sphinxes, Buddhas, floral excess, Druidical remains and standing stones. Comparisons to

Magritte or Dalí are not convincing, though a menagerie of cement animals in the manner of the American painter Edward Hicks is telling (and one admires the sheer effort made to paint all of the creatures). A reclining and naked lady (*sans* legs) on a front lawn in Worthing has suggestions of some unholy coupling of Henry Moore and Matisse; this ex-Glasgow Garden Festival item was apparently a 'snip' at £20,000, and the view of her buttocks from the front window must be a constant delight.

Every age has produced some, probably impermanent, zones in which vegetables could be grown and shelter afforded from the weather, and where their owners could reflect. It was a familiar wish of the early American fathers, like George Washington, to 'live under the shadow of my own vine & my own fig tree'.[9] Washington continues by saying that as 'a private citizen', he is free of the 'bustle of a camp & the busy scenes of public life'. The reference is biblical, but it also signals a desire for the private man or woman to find peace under a simple tree or pergola. For Washington it was a retreat from war and politics, and gardens can still afford a time out of work, war and businesses of many kinds. But vernacular gardening has also – and this is a direct response to current social conditions – become radicalized; politics can be a call to action in a garden as well as a refuge from it.

This is clear in many urban centres, but New York City offers a considerable cluster within Manhattan alone, and the discussion of them constitute an impressive bibliography.[10] Perspectives vary widely, as will be seen: from political activism to urban farming, and even to questions of aesthetics. Some of these have been termed 'transitory gardens' by Diana Balmori and Margaret Morton.[11] They are not transitory in the way of festival gardens (there by design this summer and gone the next) and some, but not all, give a sense of well-established places. The authors' topic is rich in both photographs and commentary (with quotations from the gardeners themselves). But what seems important to this making of place is not so much that vernacular gardens are temporary – some can be very long lived, and gardens anyway are essentially short-lived in comparison with

buildings – but how they relate to other forms of place-making: in other words, what dialogue is established between this topic and the works of professional landscape architects, of elite and bourgeois gardeners who make domestic habitats, or of those who contribute to festival gardens. The temptation to make comparisons, as Balmori does, with 'Japanese Zen gardens' seems beside the point, and her need to situate this work within 'the historical tradition' has her scrambling to fashion a 'new picturesque', even while a page later she seeks to divest the volume of 'any predisposition to a past critical framework'. The 'power' of these gardens certainly await, as she wrote twenty years ago, 'new interpretations'; but they will be less about the anonymity of a folk tradition than a mixture of self-identity and self-promotion in parts of society where it is hard to have an identity that can matter to others outside these transitory gardens.

All gardens are *made*, and their making proclaims both the maker and the need to show off to others (rivalry between neighbouring 'transitory' gardens is sometimes as strong as in suburbia). These generally involve ephemeral constructions – 'found objects arranged in found places', but the ephemerality has as much to do with these peoples' lives as with the gardens as such. They are often said to be composed, and the book's photographs bring this kind of 'composition' to light; in fact, they share with many other types of gardens an eye for organization and effect, opportunities for regeneration and, for the uprooted especially, a chance to hope and find their own fulfilment in some new, even if marginalized, social 'composition'. They are as much cultural, even political, as aesthetic.

In the slums of Tehran the juxtaposition of unofficial settlements with the posh and Western-looking high-rises is a familiar scene in cultures where wealth confronts extreme poverty (illus. 51).[12] Most of the slum residents are poor hawk-

ers who sell flowers and other goods in the city; they grow some vegetables and fruits – tomatoes, melons, sunflowers – for themselves; scarecrows made from discarded dolls deter the birds; hoses for irrigation are draped over discarded and now cherished easy chairs and along the paths; the path-ways themselves are lined with stones, painted

51 Workers' gardens in Tehran, 2010.

blue and white; and the occasional sawn-off tree trunk adds a sense of calculated ornamentation. These green spaces between the huts and vernacular garden plots were established in what was once a village along the river valley of Darakeh but are now absorbed into Tehran's northward expansion, though some original garden plots survive. They are places to hide and to settle without being, for the moment, noticed.

The range of 'vernacular' types covers many modes of place-making but also of many different ideological positions, the least of which tends to be the aesthetic (though it need not be). A book entitled *Radical Gardening* by George McKay (2011) raises the issue, precisely, of what is radical. Its subtitle directs us to ideas of 'politics, idealism and rebellion', and its opening chapter plays fondly with the triple idea of 'plot': narrative plots, plots of land, and (though he does not mention this example) plots like that of Guy Fawkes. The radical stance of the book is a forceful counter to the idea that a garden 'plot' is a life of patio, barbecue, picket fence and herbaceous border. And McKay's own 'plots' are well laid (he has also written on DIY culture, jazz and protests in 1990s Britain). Here he tackles gardens in the city (a *new* 'machine in the garden'), the politics of organics, peace gardens, flower power and social liberation, and then finally allotments and community gardens, though here he extends this into 'guerrilla gardening'.[13] It makes for a stimulating, if at times uneven, book focused largely on British examples; but the idea and significance of the garden type seems to get lost in his 'act of

politicking', with its emphasis on those who are descendants of 'feminists and suffragettes, socialists, anarchists, simple lifers, vegetarians, anti-vivisectionists', along with many attacked for 'fanaticism and crankiness'.

The type, as he allows, is diverse, and the 'act of gardening can be ideologically fluid'. Yet he neglects what can be achieved, as opposed to what can be protested, perhaps by avoiding the base meaning of radical as *radix*, the Latin for roots. For what the community garden does at its best is to grow things – returning to the distant origin of the garden in agriculture and cultivation, colonizing the land to yield food and the opportunity to find aesthetic delight in flowers or even how things grow.[14] Roof gardens, 'edible schoolyards' and vacant lots are types of garden, and they also lead us out of it into larger ventures beyond the scope of this book. No community garden can feed its community, for sure; and no urban farm will ever supply what the local Co-op does, let alone the Giant, Safeway or M&S. But the inspiration of community gardens has allowed others to extend their limited scope into small farms that 'fit the fabric of a neighbourhood'. Detroit, wasted with foreclosures and demolitions and with roughly 40 sq. miles of acreage lying vacant, is a huge 'neighbourhood'; the spirit that promotes and sustains community enterprise, the joy and satisfaction in growing things, can be annexed there for smaller holdings, without the need in a city for heavy mechanization. It is not always easy; unease and resentment among African Americans collide with efforts by the Michigan Urban

Farming Initiative, founded by young, white graduate students, so that the effort at making a new community can be initially more difficult than the cultivation of vegetables.[15]

Radical gardens do not always live up to what their name implies. Some 'radical' ones are authorized, established and overseen by a local municipality; while importantly useful to those who use it, it is a kind of *noblesse oblige*, a gesture *de haut en bas*. This can be compared – not with the transitory gardens seized temporally in cities, garden squats, nor the privatization of public space for a 'pre-ordained "publicness"' – but with a community that actually took it into its own hands to make a garden they wanted and which served their interests, as well as provided an amenity to those around it. Grass-roots, literally. Some instances, but not many, are available. A community garden

in Haiti (Jaden Tap Tap), where its philosophical director argues that 'Making a garden is about more than cultivating plants, it's about cultivating people',[16] was created on landfill, and neighbours recycle materials and decorate waste, like tyres for pots; visitors have started their own gardens elsewhere. Miami's Center for Community Enterprise has been cooperating with neighbourhoods in Cincinnati with site-specific installations, called Agit/Prop. Penn State University has been engaged with Cheyenne reservations to use landscape as a means to foster identity for younger members and to restore once again a sense of 'placefulness'. Designers, above all, need to see themselves as what Peter Aeschbacher and Michael Rios call 'citizen-designers'.[17]

Ken Smith's Lola Bryant Community Garden in Brooklyn, New York (from 2005) was a pro

52 Lola Bryant Community Garden, Brooklyn, originally designed by Ken Smith, photograph June 2014.

bono design for a small 40 x 90 ft lot between houses; it offers plots for local residents, herb gardens and trees for fruit and nuts; along the sides, against the houses, are torque panels where vines could grow – Smith's 'continuing interest in vertical gardening'.[18] It still exists (illus. 52), but the panels have gone, to make room for more planting beds: 'The fence was idiotic, nobody wanted it', said the son of the late Lola Bryant, a crucial reminder that designers and communities will have different perspectives; nonetheless, the main stone path exists, the geometry of planting beds is intact and in good shape with lush plantings of crops and fruit trees.

Another site that seems to have accepted the notion of 'citizen-designers' was created in Pico-Union, home to many immigrant families from Mexico and South America, on Union Avenue in Los Angeles, between 11th Place and 12th Street; it is the second-oldest community garden in the city

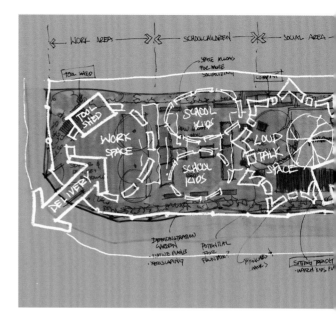

(illus. 53). It began in 1980 with children in Pico-Union inspiring their mothers to make a garden in the heart of the community. The mothers located a vacant lot and cleared it at night under the light of street-lamps, since when students, par-

53 People working in the Cesar Chavez community garden in Pico-Union, Los Angeles.

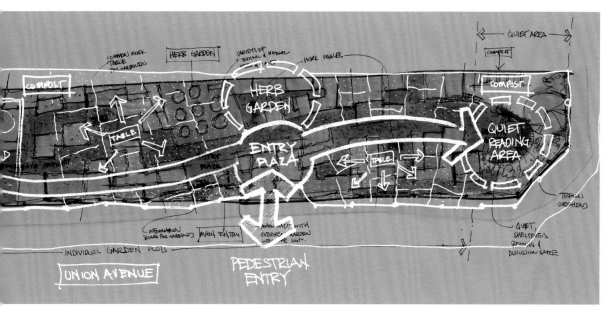

54 Annotated plan of Union Avenue Cesar Chavez Community Garden, Los Angeles, 1980s.

ents, grandparents and teachers have harvested beans, carrots, coriander, chillies, tomatoes, corn, squash, medicinal plants, citrus and fruit trees. Those with experience laid water pipes and built a tool shed and a play area.

A decade later, when the garden faced challenges and its fortune waned, more volunteers and at-risk youth revitalized the garden, and designer-builders proposed a new plan and entry, a shade area, a labyrinth for meditation, a herb garden, a native plant demonstration garden, spaces for kids to garden, a barbecue and 35 garden plots (illus. 54). The cost of materials was $10,000, and all labour and time was volunteered. It has encouraged inter-generational interaction, with space for both work and relaxation; a threshold welcomes one under an archway into the Cesar Chavez garden, and a low wall outside allows passers-by to sit, for such opportunity had not been available locally. Such gardens as the Cesar Chavez are far removed in location, size, use, public amenities and financial funding from large public parks, but they celebrate the resilience of those who make a garden in a place where they want and need it.

55 Mario Schjetnan, Parque Ecólogico de Xochimilco, Mexico City, late 1980s, completed 1993.

FIVE

PARKS

'Thinking in a garden is an essential activity.
What is a green space, if not for slowness?'
CHARLES JENCKS[1]

Modern parks seem, on the one hand, to perpetuate traditional elements from over 200 years of park-making that we don't wish to lose. On the other hand, paradoxically, there is a strong urge among designers to make them new, with both formal invention and contemporary activities. Early parks were royal, opened occasionally for public use, like Hyde Park or the Tuileries; between the late eighteenth and mid-nineteenth centuries came public parks, like the Englischer Garten in Munich, or the 'peoples' park' in Birkenhead. As they grew in both frequency and use, they were required, or needed, to absorb a host of new activities or enlarge on them, without obviously jettisoning older ones. Many contemporary parks have expanded their primary functions and incorporated zoos, athletics, boating, *manège*, outdoor theatres or concert shells, restaurants, even memorials. And other garden types, like botanical gardens, arboreta, sites for Olympics Games and sculpture gardens, have to all intents and purposes become –

or been changed into – public parklands, sometimes even requiring a fee for admission.[2]

One major contribution of new parks has been to create them on waste- or derelict land. Central Park was an early example, when its rubbish-strewn, muddy and virtually treeless wasteland, with squatters' huts and their rampaging goats, was transformed by Frederick Law Olmsted and Calvert Vaux with their 'Greensward' project, a large and varied landscape that has been the inspiration for parks worldwide, yet sometimes the despair of designers who want to do something different. Reviving and reusing defunct industrial land, whether former factories, railway lands, airfields, harbours, garbage dumps and other toxic landfills, or draining and filling marshlands, has produced many exciting new parklands. Some of these are better discussed in chapters Eleven or Twelve, which focus respectively on remaking useless or unwelcoming territories, or reinventing new gardens; but even a partial list is bewildering. These include everything from the Duisburg-Nord Park by Peter Latz + Partner (see illus. 143, 144), the 100-hectare Zeche Zollverein in Essen by OMA, the Zhongshan Shipyard Park by Turenscape, the Queen Elizabeth Olympic Park in London envisaged by Field Operations on the site of the 2012 Olympics in the Lower Lea Valley, Splash Pad Park in Oakland, California, by Walter Hood, the Brick Works site in Toronto organized by Evergreen (a not-for-profit organization), to Millennium Park in Chicago (see illus. 28), Southeast Coastal Park in Barcelona by Foreign Office Architects, Les Jardins de l'Imaginaire in the Périgord by Kathryn Gustafson, a cluster of projected insertions into the urban fabric of Hannover to augment the legacy of Baroque gardens like Herrenhausen or the land around the Maschpark behind the city's neo-Gothic Rathaus, and the Al-Azhar Park in Cairo by Sasaki Associates sponsored by the Aga Khan Trust for Culture.[3] In all these we find not only opportunities for walking, but bicycle and jogging trails, cafés, museums, memorials, opportunities for public art (sound pieces, waterfalls, light shows, follies, even imitations of derelict concrete sheds), and also attempts to rethink entirely the hybridity of modern parks and gardens. Park-making has became the *sine qua non* of landscape architectural success, what the 2005 MOMA exhibition called a 'Groundswell'. New parks sought fresh programmes and design possibilities, which competitions seem to have provided, like those for Freshkills, won by James Corner and Field Operations, for Downsview Park in Toronto, awarded to a team led by Rem Koolhaas, and a cluster of parks established in Paris (La Villette, André Citroën, Bercy, Diderot, Eole, all won by different teams).[4] While competitions became

more and more common, architects responded with new agendas, clients with more elaborate briefs and demands for fresh programmes and, above all, new designs: the classic case being perhaps Parc de la Villette, a competition (if not the park itself) that effectively upended some older assumptions about parks.

Park discussion and, inevitably, park theory have become the modern *furor hortensis* that had raged in the eighteenth century. The issue of what is, or can now be, a contemporary park tends to be focused on getting rid of the old assumption that parks have to be 'pastoral' and, at least in the United States, Olmstedian: 'the pastoral park is obsolete', writes John Beardsley. Another American critic complained, in the same vein, that 'Conventions of landscape practice and representation are thick with the sediment of habit and tradition', identifying the culprits as 'the early eighteenth-century English garden, the harbinger of the picturesque landscape'. A sediment of habit and tradition is one thing; a use of traditions and social habits is another, and the two have engaged in several skirmishes. The Dutch landscape architect Adriaan Geuze argued that 'there is absolutely no need for parks anymore, because all the nineteenth-century problems have been solved and a new type of city has been created. The park and greenery have become worn-out clichés.'[5] That modernist bravado has been challenged, at least implicitly, by different and ingenious 'takes' on 'worn-out greenery' (Downsview Park, in particular),[6] and even by Geuze's own more recent work. In 2010 he proposed an extensive, 40-acre parkland for Governor's Island in New York Harbor that includes 'green' lawns and sheep (so much for the obsolescence of the pastoral), a grand promenade that will eventually encircle the island, flowerbeds, the by-now customary playing fields, artificial hillocks and a veritable anthology of up-to-date modern follies – a 'hammock grove' where people can take a nap, a grotto, marshlands, a café, large areas set aside for private development and carefully plotted vistas towards landmarks around the island, like the Statue of Liberty. This ambitious design will apparently require a huge budget ($41.5 million for the first phase and $220 million for the second). Beyond the finances is also the issue of whom it will serve – are we talking New Yorkers, tourists or landscape architects needing a fresh field to hoe?[7] By contrast, the Parque Ecológico de Xochimilco in Mexico City by Mario Schjetnan (illus. 55), from the late 1980s, clearly addresses both its local culture and those who will use it, with a visitors' centre, shops, sports, commercial nurseries, demonstration gardens for locally grown plants and the largest flower garden in Mexico City. The design is bold, its formal elements decisive and brightly coloured, and it has restored canals and 3,000 hectares of surviving islands, through which yellow and red coloured *trajineras*, or gondolas, are poled between the *chinampas* or man-made islands (Xochimilco means 'the fertile terrain where flowers grow').[8] These canals and rectangular islands (constructed by anchoring reed mats on which soil is piled) date back to the tenth century and were declared a UNESCO World Heritage site in 1987. The park has also restored wetlands that provide diverse habitats for birds, while seven stone aqueducts release recycled, cleansed water into its lake. It is, despite its antiquity, a park of astonishing modernity.

Yet no lists, even severely limited ones, nor yet theoretical pronouncements, can do more than signal the immense effort that has been put into contemporary park-making. What, then, is useful is to focus on a cluster of six very different parks that reveal recent formulations of this type of garden: two parks in New York: Four Freedoms Park, Brooklyn Bridge Park; then Freshkills on Staten Island, Parco Portello in Milan, Parc del Clot in Barcelona and Parc du Sausset outside Paris. They all involve public and private financing as well as encouraging individuals or communities to find appropriate spaces, for they respond to locality and therefore to frequent visitations. They also confront many of the old and new possibilities of garden-making, and all play with the inherited legacies and forms of garden-making (earthworks, *allées*, geometry, narratives). Four Freedoms Park opened in 2012, though it was long in the making; the Brooklyn Bridge Park came into use gradually from 2009. Neither are particularly large sites, unlike Freshkills, Downsview or the earlier example of Bos Park in Amsterdam; yet size somehow seems of great importance to designers, not least because an extent of territory offers opportunities for innovation.[9] Four Freedoms is 4 acres, Brooklyn Bridge Park is 85 acres; however, size does not necessarily ensure an innovative and imaginative design.

Brooklyn Bridge Park, designed by Michael Van Valkenburgh in collaboration with the

Brooklyn Bridge Park Corporation, occupies over a mile along the East River facing lower Manhattan; it has been opening in stages since 2009 and in the summer of 2014 was two-thirds complete. By the end of the twentieth century the site had become a land of rotting piers and muddy wasteland below Brooklyn Heights, but before that it was a vibrant port, where Herman Melville, Walt Whitman and other 'crowds of water-gazers' enjoyed the sea. The new park reclaims five piers south of the Bridge for a soccer field, a rollerskating rink, a small sandy beach, a bird sanctuary, a picnic peninsula and a cove to welcome kayaks. There are lawns, long benches, tables, eat-ing places, shady spots, trails through a freshwa-ter marsh created from rainwater, a constructed New England meadow (still in process), a water hole with plashing jets (illus. 56) and a water slide for children, a spiral pool, large boulders at the water's edge, still some former piles jutting out of the water (illus. 57) and, above all, views over the water towards Ellis Island, the Statue of Liberty and, closer, to Manhattan. A sign says 'No swim-ming or wading', but the kids (apparently) ignore it. The park is wholly 'artificial', an impressive act of imagination and invention; but as a neighbour said, 'I want a bit of nature that feels like nature even if it's man-made nature'. A bouncing Squibb

56 Brooklyn Bridge Park, photograph 2014.

57 Brooklyn Bridge Park.

Bridge of planks and cables leads high over the expressway to Brooklyn Heights (though when I was there it had been closed for repair – too much bouncing?).

Connected with the variety of activities here, Brooklyn Bridge Park also planned to establish some residential housing at the southern end of the park near Pier 6; in a complex hybrid of public–private financing, the city and the state required the park to be self-financing, and these residential, along with commercial, developments would produce the revenue for operating costs and long-term maintenance. But it transpired that New York finances turned out to be better than expect-

ed and not all the high-end residential income would be needed for the park, so it was decided to bring in some affordable housing (which heaven knows is needed in that city). But the move has prompted a battle between those who argue for a 'community . . . to look more like [the one] we're in' and a Foundation called 'People for Green Space' that looks more to the affluent who value their equity as well as the views ('the wrong [low-income housing] in the wrong place'). The lawsuits – this America, after all – continue; but it is sad that just when park-makers have, after 150 years, managed to achieve parks for everybody through strategic design thinking and social

58 Four Freedoms Park, Roosevelt Island, New York City, photograph 2014.

advocacy, the debate resumes; as a supporter said, 'the debate is at times like the park. Sometimes it's a little loud, sometimes it is a little raucous, but at the end of the day, it's necessary.'[10]

The design for a very different site, Four Freedoms Park, dates to 1973–4 when it was designed by Louis I. Kahn. Built posthumously and opened almost 40 years later, it occupies the southern end of Roosevelt Island in the East River, and is dedicated, as was Lawrence Halprin's FDR Memorial in Washington, DC, to Franklin D. Roosevelt.[11] Aerial views of Four Freedoms Park show an elongated, tight wedge of lawn, flanked by lines of trees, descending to a box-like platform

of white granite; the whole park is seated in an apron of boulders down both sides of the island. But the problem with aerial views is that nobody experiences parks that way unless they are in a helicopter (illus. 58, 59).

At the north entrance, past the ruins of the nineteenth-century Renwick quarantine hospital, visitors see a line of five copper beeches between the fenced-off ruin and an impressive granite staircase, 100 ft wide, leading upwards; tops of linden trees in pairs can be glimpsed atop the structure before you climb the steps. On either side of the stairs are level walkways that lead down on each side of the main structure, which descends to meet

59 Four Freedoms Park, Roosevelt Island, New York City.

the two pairs of walks at the far end (so it can be accessed by the disabled, suitably given FDR's polio). At the top of the stairway you discover the base of the narrow triangle of grass, and then walk down one of the gravel *allées* under the trees to the box-like structure. Here a gigantic head of Roosevelt in a niche greets you. Once inside the three-sided box of towering 36-ton blocks, the rear wall of that niche is inscribed with the speech in which Roosevelt promised the four freedoms – freedom of speech and worship, freedom from want and fear. Turning from the inscription, not cut deeply enough to be read from very far away, the visitor confronts a view of downtown

Manhattan and, to the right, the tower of the United Nations Headquarters, where one hopes that the same four freedoms are sustained. The final element is a kind of haha, over which the river is seen; when I was there it was roped off and guards prevented people from descending to that last platform (a railing would spoil the view but it would also make it safer and be in line with current codes).

It is an unusual park for New York, small yet not exactly a pocket park – though inserted into the river, as the island is into the city. It is also austere in design, in the sense that within the blank walls of the box, the only invitation is to meditate on the inscription and its four freedoms (for nothing else is there); maybe one recognizes its adjacency to the United Nations. The blocks of granite that form the room are separated by only a 1-inch gap, not enough to glimpse the river outside. (Granite was not Kahn's first thought: he had projected steel and then concrete before being required to accept granite). The lawn itself does not invite strollers, though there is no prohibition against it, yet it is something of a relief to return down one of the side walkways, watch the passing boats on the river, be tempted by the gravel apron with its hint of a path along the water (this *is* prohibited, though I have seen people explore it), and be absorbed again by the Gothic ruin isolated behind steel fences with notices that say the structure is unstable; an original idea was to bring a channel of water across the island at this point to make the park itself an island.

Forty years between design and implementation make Four Freedoms Park almost seem like an 'exercise in conservation'.[12] The 'Room and a Garden', in Kahn's words from 1973, had at first been much more intricate – a circle inside a square – and described by Kahn as consisting of four elements: room with statue, garden, 'House of the Garden', and grove. These were modified severely as Kahn and his landscape architect, Harriet Pattison, edited the design and brought it within the designated budget. Many determinations later, the garden house below the green lawn has gone, but the minimalist wedge of grass and the *allées* of trees survived Kahn's ruthless deconstruction of his earlier plans, and

Pattison brought in the idea of the giant stairway (inspired by Versailles).

The saga of this park that the archives at the University of Pennsylvania narrate, and the process by which it passed through the hands of other architects and landscape architects to emerge in the present shape, including fundraising in the twenty-first century, are not of course what visitors see. What we do see, even without the benefit of the archives, is a room open to the sky, a kind of amphitheatre at the prow of the island, and a somewhat solemn silence within, first down the *allées* and the perspectival lawn that gradually focuses on the bust and then the room behind it with its theatre of private meditations.

It is a moving space, as much for its dedication to FDR as its isolation in the midst of the river (it is easily reached by inhabitants of Roosevelt Island, but takes more effort to drive from Queens or take the cable car over from Manhattan). It also raises lots of issues about modern park-making, and how garden ideas percolate through to their formation. For the park sits awkwardly between what today tends to be called the 'discourse' of park-making and how parks are appreciated by their visitors: between, on the one hand, what contemporary landscape architects need to say about parks (though not Kahn) and, on the other, the ongoing admiration and celebration of parks by many different users in many different places.

Over the last twenty years or so, architects have accumulated a dense and often arcane language (both verbal and visual) to identify and reformulate how parks should be designed, boosted by a series of major competitions and the making of contemporary parks worldwide. But almost all of their commentaries sidestep *how* the new parks might be used (for visitors respond to the place itself and not to any theoretic download or indeed, as with Four Freedoms Park, to the narrative history of its design). However, that response to the afterlife of parks is hard to access.

Attempts to chronicle visitors' reactions to the world of parks, some new but most well-established, are provided in Sarah Pickstone's *Park Notes* (2014) and by Catie Marron's *City Parks: Public Places, Private Thoughts* (2013). The first anthologizes responses to just one site, Regent's Park in London, and chronicles women who walked there (Virginia Woolf, Elizabeth Bowen, Stevie Smith) and their writings about it: its 'magical strangeness' for Angela Carter, how time changes rhythm for Marina Warner, or how there are 'patterns everywhere' for Ali Smith. Marron's anthology, alongside some often elegant photographs by Oberto Gili (though on his own confession, not one to photograph exteriors, and not always images that tell you much about the park if you don't already know it), invites reflections on a variety of parks from famous people, not always the clientele that parkmakers might envisage (Bill and Hillary Clinton in Dumbarton Oaks). The reader is not given any indication of who the various designers were; this total avoidance of issues of design makes *City Parks*, and indeed *Park Notes*, starkly different from how landscape architects portray their work, but it does afford glimpses into what visitors might discover.

The parks discussed vary considerably, not least because of the range of cultural examples invoked, yet are unsurprising in the options that groups or individuals desire and the range of their associations, like the strong sense of 'humanity' in gardens – observed in Cairo by Ahdaf Soueif, but registered by many others – or in paintings of people by John Soane or Edward Hopper, invoked by André Aciman on the High Line in New York. Sometimes, but rarely, you have to pay a fee to enter: Cairo is one, as likewise the Temple of Heaven in Beijing and the Jardins de l'Imaginaire in France. Otherwise things are what you might expect – in Cairo there are bubbling fountains, necessary in the heat; in some parks you can get pleasantly but not hopelessly lost; security is now conspicuous and necessary. Some recommendations on park use are offered: in cities where other green spaces have been ruthlessly eroded, parks should be of easy access; the absence of traffic is vital, as is the chance to go slow, to attend to scents and different sounds, many changes of light, or places from which to take a view. Spaces should satisfy the introverted, but for extrovert visitors there will be amphitheatres and the chance of various entertainments. Statues of eminent worthies are almost mandatory.

But the responses to other, older parks in Marron's *City Parks* (for example, Gorky Park, Moscow; Berlin's Tiergarten; Calcutta's Maidan military ground, cleared by the British so nobody could hide;[13] or Prospect Park in Brooklyn) suggest that parks of any period can be inventive and resourceful, and that different cultures do similar things differently. People coming from urban or rural living spaces have a very varied 'take' on how parks are to be read. In *I Capture the Castle* (1948), Dodie Smith wrote that 'It came to me that Hyde Park has never belonged to London – that it has always been, in spirit, a stretch of countryside; and that it links the London of all periods together most magically – by remaining forever unchanged at the heart of an ever-changing town.' The Luxembourg Gardens in Paris, we read in *City Parks*, is neither 'a garden, nor is it a municipal park', which seems odd, as both garden effects – fountains, *allées*, even planting – are there and they serve the locality (as well as visiting tourists) with tennis players, t'ai chi and children sailing model ships around the pond.

The city motto of Chicago is 'Urbs in Horto' rather than 'the garden in the city'. Today our conventional understanding of the dialogues between nature and culture is complicated by formal inventions in modern technology or ecology and by misunderstandings of landscape architecture itself. People may think that a visit to Central Park is an immersion in 'nature'; it could well be that, since for utter urbanists the only 'nature' they see is on the TV screen; some may even glimpse countryside and indulge in its facsimile of rurality. Geuze's vision for Governor's Island is a wholly factitious world of invented nature, and (if it gets built) people in 50 years may think – and why not? – that it is a stretch of countryside, as Central Park seemed to be in the late nineteenth century.

But nothing that I read in park responses or in architectural proposals makes me really think that 'people don't want parks.' A larger and more demographic sampling of experience in parks (of all sorts) suggests a cluster of elements and even requirements. One expects trees and grass, shrubs and plants, and sometimes these can be more than just routine, municipal planting; indeed it is impossible to think of a park without these elements. Water always makes a park, whether as a lake or with fountains; one wishes for adequate, even inviting, park furniture – from benches and individual chairs to good lighting and elegant rubbish receptacles, and with paths that allow access for the disabled, legally mandated now in many countries. While parks may be clearly separated from their urban surroundings, we value thresholds and entrances that signal our entry into them; in large parks, it is always good to see beyond their bounds, for prospects outside make one register where visitors are; but equally, different views and prospects within, different glimpses or invitations to explore, are important for they endorse our recognition of variety in large parklands. While Olmsted, and the makers of the smaller late nineteenth-century parks in New York City, made fresh milk available for nursing mothers, these days the provision of food is almost essential, whether within the park itself, or adjacent to it (in Paris, parcs Bercy and André Citroën have eating places in their immediate vicinity). Sometimes people are allowed to cook for themselves; barbecues in Berlin's Tiergarten, though supposedly confined to certain areas, get wildly out of hand.[14]

There are in fact rules for parks, many of which are posted at the entrance – an ancient system that dates to Roman times, when parks displayed by-laws for their use, known as the *lex hortorum*.[15] One expects a variety of opportunities as well as prohibitions (not walking on the grass – a boring impediment in the Luxembourg Gardens in Paris, but actively encouraged in Bercy and André Citroën); instructions of where to let dogs roam freely. We want places or areas that are more public, where the elements of the landscape promote or even shape behaviour, and occasions for privacy: thus spaces for solitary introspection as well as spaces where we can watch others in the park – that fascinating exchange between us watching others and them watching us, an informal and improvised theatre. The variety of activity and social interchange is vital: walking, jogging, skating, birdwatching and other impromptu activities beyond tennis, foot- and volleyball, cricket and baseball. None of those are likely to be accomplished or enjoyed on concrete or asphalt, and they should take place without pre-empting others' enjoyment (occasionally areas of large parks are reserved for special events, like concerts, fashion shows and theatrical performances). And in large parks with multiple entrances, it is always useful to offer plans at entrances to orientate new visitors, a subtle but important way in which the educational value of park use can be deployed. For the educational impulse behind making parks was foremost in Olmsted's work to encourage good citizenship in a country of immigrants,[16] and this idea still constitutes, often very deliberately, a major role in modern park-making: it can promote the importance of physical activity, learning

about plants and how they change in different hours of the day or flourish in different ecological zones, and (sometimes) seeing public art, even learning to respond, if you are not a designer, to the designs themselves. One also hopes that new parks are positioned to encourage access from surrounding neighbourhoods that lack them – the Jardin Atlantique, established over the Gare Montparnasse in Paris, provided an open space that was lacking in that *arrondissement*, as did the latest public park, Parc Clichy-Batignolles in the north of the city. Parcs Bercy and André Citroën were established at opposite ends of the city (in the same way that the bois de Boulogne and de Vincennes were exploited to the west and the east of the city) with very different user demographics in mind.

Large parks outside cities have room for various activities and, perhaps strangely, less interest in new inventions. Freshkills on the eastern edge of Staten Island is, however, adventurous in two respects:[17] it deliberately envisages the development of the former landfill over 50 years and responds to the local landscape of creeks, wetlands and lowland; and it embraces historical as well as topographical circumstances. The landfill was in fact reopened to take the debris from the Twin Towers after 9/11 and that material was sculptured into a pair of long ridges or mounds for the September 11 Earthwork Monument; from the new parkland there are views of new towers rising at Ground Zero. The envisaged *longue durée* of the park's design – a tactic that Field Operations also employed for their unsuccessful proposal for

Downsview – makes sense, for it involves visitors in understanding landscape architecture, for even 'nature' cannot be established overnight. Equally it allows a significant wildlife to establish itself; it gives occasion for the designers to respond to community wishes as it establishes boardwalks, sports fields and tracks for walkers and routes for bicycles; it allows time to search for funding, and to test the overall vision against the developing uses of the site's visitors. But it also casts its bread on the political waters of New York's administration that is unable, alas, to see 50 years ahead or to protect that perspective.

Large parks pose both managerial and ecological challenges, which necessarily concern designers. This was faced deliberately by the large-scale Parc Départementale du Sausset (200 hectares) to the north of Paris, through which pass the trains to Charles de Gaulle airport. It was created by Michel and Claire Corajoud from 1980,

on a vast agricultural plateau, to include forests, meadows, lakes, herds of grazing goats and rare birds (illus. 60). Close to the city (30 minutes by train) at the town of Aulnay-sous-Bois, it offers millions the chance to respond to its environmental and historical riches. The overall plan shows an intricate network of paths, many aligned on the boundaries of fields and old roads, one of which marked a former route that took workers from these villages to the centre of Paris; 'it reawakens', writes Corajoud, 'at each step the memory of the old earth' (illus. 61). The forest edges are irregular and strangely un-French when you are down in them, though the overall plan looks like a seventeenth-century estate with a Baroque play of geometry, clearings within clearings of woodland (illus. 62). On the edges of the forested zones are some usual features of a country estate – a labyrinth, *potager*, vineyards, marshlands and lake, a garden of American plants brought to Europe or

60 Parc du Sausset, north of Paris, photograph 2014.

61 Parc du Sausset.

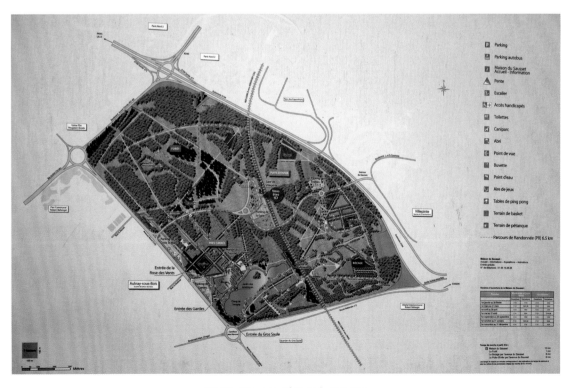

62 On-site map of Parc du Sausset.

deposited here by birds, a *bocage* (grove or copse) – a historical reminder of how gardens emerged out of an agriculture of small fields, hedgerows and ponds. But there is also an experimental forestry station, with a cluster of water towers like a modern château in the distance. Many of the pathways are given names, a hint too of earlier usages, but they can also guide modern visitors through the huge site; some dotted lines specifically mark routes on maps and are marked with their various distances. Amenities are signalled throughout: see-saws, water fountains, toilets, cafés (*buvettes*), dog-parks, vistas, *parkings* and places where steps have to be negotiated or slopes are

steep; also indicated are various areas for sport: ping-pong, basketball, *pétanque*.

Among the extensive new urbanism of Barcelona, where architects, landscape architects and artists have created a series of new parks following neglect under General Franco and in anticipation of the 1992 Olympic Games, is the small municipal Parc del Clot, created in 1985–6.[18] The city itself is a mix of medieval, Baroque and neoclassical buildings, streets are lined by plane trees or palms, there are flowers and shrubs everywhere (a 'mixture of formality and spontaneity'), and the park spaces are part streets, part outdoor rooms. There are so many

63 Parc del Clot, Barcelona, 1985–6.

parks – from Antoni Gaudí's startling and restored Parc Güell to Richard Serra's Plaça de la Palmera, created with architects Pedro Barragán and Bernardo de Sola – where radical and often abstract forms and modern materials usurp and transform traditional garden elements of pools, labyrinths, gravel walks, ruins, terracing, groves, amphitheatres and playgrounds.

The revitalized space for Parc del Clot, small as it is (27,000 sq. metres), does the same. It takes over, as have many new parks, some railway workshops on the edge of a village that has now been absorbed into the city. A factory chimney, a dramatic facade of arches, sometimes curtained off with falling water (illus. 63), and a ruined industrial hallway without its roof, with a modern sculpture of the 'Rites of Spring' by the American Bryan Hunt (illus. 64) – these form the northern, garden segment; from benches spectators watch the game of *petanca* (or *pétanque* in Catalan) under the trees. An artificial grassy mound skirted by a belt of umbrella pines shares this landscaped area. And this is separated by a diagonal, raised walkway with steel pergola arches from the square, into which two flights of steps descend to the original basement level of the factory. Tall lamp pillars illuminate the square for football at all hours.

There is much to learn from Parco Portello in Milan. Created by Charles Jencks, along with landscape architects Andreas Kipar and Margherita Brianza of the Milan-based office LAND, this is Jencks's first public park.[19] Begun in 2002, it has evolved over ten years, and Jencks's narration of the stages of his thinking, his necessary dialogues

64 Parc del Clot, Barcelona.

with patrons and the changes he made in the design are recorded in sketches, drawings and text. These are essential to an understanding of his achievement, but they also engage with why and how we respond to the site itself, even if forearmed with his own account of its process and its final spatial clarity.

During that ten-year process, Jencks composed 'Some Lessons of City Parks' (p. 66); most are similar to ideas touted in this chapter, but some seem particularly relevant here and local. Beyond getting people of all sorts, locals above all, to visit the park frequently ('high public use'), there was the need to supply composure and security, which can be ensured by visibility within an urban park ('seeing ways into and out of a space') and with many entrances and exits; the 'formal layout of the whole should be clear', but small sections of 'different character and quality' are essential. A park must be a 'good theatre', where the 'art of nature and the nature of art' should make it 'an institution essential to spiritual and communal life'.

For this 'theatre', Jencks has devised a scenario of forms, narratives and metaphors. Some of this is strong, visible and palpable: the park is raised on a platform and, after ascending the staircase, we are confronted with three artificial mounds: one cone-shaped with ascending paths, facing a curving ridge which holds within its embrace an elliptical basin of water; this then turns in a counter curve towards the city to the south. Below the ridge and between it and the city is the straight line of the 'Time Garden', as well as a children's garden.

The rising mounds in a flat Milanese topography are conspicuous – Milan's Gothic cathedral has been compared to a dolomitic outcrop, so Jencks's mounds might prefigure the Alpine hills to the north, for Portello is sited on the northern ring road from where travellers may head northwards. More specifically, as Federico de Molfetta notes, it echoes another – Monte Stella, less than a kilometre away from Portello: both were landfills. Pietro Bottoni made his a mountain of rubble from the buildings destroyed in the war, while Jencks used excess earth and rubble from an indus-

trial site and excavations for a new neighbourhood.

The park, raised above the busy city, provides an acoustic buffer within the mounds against the adjacent ring-road traffic and the nearby housing, so one of its hopes is to encourage peace, time for reflection and slowness. The slowness is apt in many ways, for the park is raised on the former Alfa Romeo works, where speed was of the essence, and the busy, frantic, industrial city is also a context against which the park needs to respond, to hold itself apart, to give humans time to slow down. This is achieved in part by inviting walkers to climb and descend the mounds, guarded by fences that steer their ascents, and to discover and pause to ponder on the summit of the conical mound a steel sculpture of DNA (a similar sculpture can be found at Jencks's The Garden of Cosmic Speculation in Scotland).

So the forms are clear and striking, but the metaphors are either occluded or, down the 'Time Walk', richly articulated: slowness as well as thinking are essential, along with a constant exposure to the park to learn how to respond to it. The park's theme is *ritmo del tempo* (rhythm of time), time in its many aspects. It is easy enough to ponder, when climbing the mounds, what lies underneath them – not just the rubble, but the stories that go with the decline and fall of local industry. The conical mound is thus denominated Present Time (illus. 65). The first section of the double curve is Prehistory (illus. 66), and the final counter curve is History, for it confronts the long narrative of the city of Milan.

65 Parco Portello, Milan: the Present Time Mound, 2002–12.

So history as time is clearly present, if unmarked. By contrast the 'Time Walk' situated below History is busy and 'talkative'. Time here is strongly linear, but it passes through five circles (illus. 67) that echo the circular pathways up the cone and the zigzag ascent towards Prehistory. Both the straight 'corridor' and the circles it crosses are labelled with clusters of ideas inscribed underfoot, on bright red benches and on steel dividers along the time line. The central pathway is formed by a dizzy mixture of black-and-white rectangles that 'mark the rotation of the earth,

66 Parco Portello, Milan: the Prehistory Time Mound.

turning every 24 hours in its night and day cycle'; alongside it, black and white pebbles like a Zen-like 'dry water' are laid in a zigzag (*rizzada*) down the long 'corridor'; they are the heartbeats of individual human time. Underfoot, too, are rebuses that signal the different rhythms of linear and cyclical time – geological, yearly, seasonal, moon cycles, sun and moon – a chance to condense time by offering visual representations of *ritmi del tempo* and their syncopation.

To 'venture on this metaphorical walk in time' invites two kinds of walking: one is simply to be dazzled by the poetry and ingenuity of ornament, pattern, colour, planting; an alternative is to ponder and decipher the metaphors to be found there. One approach is obvious and striking; the other dense and time-consuming. One is quick enough, the other slow. Jencks cites the Latin adage *Festina lente* (make haste slowly), and the assumption is that the best parks rely on this double strategy, however busy and 'talkative' they may be. There is always, with any design, a need to respond, to think, to recognize what would not be there if the designer had not intervened, to find what is implicit in his/her inventions. But there is also, especially for the visitor with but one opportunity to be there, a relish for the immediate impact.

67 Parco Portello: the Time Walk.

Portello packs a lot into a relatively small space and much into the mind. When large spaces are either not available or are far too expensive to fund, small parks, whether linear or pocket, are more plausible these days; the extent of some more recent parks is also less than 'big'. We can continue to enjoy the Bos Park in Amsterdam, or Central Park in New York; but the future – give or take the money that can fund and complete Freshkills, Downsview or Portello – is unlikely to be with the 'large parks'. So what of small parks – pocket, linear and even vertical?

68, 69 Promenade Plantée, Paris, and the High Line, New York City.

SIX

SMALL PARKS: POCKETS, LINEAR AND VERTICAL

It is perhaps pointless to decide when a park is small (pockets as opposed to portmanteaux). Small parks discussed here, as well as things like roof gardens, are not on the scale of Richmond Park, Central Park or Bos Park in Amsterdam; the acreage of parks can, in part, determine size, but they depend ultimately on the activities they accommodate, the variety of experience on offer and those who are their intended users. It is unlikely that pocket or linear parks will feature courts for basketball, baseball or tennis or pitches for cricket; jogging may be feasible, but crowds on the High Line in New York militate against it, though the much longer Promenade Plantée in Paris makes that possible (illus. 68, 69). The Jardin Atlantique in the same city, constructed over the Gare Montparnasse (so, in effect, a roof garden), has tennis courts on two of its edges, but the middle-aged couple I saw jogging there had to circulate every five minutes; yet it is, for its size and location between high-rise apartment blocks, pocket-sized, even while its scenario of Atlantique-focused activities – children's games, 'caves' to explore, a walkway behind the 'cliffs' – provides residents of this *arrondissement* with a welcome interlude in a busy part of Paris.[1]

There are basically three kinds of small parks. 'Pocket parks', as we shall see, was the term devised to describe a couple of urban infills in New York City in 1967 and 1971, where a gap-tooth effect between houses was remedied by creating small parklets to fill the empty spaces. More recently, a different mode of infilling has proved attractive: a necklace or string of small linear parks that may take back a disused railway line, or bring together a sequence of small urban areas by linking them together in a system of open spaces and zones for various activities. Given that big parks are less and less likely to be created (finances proving a problem, even when sufficient open space is available), the resumption of useful, but currently moribund, city lots to create a string of multi-purpose open spaces can both regenerate small neighbourhoods and tie them together. Another kind of small park is vertical – non-enterable, obviously – but a green relief in the cliffs of modern city blocks, and somewhat of a surprise to find that a garden can climb up a facade.

What perhaps started the modern interest in these small insertions into urban life was two pockets parks in New York City: Paley Park on 53rd

Street between Madison and Fifth Avenues, designed by Zion & Breen in 1967, and Greenacre Park on 51st Street between Second and Third Avenues in 1971, designed by Sasaki, Dawson, DeMay Associates, with Masao Kinoshita as lead designer and involving Hideo Sasaki and Tom Wirth. An American friend in New York also calls them 'vest' parks (that is, waistcoats with pockets). Though different, each is inserted into the street fabric where a building would have stood.[2] Steps at Greenacre rise from the street under a heavy pergola (illus. 70); inside are plants in pots, green chairs and tables between the pseudo-quincunx of twelve trees. The right-hand wall of heavy granite blocks, with low benches, overlooks a rill that cascades from the street down to the pool below the wall of water that plashes over irregular lumps of granite, bounding off others, and descends into the basin. This pool is lower than the main space, with a line of plants across the top, and steps down one side lead to seats in front of the waterfall. A raised area down the left-hand side of the park under another pergola allows one to observe the falls and the plaza below, and find some shelter if it rains. There is a strong sense of theatre about Greenacre: the scenery of the falls, the sunken 'orchestra pit' and the 'balcony' along one side.

70 Greenacre Park, New York, 1971.

71 Paley Park, New York, 1967.

Paley Park is more simple (illus. 71), with its waterfall occupying most of the rear wall and 'framed' like a painting; it blocks more of the apartments behind it than at Greenacre, where one saw the balconies of adjacent buildings immediately above the waterfall. Four steps at Paley lead *up* to the pool, so the waterfall is seen as the climax of the space. Plants climb both lateral walls; on the cobbled floor are low pots, wire chairs and tables beneath the trees. A small refreshment kiosk at the rear, by the street, provides refreshment, and in general both spaces are used for local workers taking their lunch. Once you enter the pocket

at either Greenacre or Paley Park, the sound of the rushing water drowns out the Manhattan street noise.

Another key feature of both the New York pockets is the adoption of individual seating that lets people sit alone or in groups for conversation, a more flexible arrangement than long lengths of benches, however elegant – as on either side of the Mall in Central Park, or the curving green imitations of Olmsted's benches by Martha Schwartz in Jacob Javits Plaza. (These have been replaced, but it was a design I liked: because the benches looked outward around a circle, one sat with neighbours slightly behind to left and right, which encouraged either aloofness or active participation as one had to turn sideways to talk). The idea of individual chairs came originally from the movable items in French gardens like the Luxembourg in Paris, but was brilliantly adopted by Hanna/Olin when they refurbished Bryant Park in New York; for, as well as opening that park to the street and establishing a threshold that both welcomed visitors and made the place safer than it had once been, the simple and easily moveable chairs have allowed a wonderful range of social activity (illus. 72).

Pocket parks have spurred many imitations, or what the *New York Times* called 'urban oases': subway entrances and sunken plazas, passageways in trouble spots, even Bryant Park.[3] Inspired by Paley Park and following a competition in 1979, a former parking lot in Philadelphia was designed by Delta Group and John Collins, a local landscape architect and professor, whose name was

72 Moveable chairs in Bryant Park, New York, 1991.

given to the park: the small space celebrates the native landscape of the Delaware River Basin, with fountain, pavements, entry, and sculptures of migrating birds and turtles to represent marshlands; rectangular pools reflect the sky. In Glendale, California, a Chess Park took over an underused passageway between retail stores and a parking garage: five giant lamps, abstractions of five chess pieces (King, Bishop, Pawn and so on) illuminate the 4,500 sq. ft after dark, but the space is available for others as well as members of the local chess club. In New York the Tudor City Greens, originally a common area surrounded by apartments, after trials and tribulations (par for the course in Manhattan real estate) was gifted to the

Trust for Public Land and since 1988 has been restored (new lighting, pathways, seating and the original wrought-iron fencing) and volunteers, along with professional landscape care, sustain it. A similar insertion between new apartments in lower Manhattan is Tear Drop Park (2004), by Michael Van Valkenburgh (illus. 73); it seems more extensive than the original space would have been if left empty, with its children's playground, a lawn, rock slabs lining the pathways, and the huge bluestone/ice wall, reminiscent of the throughways cut through upstate New York, that freezes in winter. Isamu Noguchi's California Scenario (early 1980s) was inserted between skyscrapers and blank garage walls to offer an abstract

representation of California landscapes: an epitome of desert lands, a forest walk, a waterfall or
'Water Source' that feeds a river winding across
the small plaza, sculptures in homage to the lima
bean (the original agriculture on the site) or to
the pulsing energy of 'Water Use' (a celebratory,
maybe ironic, homage to California's much-
needed water); this 'scenario' allows visitors to
stage their own understanding of the state. In
Dallas, Dan Kiley's Fountain Place (1985) is a
cool oasis within clusters of banks and hotels,
where a foaming sequence of water runs down
the slope, past bald cypresses in planting pods
to a plaza with tables and chairs. Kiley saw this,

in his own words, as an 'urban swamp', or 'a
complicated experience of nature so intense that
it would be almost super-natural'; it too provides
a 'scenario' of a Texan landscape. Water can always
enliven small spaces, and many small parks, like
Waterfall Park in Seattle by Sasaki, Dawson and
DeMay, manage to do so. The small garden in
Paris, though now renamed Parc Diderot, in the
vast and uncompromising high-rises of HQs,
corporate offices and apartments of La Défense
in Paris, has an abundance of (recirculating) water
that plunges down the hillside, under two bridges
where visitors can sit and dangle their legs in it
(illus. 74).

73 Michael Van Valkenburg, Tear Drop Park, Lower Manhattan, New York, 2004.

74 Parc Diderot at La Défense, Paris.

But so-called 'pocket parks' were not entirely new, though the sartorial reference may be. Crowded urban towns and cities from the Middle Ages onwards sponsored courtyards, both utilitarian and social: Venice has its *cortile*, usually with a wellhead through which to draw water from a cistern below that would be gathered from surrounding rooftops; each Venetian parish also enjoyed a square, called a *campo* (that is, a meadow, and most not paved until the nineteenth century).[4] In the eighteenth century Abbé Marc-Antoine Laugier recommended that every public place should be like a clearing in a forest. Since Laugier saw 'nature' as the origin of all architectures (like the primitive hut), his idea of a 'forest clearing' finds its recent counterpart in those small urban insertions where trees and flowers and other garden-like elements flourish within the city 'forest'. Major edifices often enjoy open spaces in front of them: we see it in Rome before the Pantheon (with a fountain but no garden), and today it has become ubiquitous in modern cities, where designers like Martha Schwartz's square before the Law Courts in Minnesota, or that in Jacob Javits (reworked now by Michael Van Valkenburgh), have filled the spaces with gardens or references to them.

In the late nineteenth century New York sought to create small parks in the darkest, most impoverished ghettos of the city to combat typhus and tempt young people out from cramped and overcrowded tenements.[5] The Small Parks Act of 1887 allocated $1,000,000 annually to clear and form small parks in immigrant neighbourhoods; these were mainly situated in lower Manhattan – at Corlears Hook (8.3 acres) and Hamilton Fish, with, further north, East River and Jefferson Parks (12.5 and 15.4 acres respectively) and Mulberry Bend designed by Calvert Vaux (2.7 acres) – the 'most dangerous and pestiferous ulcer' in the city according to the Sanitary Super-intendant. Their main function was to provide opportunities for exercise and relaxation around a central lawn or lawns, which were scattered with trees or flowerbeds and separated, if not protect-ed, from the surrounding streets. Long lines of individual benches backed onto the lawns, pro-tected by low wire fences, for there was no 'walking on the grass'. Most offered opportunities for 'play' or recreation – basketball or football were indicated on the City Parks department plan for Mulberry Bend Park; Tompkins Square Park in the East Village had separate playgrounds for girls and boys. Some eventually had band-stands and concerts. Seward Park, designed by Samuel Parsons with a Roman-inspired gymnasium hippodrome, was deemed the 'Best Equipped in the World', according to *Munsey's Magazine* in 1904. In the early twentieth century, Jefferson Park, unsurprisingly given its name, boasted a farm school, while De Witt Clinton Park had extensive gardens for children to tend. By the late 1890s public baths were incorporated, and by 1906 'mothers' corners' promoted better nursing and nurturing especially for 'young mothers', and milk stations were provided.

Most of these small park designs eschewed anything rectangular, even within oblong city blocks, but over-indulged in elliptical or squished ovals, a gesture, one supposes, to an ill-understood idea of the Picturesque, but a scheme that pro-moted slightly more extensive walks through the park. It is clear from the research by Rachel Iannacone that the design impetus for the New York projects, if not its social thinking, came from Paris, for the issue of *Garden and Forest* from August 1888 contained a plan of a Parisian 'square' – a rectangular space edged with borders of shrubs and flowers and containing two elliptical lawns, each with flowerbeds and a walkway around the paths, that has been illustrated in Adolphe Alphand's *Les Promenades de Paris*.

Parisian 'squares' were one of the most suc-cessful of urban interventions, and they are still being copied. The term derives from Napoleon III, who, after being exiled in London and liking the squares there, asked Baron Haussmann and the landscape architect Alphand to create during the 1860s and '70s similar pockets within the city between the larger system of boulevards. The word 'square' was retained, though it acquired new pro-nunciation and a radically different aspect in the French capital: they were generally smaller than

London squares (see for instance illus. 43) and also less intimate, because London squares were used mainly by the residents of the surrounding houses; in Paris they were more open to the streets and local French inhabitants, which meant that *arrondissements* tended to have their own distinct social feel and quality. Alphand's large folio of his Paris work, *Les Promenades de Paris*, illustrated many of them, and in one engraving (unnumbered) showed six different formats within the larger metropolitan infrastructure; Antoine Grumbach calls these 'squares' the 'leftovers' of Paris, a suitably gastronomic flavour, and they often seemed more congenial than the *grands boulevards*.

The practice of making 'squares' has continued to address areas of cities like Paris that enjoyed few such opportunities: the Square Montholon, south of the Gare du Nord from the 1930s, or in 2000s the recent 'square', though called a garden, the Jardin Damia in the 11th *arrondissement*, designed by Bernard Lassus. Kathryn Gustafson has made two 'squares', the Jardin Rachmaninov at the Quartier de l'Evangile, an early work, and the other in Evry, the Rights of Man Square (illus. 75, 76).[6] All the last three designs bring to the original idea of Paris 'squares' a rich Gardenesque feeling: Lassus, inheriting a much neglected site, took a chance and filled it with curving paths and rich picturesque planting rather than an open

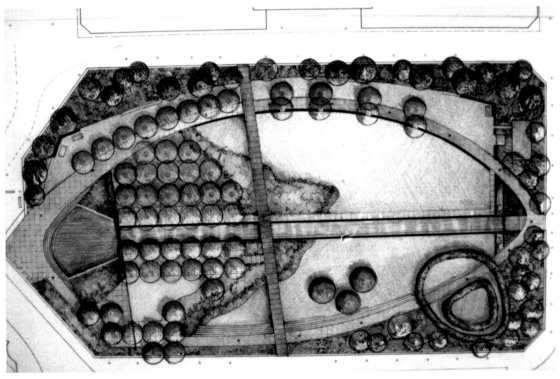

75 Kathryn Gustafson, design for Square Rachmaninov, Quartier de l'Evangile, Paris, 1991.

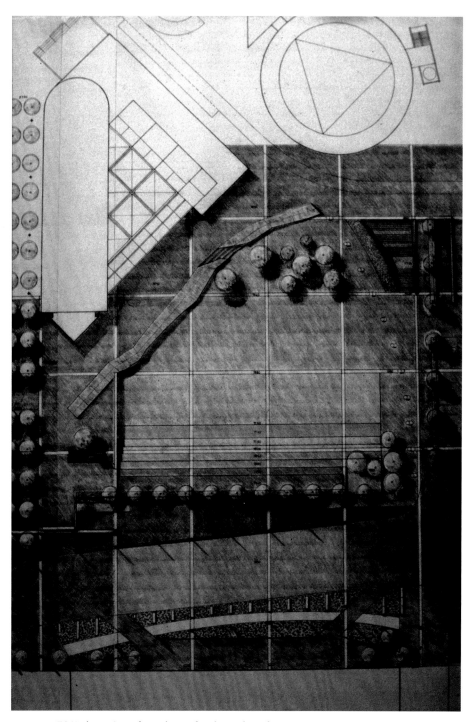

76 Kathryn Gustafson, design for the Rights of Man square, Evry, France, 1991.

and 'safer' park; it has been much respected by its users in a section of Paris without parks. Jardin Rachmaninov, not far from Parc de la Villette and contemporary with both it and Parc de Bercy, invoked geometrical forms – a canal that bisects the space of the slightly squeezed oval and with a deliberately skewed cross axis, jets that spurt horizontally across a water channel, a small pond and a regular *bosquet* (though partly fractured at one point), but with lawns, some hardscape and seating around it that allows the space to function as an amphitheatre. In Evry, a competition in 1989 required a complex insertion into a multi-levelled site with parking, a train station, the city hall and Mario Botta's new cathedral. This 'square' is even more elaborate in its geometry, though still simple and honouring the eponymous 'freedom of expression' in the French constitution, Rights of Man: a long zigzag water-trough, like a Chinese dragon, cuts across the north of the square, with stairs crossing it from the city hall to the station; single lines of trees mark its west and east sides, an equally straight canal crosses at midpoint, while at the southern end a plaza – a *plage des jets* – also features a zone of jetting water or, when empty, a space to be used. One may sit on the edges of the zigzag trough or lean on the *siège* (seat/guard rail) and gaze into the pool and its fountains. Sounds of the fountains can be heard in the parking space below, before motorists climb the stairs and emerge in the southwest corner before the cathedral.

The idea of a 'pocket' has, however, taken on a wholly new life and format – not as small quieter zones within busy cities, but as a thread

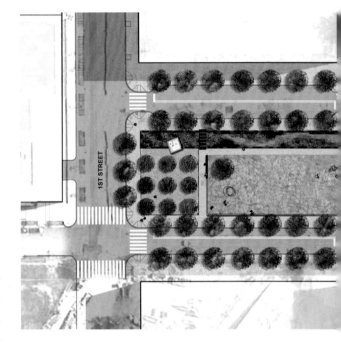

running through them, often on disused railway lines or through derelict and diminished neighbourhoods, along waterfronts, beside disused canals, and even on piers jutting into less frequented waterways. Most are, for size and even opportunities, modest. Early examples were the sequence of three parks that Lawrence Halprin designed for Portland, Oregon, where his different representations of water among groves or in open plazas make the sequence rich and intricate. Yorkville Park in Toronto (minute when compared to the grandiose plans for Downsview) was formed over an excavation for a subway line for which a line of houses was removed. The footprints of the former buildings are rehearsed in a series of 'cabinets', or what one of the designers called 'caskets', where elements of the Ontario landscape are captured in segments of marshlands, botanical collections,

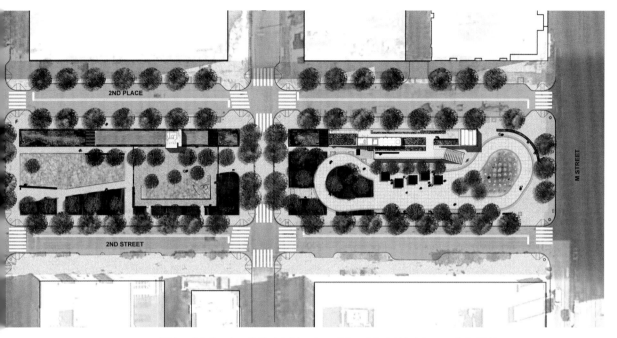

77 Land Collective, Philadelphia, plan of Canal Park, Washington, DC, 2013.

even a huge rock on which people can climb with their portable chairs. No fountain here, except in winter a pergola captures and freezes water descending the wires.

About the same length as Yorkville Park, which occupied a single block, Canal Park fills three blocks over a canal that linked the Anacostia and Potomac Rivers in southeast Washington, DC, and which was eventually paved over (illus. 77). A tedious parking area for idling buses and a contaminated brownfield site has now been transformed into a sequence of three zones: a large lawn for performances and concerts at the northern end, with rental lawn chairs for people to situate themselves where they wish, then a central segment where children can play or markets and fairs can be set up, and finally a fountain and (in winter) a skating area

that can also offer a large gathering place when the fountains are off; adjacent to this is a tavern. Like so many early big parks, created specifically to encourage an emerging citizenship, this part of Washington is looking to define its local inhabitants; for its designer, David Rubin, it would be a park that 'drives development of a neighbourhood', but flexible enough to engage whomever wanted to go there. The design has garnered awards for its embrace of sustainability and its complex infrastructure (an elaborate engineering system that collects and filters water from roofs and other facilities) and it has also raised $28,000,000 from local developers, local associations, corporate donors and federal funds:[7] both are nowadays the measure of financial inventiveness and design success. But what the users see, what they relish in the afterlife of its design and promotion, are the ways it connects people, a new 'machine' (Rubin again) in the garden.

Both Halprin in Portland and Canal Park in Washington extend their narrow insertions through the city in different ways, like small corridors that sometimes open out on either side to pull in, or take views into, adjacent urban 'rooms'. The technique is not entirely new, as Karl Kullmann demonstrates with his twenty scaled maps of examples as small as the Topographie des Terrors, Berlin, to the One North Park, Singapore, or Guadalupe River Park, San Jose, California;[8] some are extremely thin, though they may be thicker at certain points; their lengths range from 0.2 km in Berlin to 3 km in San Jose; also included are the Passeig Marítim, Barcelona, the Mall in Washington, DC, and the Central Waterfront in Toronto. Kullmann terms these parks 'thin', but also says that they have 'thick edges'; indeed, some are 'all edge and no middle'. These long and often narrow threads can be connected to spaces on either side, so he notices how frequent such sideway excursions can be on the different trajectories ('cross-street fragmentation'), as well as what roads cross them from surrounding areas ('side access'). He also notes the different typologies that may inform them, some formal (thickets, stages, other programmatic incidents), and explains them metaphorically as sutures, filters or conduits. While Central Park or Hyde Park accommodate many activities within their large spaces (boating, swimming, ballgames, walking, bicycling and jogging, theatre and entertainment), linear parks tend to be more selective in what events they provide or allow, though they can still continue to draw on some of the usual agenda of park activities. Perhaps more importantly, they initiate fresh social roles: they join city locations hitherto cut off from each other until a linear pathway connects them, emphasize local contexts, encourage businesses just off the pathway, reward local initiatives, in short, find new ways to do what the big nineteenth-century parks aimed to do: embody civic ideas.[9] Such is the mode of the Sagrera Linear Urban park in Barcelona, by West 8, where the 4 km diagonal corridor connects the city to the ocean and widens twice to incorporate orchards and sports facilities and shady gardens, fountains and nodes and points of attraction. The high-speed train route into France is now underground and no longer divides the city, and is especially capable of absorbing historical neighbourhoods, so that small micro parks bring in Sant Andreu, Sant Martí and Parc del Clot.[10]

Linear parks, writes Diana Balmori, are 'the poster child of . . . ecological transformations'.[11] They are not, however, simply a greening of the city or its derelict infrastructure, nor yet a 'return to nature', because much reworking needs to take place – on railway lines the removal of ballast, pollution and illegal dumping, the planting of new trees, and the acknowledgement of a long previous use of herbicides, invasive plants and migrating animals, as described by Balmori in the Farmington Canal master plan for New Haven or that for the Gwynns Falls Trail in Baltimore. The aim is to create a biologically but also socially diverse neighbourhood, responding to the different local cultural and geographical conditions, since a pedestrian or cycle trail can now link what had been discrete sectors. As much effort goes into funding, into growing the relevant communities, both professional and private, as into the landscape work. The same is true, if more so, along denser urban trails.

Edges are, as Kullmann argues, spatially and temporally dynamic. On both the High Line or the Promenade Plantée, both of which raise walkers above the city, our attention is called to left and to right, to distant views or details of adjacent buildings, but in both we have some opportunities to escape the city below but also descend into it at various places. On ground-level routes, there is more flexibility, boundaries between the linear and the adjacent thick edges are blurred, invitations and distractions are more frequent, the line between park and city ambiguous and inviting.

An abandoned and elevated rail track in Chicago, first built in 1872, drew a design for it by Michael Van Valkenburgh, and some alternative proposals; these highlight the challenges of this new kind of park.[12] What was proposed by the Van Valkenburgh scheme took an elevated pedestrian path and bike trail through an 'urban oasis' within 'lush plantings'; no remnants or relics of the former railtrack were indicated in his renderings, and only two ways in which access to and from the ground was implied. Rival student proposals for the Trail ranged from conventional (ecological urbanism with a focus on farms, nurseries and restoration of native flora) to ones that urged

recycling of paper or rubber tyres, greenhouses with solar power, and an aqueduct with 'wetlands that treat sewage water' and a high-speed walkway to O'Hare airport.

These landscape students had envisaged a somewhat different need for the Bloomingdale Line that passes through four Chicago neighbourhoods and crosses 36 blocks of the city. In such an urban environment the current dialogue is between biocentric and anthropocentric perspectives: on the one hand, between nature that enjoys a fundamental role by offering forms of relief to the city (exactly the ideas that Adriaan Geuze denounced in 1992) and, on the other, a trendy emphasis on ecological planning and sustainability. These views can be strangely confrontational, for both positions tend to privilege rhetoric over community values, and landscape professionals (established and newly minted) can be at extreme odds; meanwhile the psychological and cultural imperatives of humans that suggest a 'social rather than natural ecology' get lost. But that is what students at Illinois focused on: using adjacent green spaces like Humboldt Park and adding greenery to make a continuous open green space of 30 acres for the whole site; at the same time both enlarging the visibility from the trail as it crossed streets below and opening more access routes to the ground with ramps, fire-poles and ladders (illus. 78, 79).

Another even more intriguing project, submitted to a competition for the city of Toronto by Karl Kullmann, realized his thin line/thick edge typology in a more concrete form, with a subtle variation of the corridor. The route of the staggered

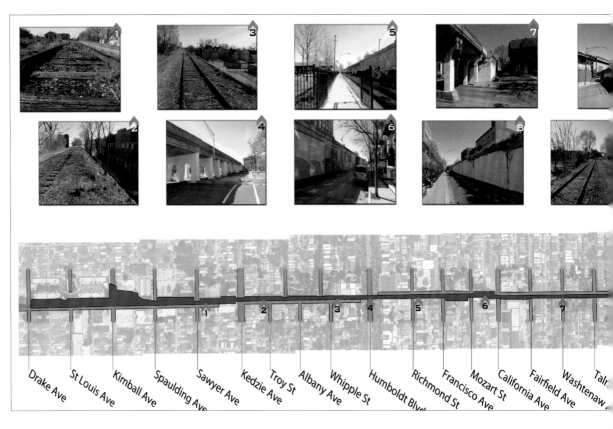

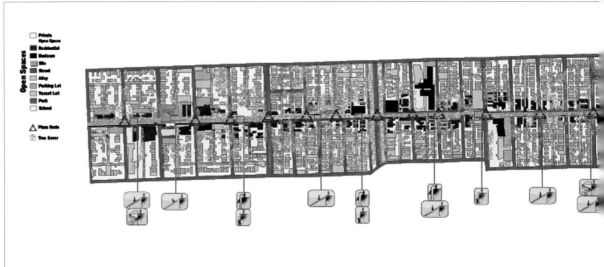

78, 79 Two proposals for linear parks in Chicago by William Lingel and David Hunter.

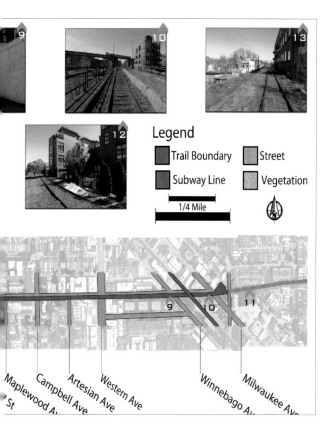

Legend

■ Trail Boundary   ■ Street

■ Subway Line   ▨ Vegetation

1/4 Mile

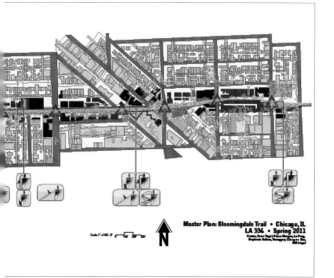

Master Plan: Bloomingdale Trail • Chicago, IL
LA 336 • Spring 2011

park traced easements required for high-voltage power lines that run through residential Toronto. The obviously 'thin' power line encouraged more attention to the thick edges of the neighbouring suburban fabric; so while the trail for pedestrians and cyclists seemed to hop, skip and jump over many roads through the suburb (illus. 80), the cross connections allowed Kullmann to exploit his series of metaphors to mark different responses to them: the straighter parts were 'conduits', with commercial, industrial and business opportunities, while 'stitch' and 'filter' brought in neighbouring green spaces to close the divide.[13] Such linear parks offer, for the most part, not destinations so much as ways for walkers, cyclists or wanderers. You can go as far as you want, then return or loop back to where you started from.

Similarly, piers at the seaside or on large rivers offer the same unproblematic relaxation of knowing you had to walk to the end and back, and as more inland harbours and waterways are in the process of being rehabilitated, this opportunity returns. Kullmann called these 'peninsular effects'. Municipal Pier 11 (illus. 82), which sticks into the Delaware River in Philadelphia under the huge span of the Franklin Bridge, replaced an early two-storey pavilion (shipping business below, sightseeing for citizens who couldn't actually take river trips above). The design of the pier by Field Operations found a simple equivalent to the original building: you can walk out above the water – the railings copy handrails on ocean liners – but at the end you descend close to the water and head back along a lower level with a thin lawn and trees.

The massive bridge above makes the pier a space both intimate and passive and yet active and strenuous as you envisage how the river beckons.

Other new small insertions into urban space join walks with some peninsular effects: CityDeck on the Fox River, Wisconsin, by Stoss Landscape Urbanism, a firm that also designed the Minneapolis Riverfront, is a small, linear park along what had been an unnoticed and unloved waterfront. Now with wooden benches and street lighting, it also has small jetties or mini-piers that stick out in the water – what the firm calls 'giving water its space'.[14] By thickening the thin water's edge by piers jutting into the water, whether busy or empty, the small insertions gain amplitude and diversity.

Some of these small garden places are found – such is the necessity of urban insertions – on subways or filled-in waterways, piers or roofs of parking garages. It is no huge leap to see roof gardens lowered to become building facades, as dense cities, or otherwise unsightly or uninteresting buildings, can be enlivened with a rich carpet of plants and small shrubs, rising and falling up and down the wall.

They are not easy to maintain, as a newspaper article under the title of 'Please Weed the Wallpaper' argued; but they transform a building. Arquitectonica wrapped vertical gardens around parking garages in Miami Beach. Patrick Blanc clothed the museum at Quai Branly in Paris with a glorious tapestry (illus. 81); and he did the same, far less conspicuously, on a blank wall high above the pavement to the left of the Gare du Nord.[15] Longwood Gardens in Delaware has a curving wall of plantings on a corridor that leads to the rest rooms, and the interior hallway of a new scientific building at Drexel University in Philadelphia fills the whole wall that faces the entry with plants. Gardens have learned, these days, to colonize leftover spaces, many of which were hitherto ignored, unnoticed, too small to bother with or just abandoned.

80 Karl Kullmann, proposal for a Green Line in Toronto, Canada, 2013.

81 The vertical or hanging gardens at the Musée du quai Branly, Paris, 2006.

82 Pier 11, Philadelphia, by Field Operations, 2011.

83 Clark Art Institute, Massachusetts, designed by Reed Hilderbrand, commenced 2001, photograph 2014.

SEVEN

CAMPUSES

Campus is an American term, first applied to universities and colleges, and by extension to other non-academic institutions, like Google and other corporate HQs, or even large museums like the J. Paul Getty in Los Angeles or the Clark Art Institute in Massachusetts (illus. 83). It was not a word used in Britain until the foundation of the 'new' universities in the 1960s – Sussex, York, East Anglia, Warwick, Kent at Canterbury, Essex – when the American term became acceptable. The term does not appear in early editions of the *Oxford English Dictionary*; however, the obsolete term *campo* does, and means a school playground (a usage first recorded in 1612). The Latin echo in 'campus' or the Italian word for meadow, *campo* (what Venetians call a *piazza*), suggests that many land-grant universities in the United States were established in agricultural land outside towns, which then grew up around them.

Early American academic institutions like Harvard, Yale, the College of William and Mary, or the College (later University) of Philadelphia took up variant forms of the quadrangle or court used at Oxford or Cambridge: Harvard has its Yard, and buildings would often be grouped to suggest an enclosure, like the triad of buildings at William and Mary, or the Lawn at the University of Virginia. Many late nineteenth- and twentieth-century American campuses formally adopted the quadrangle: for colleges at Yale, or for dormitories like the so-called Quadrangle Dormitory at the University of Pennsylvania. Campuses, of whatever shape or usage, drew on a mixture of landscape forms and garden elements – the medieval cloister with an adjacent garden (usually for simples), the park and garden, and the 'English' or pastoral landscape. In front of Nassau Hall at the College of New Jersey (later Princeton University) there was an enclosed lawn with a few trees that by the 1770s was called a 'campus'. The 1813 plan for Union College, Schenectady, New York, placed a Palladian-type villa layout (central rotunda linked with arcades to lateral wings as dormitories) within a wooded landscape of wandering paths and open meadows, geometrical forms (a lake and *allées* of trees), plus a large vegetable garden with a central cross axis and long parallel beds for planting. Trees frequently graced universities like that of North Carolina at Chapel Hill or the elm-lined avenues at Penn State University; a relict grove of forest trees was incorporated into a garden dedicated to Edvard Grieg at the University of Washington (illus. 84).[1]

By the twenty-first century even large urban campuses endeavoured to include or develop garden pockets and grass courtyards, and new ideas of what a campus could be have emerged, in part by the extension of the term to non-college sites where those elements are invoked.[2] Many, but not all, of these paradigms invoke garden and garden elements. The master plan by George Hargreaves for the University of Cincinnati required many 'greenscapes' (the designer's word). Plans for the Cornell Tech institute on Roosevelt Island in New York include lawns – which may answer the triangular lawn of Four Freedoms Park at the southern end of the island. Turenscape's Shenyang Jianzhu University Campus in China, from 2004, has been much published and discussed, and the idea of this working landscape combines form with programmatic properties; students and faculty harvest the rice in the paddies which are flooded from a pond that collects rainwater, and after the wheat and buckwheat are harvested goats roam to eat what is left in the dry areas. The geometry of paths across the fields is designed to connect classrooms and dormitories, but is primarily a celebration of its cultivation; benches and 'cul-de-sac' study platforms are interspersed within the square fields throughout the campus.[3]

Not all campuses are academic, though some fit the traditional typology of an urban university: for the Gates Foundation in Seattle, the landscape architects Gustafson Guthrie Nichol have devised a series of courtyards, reflecting pools, and vista or sight lines, with a firm commitment to sustainability. By contrast, Norman Foster's vision of the campus for Apple, a 'glistening donut' or ring of glass and steel looping through suburbs in a north California pastoral setting, says little useful about landscape but much about its architecture. Many more campuses are envisioned – in Dubai, in Singapore – but whether they will develop any new sense of campus as 'field' or 'meadow' is unclear.

84 Laurie Olin, drawing of a relict grove incorporated into a garden dedicated to the composer Edvard Grieg at the University of Washington, Seattle, 1985.

85 Louis Kahn, Salk Institute for Biological Studies, La Jolla, California, 1959–65.

Louis Kahn's Salk Institute for Biological Studies, La Jolla, California, is a remarkable campus, not least because its main plaza is utterly devoid of planting. The westward view towards the Pacific Ocean is an austere platform of stone between laboratory and study towers. It is exposed to the midday sun, and not a space where anyone but photographers would wish to linger, as they train their cameras down the narrow channel of water at its centre (illus. 85) – the one element that might suggest the *catena d'acqua* in Italian gardens (one of Kahn's 1960 sketches for the Salk includes a partial plan of Hadrian's Villa) or the landscape work of Luis Barragán. However this plaza exists between an informal landscape to the east and the rocky coastline where the residential buildings are situated, thus suggesting a long-standing relationship of the wild and fields to the 'garden', which other early sketches of Kahn reveal. Salk himself had envisaged an arcaded, monastic cloister.[4] Kahn's other work for both universities and museums, the Richards and Goddard building at the University of Pennsylvania, the Erdman Hall at Bryn Mawr College, the Indian Institute of Management at Ahmedabad, or the Kimbell Art Museum, were never dissociated from their landscapes, whether gardens, ponds, lakes, informal planting or groves of trees. The sunken grass

86 Louis Kahn, courtyard at one side of the Kimbell Art Museum, 1972.

courtyard to the side of the Kimbell, with its four isolated stones, is a splendid foil to the six cycloid shells on the roof of the museum itself (illus. 86).

Museums do not always enjoy or need campuses: we enter London's National Gallery or New York's MOMA straight from the street, though the latter has a famous, but much reworked, garden court inside. But both the Getty Museum in Los Angeles and the Calouste Gulbenkian Foundation in Lisbon have extensive parklands, while new gardens and landscapes have been designed by I. M. Pei in Suzhou, or by Catherine Mosbach for the Louvre Lens project in northern France. At the Getty, its campus surrounds the stark white buildings by Richard Meier, grouped on the hillside like some Tuscan village – a modern San Gimignano; the landscape was designed by the Olin Studio, who were later also engaged to set out the sculpture garden on the hilltop (see chapter Ten). It contains plazas, fountains and a wonderful cactus garden jutting out towards downtown LA, as well as another garden designed by Robert Irwin, an inaccessible labyrinth set on an island in a pool at the foot of rings of gardens that descend through an intricate circuit of Corten steel-lined terraces and pergola arches.[5] In his home town of Suzhou, I. M. Pei created an inner courtyard of Chinese garden forms for the museum, abstracted (as with all Chinese garden art) from the world outside: zigzag walkways over ponds, a representation of mountain peaks against a white wall of 'sky', and stepping stones on the ground through bamboo groves (illus. 87).

The Lisbon site was designed by Francisco Caldeira Cabral, a leader of modern Portuguese landscape architecture,[6] and its landscape, courtyards, fountains and paths consort, tactfully and richly, with the modernist lines of the low, central building, its balconies abrim with flowers and trees. Remove the main building from the campus,

and it is still an eloquent and unmistakably modern landscape (illus. 88). The ground texture is striking: the paths around the lake or through the shrubbery take the form of staggered squares of concrete, some with geometric patterns, and lead visitors across lawns or through stands of bamboo and across pools fringed with pebbles (illus. 89). The pathways throughout are fractured, either breaking up the ground plane with cobblestones, or by individual slabs slipping sideways through the landscape, as they do across the pool beside the Centro de Arte Moderna – with more gardens

87 Courtyard garden at the Suzhou Museum, designed by I. M. Pei, opened 2006.

88 Francisco Caldeira Cabral, gardens of the Gulbenkian Foundation, Lisbon, 1960s.

89 Path through a grove of the gardens of the Gulbenkian Foundation, Lisbon.

on its sloping roof terraces. These discrete concrete squares are reminiscent of Japanese stepping stones, something often invoked by modern garden-makers like Christopher Tunnard, or Lawrence Halprin for his Auditorium Forecourt in Portland, Oregon, and the Heritage Park at Fort Worth, Texas.

Catherine Mosback's design of the park for the Louvre Lens, considered by the museum as an 'essential component of the museum's identity', seeks to interpret the territory of the former coal mine (so yet another example of parkland made on dysfunctional land). Traces of mining, shafts and rail lines that took coal to the station are revealed, as well as highlighted, within the park, to which entry is free and open even when the museum is closed; collections of local and rare plants will create conditions for a long-lasting landscape garden. The parkland is abruptly juxtaposed to the clear glass walls of the museum itself, a now familiar aspect of modern institutions where major architects (here SANAA) are paired with equally prestigious landscape architects; gone are the days, fortunately, when architects surrounded their work with a basic and generally bland 'green' apron.

Where space allows, museums gain considerably by providing themselves with gardens and landscapes (these can also be used to accommodate sculptures). The stylistic range of campuses is various and the forms eclectic, even arbitrary – from the austerity of Kahn's Salk or Dan Kiley's parade grounds at the Air Force Academy in Colorado Springs (1968), where the mountain slides across the edges of the immense platform, to the classical geometries of Kiley's Nelson-Atkins Museum of Art in Kansas City, Missouri, and to the hanging gardens both at Lisbon and on the terraces of Kiley's Oakland Museum. Kiley's museums exploit, at Oakland, a series of descending gardens over the interior galleries, where overhangs cast shadows of pergolas onto the connecting corridors (illus. 90); or, at Nelson-Atkins, a sloping and open lawn carefully plotted with a rhythm of trees and then edged by meandering paths in the lateral groves where sculptures have been inserted. Kathryn Gustafson's plain garden lawn for the American Museum of Natural History in New York is far from either of Laurie Olin's two very different insertions on the Ohio State University Campus (a representation of prairie grasslands) and at the new Barnes Collection in central Philadelphia.[7]

Though the campus *type*, even for different institutions, is recognizable, their invention of forms and uses is often surprising. For museums, it is also perhaps a need to signal their holdings across a spread of cultures and periods, so settings do not impose one particular format: Peter Walker at the Nasher Sculpture Garden in Dallas, or Kiley at the Nelson-Atkins, acknowledge how minimal, and usually geometric, forms will set off the richness of collections; and if this is modern sculpture, the contrast of geometry with modernist asymmetries is telling. For some institutions, it is perhaps as much a concern to present themselves clearly to outsiders and/or to those who work there:[8] the austerity of Salk, the open parade

90 Dan Kiley, planting on the terraces of the Oakland Museum, California, 1969.

grounds at the Air Force Academy, or the new Barnes are each attentive to their focus on science, to military precision, or an attempt to honour the original Barnes arboretum on the Main Line. Other non-museum sites suggest a similar concern for self-representation. At Lisbon, the buildings by Charles Correa for the campus of the Champalimaud Center for the Unknown (a neuroscience and cancer institute) has a landscape designed by PROAP: lawns and paths, with benches, lead towards the buildings, largely blank on the city side, except for some huge, but tilted, oval windows; the two buildings are joined by an overhead glass walkway under which, now on marble, we rise slightly towards two gigantic pillars that dwarf the human visitors (illus. 91). Below is a pool, fringed with pebbles, that has a bubbling fountain at its centre, and this merges imperceptibly with the waters of the River Tagus beyond. The landscape and an adjacent amphitheatre invite us to contemplate both the unknown and the expectation that research can perform new miracles. The Shenzhen Stock Exchange, designed by OMA, needs its contacts with the West to be registered in a garden landscape that combines European geometry with Chinese asymmetries.[9] Campuses for industrial and commercial HQs, though a much more recent development, pose different challenges for how they are to be designed and received. Their main buildings have not always been very exciting or stirring and may even seem heavy-handed, if not scary and inhospitable to outsiders and even their employees.

A splendid example of how to confront sites of industrial activity comes from the English landscape architect Brenda Colvin, who was commissioned in the 1950s to create for a power station in Staffordshire 'a fine landscape', as she put it, 'of the future'. She was convinced, having studied carefully the history of design in her book on *Land and Landscape*, that 'Our power stations, oil refineries, factories and waterworks must take their place, in time, with the pyramids, castles and temples of the past' (p. 344). She is an important landscape architect, much in need of widespread recognition, who designed across a range of gardens and landscapes, including highways, military establishments, universities and colleges, among them the campus of the University of East Anglia, where I once taught: seen from its lakeside on a former estate, the university's residential ziggurats seem to spring from the ground as if growing there.[10]

91 Campus of the Champalimaud Center for the Unknown, Lisbon, buildings by Charles Correa and landscape by PROAP.

What is relevant here is Colvin's work for industrial complexes, the offices for Bowater Paper, a reservoir, and power stations at Didcot, Eggborough and Drakelow; this was not a question of remedying a defunct site, but of finding ways to give it presence in the landscape. You cannot hide or block out cooling towers or ignore reservoir edges that betray unsightly water levels during droughts; nor can you always try to facsimile natural events. But you can move beyond immediate economies and functional needs to create new beauties, some of which are necessarily artificial. Tall cooling towers were 'eased . . . into [an] inappropriate and resentful setting' by planting a perimeter hedge around their base to conceal their clutter, over which they rose, preternaturally, as 'giant "eye catchers"' (illus. 92). For a reservoir Colvin added

topsoil to the banks for new trees, and lined its lower edges with stones and grass edges to make a 'shingly beach'. She always sought to privilege existing trees, but nevertheless expanded adjacent facilities, introducing a duck pond near the Drakelow power station alongside the River Trent, or a sailing club beside the River Severn near the reservoir. Far more unconventionally, she used industrial residue of waste ash and shale to mould ridges and hilltops, drawing on a repertory of ancient earthworks to model new ones. Abstract landforms were preferable to naturalism, so waste could be used to relieve flat terrain – and she was not above invoking Repton's 'before' and 'after' imagery to make the point (illus. 93). There is, as Trish Gibson remarks, a poetry about her designs that meshes the novel and unexpected with the

92 Brenda Colvin, design around the base of these 'giant eye catchers', Drakelow 'C' power station, Staffordshire, 1980s.

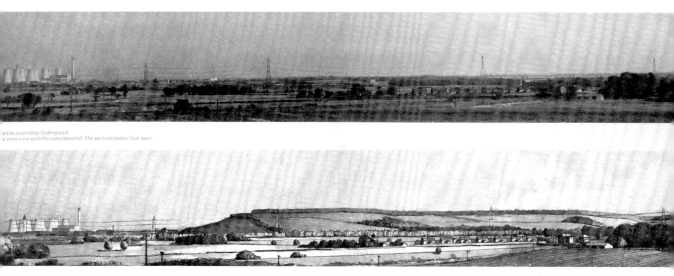

e site as existing, looking east.
e same view with the completed hill. The sections below look west.

93 Brenda Colvin, before and after images for Stage I of the Gale Common Hill, 1967.

obvious and the familiar, the obvious and inescapable modern with a timeless Englishness.

A somewhat similar aesthetic led Dan Kiley to confront an industrial site in 1965 for the Chicago Filtration Plants on a newly constructed 'pier' that juts out into Lake Michigan, supplying water for residents of Chicago.[11] Kiley often records his first impression of a site, and here 'my first thought . . . was of moon craters – huge, shallow pockmarks in the ground that would seem to fill up with water from below'. A subterranean reservoir holds 8 million gallons, and from this spout fountains at the centre of each of the five 'craters'; a double entry through the honey-locust groves allows in either workers or visitors, and a bicycle path circles the 'pier' or promontory. There is no protection on this extremely windy site (Chicago is known as the Windy City), but Kiley worked against it with the double *allées*, bosques of trees and low shrubbery of hawthorn and bar-

berry beside the lake waters. What is intimidating in scale and industrial activity is both made sublime and yet given a certain human resonance.

Large HQs, whether industrial or commercial, have felt the need to palliate and not flaunt their ugliness or capitalism. The harsh image of pushy and aggressive commercialism could be softened if it could be surrounded with pastoral meadows, lakes, vistas and seats under pergolas and around camp tables for workers. These are modernist versions of Poussin's *Et in Arcadia Ego*, where the threats of death troubled the Arcadian shepherdess and shepherds when they confronted the sarcophagus, but the classical pastoralism of the setting soothed their and the viewers' disquiet: now it is commerce, rather than death, that faces its own created arcadias within meadows, lakes and flowers. The machine in the garden, announced by Leo Marx's book of 1964, subtitled 'Technology and the Pastoral Ideal in America', now became the agent of mercantilism and commercialism in the modern corporate garden. Pastoral surroundings for both employees and visitors also soften any threat from a powerful organization, allowing its commercial clout and usually large architecture to be softened by a landscape and garden setting.[12] Alternatively, HQs could strive to surround their often massive structures with a landscape that was elegant, yet clearly a result of intervention (which 'natural'-looking pastoral scenery had always seemed to disguise). Such designs had a dual role: a way of signalling the virtues as well as the power of the companies involved and of offering attractive settings for their workers.

One of the earliest designed campuses in the United States was for the General Motors Technical Center in Warren, Michigan, a suburban corporate research centre in the northern suburbs of Detroit. It was planned initially in 1944–5, with Saarinen & Swanson as architects and Eliel Saarinen as the design leader. After a hiatus, the project was resumed in 1949 under a new agreement with Saarinen & Saarinen under the design leadership of Eero Saarinen, working with his father before the elder Saarinen's death in 1950. The Saarinen firm called on the California landscape architect Thomas D. Church, primarily in a consultant capacity, to develop a planting plan for the site, while Detroit landscape architect Edward Eichstedt developed planting lists and supervised the landscape development. Construction for the main phase was complete in 1956, and the Technical Center was dedicated in May of that year. Beginning in 1957, additions

were made to several of the building groups and the campus, but nothing adversely affecting the design of the whole and thus its integrity. The current conditions of landscape setting of the Technical Center Campus range from fair to excellent condition.[13] In its heyday the photographer Ezra Stoller took images that GM used to promote both their products and the campus setting. The 'new' art form of photography did what earlier picturesque artists and landscapers did in representing as Italianate paintings the mansions and villas of Whig gardening lords; it is a mode that translates readily into corporate America.

During the 1970s and '80s Laurie Olin, then in partnership with Robert Hanna, created a cluster of corporate HQs, many along Route 1 that led south through New Jersey. Buildings at Johnson & Johnson, Pitney Bowes, ARCO Engineering or Carnegie were surrounded by elegant meadows, lakes and engaging vistas, even rotundas and open temples (illus. 94). But in time, both designers and companies wanted more; a garden and landscape emphasis for HQs moved from providing a benign pastoral setting to ones more patterned and more abstract, more concerned to show off the firm than immerse their buildings in 'nature'. A designer's skills could be used to suggest that whatever the corporation produced or engaged in – from pharmaceuticals to videos or computers – was in fact an elaborate reworking of natural projects for human consumption, like landscape architecture itself. So pastoral settings, as antidotes to business, came to be less esteemed than when landscape architecture celebrated whatever the companies stood for – ingenuity, design elegance, invention and cutting-edge technology. SWA's garden landscapes for the SCI Technology Center at Mountain View, California, or the Kelsey-Seybold Clinic in Houston, both of which won awards from the American Society of Landscape Architects in 2001, make strong play with contrasting textures of plants, materials and forms. A conspicuous landscape design, along with impressive architecture, could draw attention to the corporation that solicited it.

Peter Walker, working with a variety of distinguished architects, has an extensive portfolio of campus work for both universities and corporations.[14] His emphasis on minimalism in his essay 'Classicism, Modernism and Minimalism in the Landscape' has always seemed a touch disingenuous, or perhaps sly: his skill and delight with pattern, repetition, grids, juxtaposition of forms, materials and colour make for a rich and conspicuous declaration of the spaces that surround the HQs for which he designs. While his ground plans are geometric, and his forms on the ground abstract, what is appealing for the users of his sites are the delight in clarity and expressiveness; what he derives from nature and from craft and technique are striking and mutually dialogic, and that is what is most striking to visitors. Yet while he

94 Robert Hanna and Laurie Olin, landscape for headquarters of Pitney Bowes, Stanford, California, *c*. 1983.

95 Peter Walker, garden for the Nasher Sculpture Center, Dallas, Texas, 2003.

salutes abstract art by Donald Judd, Carl Andre or Richard Long, when he designs – as generally he must do – for human use and occupation, his abstractions and formalism engage their users visually and as explorers of the spaces themselves and of their relationship to local topography. A dialogue of building with landscape and water, stones and lilies with contrived oblongs of grass and gravel at the IBM Clearlake site, the contrasted ground covers of the IBM Solana where rigorous rectangles are inflected with meandering water and irregular ponds, the mix of orthogonal and diagonal pathways for the Charles Tandy Foundation in Fort Worth, Texas, are prominent. The Technology Center for Sony Corporation at the Chiba Prefecture in Japan plays triangles against quincunx (a 'technological forest') and *allées*, squares of sand with squares of water. And he enjoys colour, in constructivist ornamental shapes: the Boeing Company park in Renton, Washington state, has a wetland forest, curved and coloured like Joseph's coat of many colours, and these draw in their turn on the primary colours of the earth. His fondness for the basic elements of land – water, wetlands, rocks and boulders, wood, wild flowers and grasses – are brought into his designs as yet another dialogue between the aesthetic and the actual. Though not a campus design, his festival design of 'Power Plants' at Chaumont-sur-Loire in 1993 focused entirely on that dialogue: sunflowers, deckchairs and solar panels through the plot (regularly placed, *bien sûr*) served the sunbathers in deckchairs and also illuminated the central *fluorescent* line in the centre of the garden: a pun (both verbal and visual), a linkage of technology with 'nature', a metaphor. Like some garden festival displays (see chapter Three), Walker offered an epitome of what elsewhere he explores more expansively (illus. 95).

Kathryn Gustfason is also keen to register the profile of companies – at a factory campus of the cosmetics firm L'Oréal, at Aulnay-sous-Bois near Charles de Gaulle airport, or for the HQs for both Shell and Esso, both at Rueil-Malmaison, near Paris (illus. 96). In all three designs her major contribution comes as a dialogue between formal invention and bold design with metaphorical, even subliminal, meaning.[15] Groves of trees at L'Oréal are reflected in the arching glass of the factory facade; mounds, coarse shrubs, pools and fountains give way to smooth lawn, and a wooden boardwalk that cuts straight through the geometrical forms of the garden. Boldness is necessary, with a clear sense of progression from the approaches to the buildings themselves; the folding of grass slopes, the use of water in pools, jets, emphatic treescapes, pockets of gardens where each offers its own identity, the juxtaposition of loose order with severe lines and edges to luxury of colour and foliage. Shell HQ is the more impressive, with carefully secluded private pools between the buildings, though linked overhead by glassed walkways, and a striking public approach, where a grass slope, slightly rippling, is sliced by a dozen, sharp stone walls that extend the building behind them down into the public entry; some of these sections of wall hide descents into garages beneath. Legibility, yet a sense, too, of mystery; business, yet elegance. Locality matters, too, at least for Esso on the banks of the Seine: for when the gardens meet the river there are pedestrian paths and an adjacent small public park, cantilevered over the water; its modernist steel benches and Corten steel retaining wall echo the equally modernist building by Viguier and Jodry.

Yet the careful design and planting conceals more subtle agendas. Metaphors underscore at least two of the sites, and Peter Walker has argued that metaphors are vital for any dialogue of land-scape design with users of it.[16] The pools at L'Oréal 'speak about cleansing', apt enough for a cosmetics firm, and the skin on human arms, rough outside and tender inside, is suggested by the 'refinement' of the design as one approaches the building down 'a crooked arm that speaks of freshness and fragility'. For the international petroleum HQ of Shell, a clear alliance is intimated between its industrial power and productivity and the pleasure that attends them; tall, steel lamp shafts rising out of pools look like 'giant drill bits' and they celebrate the 'on-going exploration of natural resources'.[17]

Sometimes corporate HQs and museums have little space for garden embellishments. So the Quai Branly Museum has installed a vertical garden on its exterior wall to augment the small entry garden (see illus. 81) and, also in Paris, the offices of COLAS, an enterprise that makes *autoroutes* through the French countryside, gets a similar vertical set of miniature gardens of largely artificial forms – metal hedges and trees, a steel cut-out *théâtre de verdure* on the rooftop – that truly distinguishes its offices in the anonymous *banlieue* of Boulougne-Billancourt.[18]

96 Kathryn Gustafson, landscape for the Shell headquarters at Rueil-Malmaison, near Paris, 1991.

97 Julian Bonder and Krzysztof Wodiczko, design for the memorial in Babi Yar Park, Denver, Colorado, 2011.

EIGHT

MEMORIAL GARDENS

There are many earlier examples of memorials: the Cenotaph in London's Whitehall, or the Tomb of the Unknown Soldier under the Arc de Triomphe in Paris; iconic, but little to do with landscape, unless that is understood as referring to their role in urban landscapes, or metaphorically to the territory or land of national identity. Yet the Irish Hunger Memorial in New York City does try to represent an Irish scenic setting with crofts and a working, if derelict, landscape. At the other scale, there are countless memorials to the fallen in different world wars on Western village greens and in small town squares; these are often placed in small gardens, decorated with individual tributes or communal offerings and listing the names of the fallen. Naming the dead can occupy horrifyingly lengthy lists, if we visit the Vietnam Memorial in Washington, DC, or the 9/11 Memorial in New York. Gravestones in conventional cemeteries usually commemorate either a single person or a family, so the sheer litany of names on sites of huge destruction like 9/11, or commemorating major tragedies like Vietnam, measures the extent of tragedy.

During the twentieth century – increasingly, in the later decades – memorials have become an obsession, prompted surely by the horrifying disasters that humanity has endured since at least the First World War. These days there are memorials everywhere, so much so that this has been termed a 'Memorial Mania'.[1] A notable example of excess mania is cited by Erika Doss: after Daniel Libeskind designed a fine addition to the Denver Art Museum, its staff had to determine what to do with an outdoor space, for which Libeskind immediately proposed a 'memorial'; to which the staff responded with 'Memorial to what?' At least his proposal related to outdoor space that the architect may have thought of as promising a designed garden or landscape.

There are, indeed, some odd monuments, though the impulse behind their creation is, if eccentric, not in doubt. There is a monument called 'Georgia Guidestones' in Elberton, Georgia, paid for (according to local lore) by an anonymous donor who went by the name of R. C. Christian. This huge granite structure, a slab supported by three uprights 19 ft tall, is engraved with 'teachings in eight languages' that speak of how to guide civilization after a nuclear attack and invite people to 'unite humanity with a living new language' and to keep the population down to 500 million.[2] As Elberton is the mainstay of granite production, some think it's a promotion to draw attention to that industry. The site is owned by the county, and the deed prohibits any other structure or the charging of admissions (some there would like to exploit its mysterious presence). Built in 1979 during the Cold War, it is less a memorial to the past (stockpiling of nuclear bombs) than a challenge to an unknown future. How it could 'guide' this future is much disputed, yet its vague resemblance to a megalith at Stonehenge probably augments its mystery. Another memorial, now in Alabama, commemorates a Yuchi Indian, Te-lah-nay, who walked for five years to regain her home after being displaced during the Trail of Tears (the forced relocation of Native Americans in 1830); it was constructed over 25 years, single-handedly by her great-great-grandson, as a drystone amphitheatre of sandstone and limestone rocks. Nearby, also in Alabama, a Benedictine monk carved an Ave Maria Grotto that houses a collection of miniature reproductions of religious buildings from Jerusalem and Europe.

We need to parse the profusion of this memorial mania to yield some insight into how garden landscape is used, like amphitheatres and grottoes. Many memorials address events or causes that have no specific topographical site, or are for people whose memories are not related to that place. This is not to say (setting aside crazy examples, of which Doss offers some amusing instances), that those causes and people are unimportant; but what properly concerns this type of memorial

garden is whether it honours a site where the disaster occurred, or, if it does not, how the design of a garden or landscape makes sense of its chosen locality.

All memorials should recall us to 'signs of the passage of time as well as enthusiasm for the new'.[3] But especially in a specific place, these are also 'sites where memory is crystallized'.[4] An issue of *Le Figaro* on 22–3 June 2013, in anticipation of the 100th anniversary of the Great War, acknowledged how much tourism was fed by the need to nourish memories of such events in specific places. A two-page spread on the 'L'incroyable engouement [unbelievable craze / infatuation] pour les lieux de mémoire' listed 236 sites dedicated to that war in six Départements along the French/German border; Michelin guidebooks to the Great War have already appeared recently with titles on Flanders, the Somme and Picardie. *Le Figaro* asked why young people (including Americans) needed to know about what happened to their grandparents and estimated that 6 million people visited (and paid for visiting) 'les lieux de mémoire français'. It really had no need to refer to the extraordinary success of the widely circulated work by Pierre Nora on memory places. This strong French dedication to the history of memorable sites was usefully, and predictably, an intellectual affair; part nostalgia certainly, but in part also a serious enquiry into what we could or should learn from an encounter with sites, places, landscapes and their connections with memory, both historical and personal. It therefore resisted the thrall of nostalgia *à la* Downton

Abbey and made an important plea for the *necessity* of nostalgia.[5]

It is not always easy for memorials to use landscape: many Holocaust memorials, for instance, seem to have no reason (however striking their designs) for invoking landscape or making reference to some locality, though the significance of the Holocaust does expand beyond the merely local. Yet the Babi Yar Park in Denver brings a distant past event together with a landscape that portends a future. The 27-acre park, completed in 1982, was designed by Lawrence Halprin and Satoru Nishita to commemorate the Soviet massacre of Ukranian Jews in 1941–3. A pathway through the site is configured on a Star of David and includes an amphitheatre, a grove (a familiar item in memorials: 100 deciduous trees to represent the 100,000 people killed at Babi Yar), and a ravine: the ravine, down the western side of the site, recalls the site where the victims were buried. Black granite is everywhere; a fountain, monoliths and some stones polished to mirror the visitor. It was renovated in 2011, and in the northern end a new memorial was proposed to the Victims of World Terrorism designed by Krzysztof Wodiczko and Julian Bonder (illus. 97).[6] A huge perforated 'box', open at the corner of entry, dwarfs its visitors yet offers glimpses of a bright sky above and through innumerable windows – what Bonder terms 'a frame for evocative thinking and engaging in continuing acts of re-actualization of the past'. The Memorial warns against repeating such horrors (Bonder notes that the Latin *monumentum* derives from the verb *moneo*, to warn, and that it

also refers to *momento*, 'a command to mind and remind').

Maybe for something as immense and horrible as the Holocaust there can be no landscapes that speak adequately of what was there and what we ourselves need to feel.[7] A photograph of Majdanek by James E. Young (illus. 98) does respond bleakly both to the land and to a sufficiently abstract memorial: the approach to Wiktor Tolkin's sculpture, dedicated in 1969, leads upwards from a symbolic valley of death past jagged rocks that guard the steps, at the top of which we are overwhelmed by the lintel of Tolkin's threatening work. Looking between its twin supports, and almost a mile away, are the dome over the mausoleum of ashes at the gas chambers and the crematorium chimney. Here it is indeed the landscape and its locality that speak sufficiently to our sadness, awe and our acknowledgement of the 'historical significance' of the Holocaust; the scene also offers itself as a metaphor of the horror.

It is largely through its landscape, actual and metaphorical, that Bergen-Belsen, originally the site of a concentration camp, speaks to its visitors. Old photographs of the immediate aftermath of the liberation by British troops in April 1945 are moving, but only distantly. There is a new and sobering Documentation Centre, full of documents, more photographs and memorabilia that resonate within the huge space. Yet we tend these days to be overwhelmed by too much imagery, and it is the landscape beyond the building that seems to work better. Though stripped by now of most of its erstwhile buildings, the site can be

98 The memorial by Wiktor Tolkin at Majdanek, Poland, 1969.

99 The entrance to the memorial landscape at Bergen-Belsen, where the outer edges of the whole site are kept mown.

approached through a mixture of memories and attention to the place itself. The central memory for many would be that this place marked the end of Anne Frank's life in 1945, but it also held prisoners from the Russian Front and from the Warsaw Uprising. Physically, we negotiate our route into the vestiges of the camp either by first visiting the documentation centre, or by proceeding directly down a long alley beside the blind wall of the building to the edge of the forest. The far end of the Centre itself is cantilevered ('hovers')[8] over the edge of the site to avoid trespassing on it. Those edges, including the one that passes directly under the Documentation Centre, are regularly mowed to indicate the site's boundaries (illus. 99). And this sotto voce handling of the landscape is typical: some thin steel markers in German and English mark moments in the topography, and others laid flat on the ground are similarly abstract maps of the original layout and buildings. A multi-textured path wanders through the site, passing the low mounds of the mass graves, marked in capitals HIER RUHEN 1000 TOTE APRIL 1945 (illus. 100). There are other scattered items, a cross, and a Wall of Inscriptions from 2010, but the empty and open heather landscape bordered by the forest speaks the emptiness.

One of the curious and disturbing things about the meandering path around Bergen-Belsen was that it was designed and laid out after the war by the architect Werner Bauch. But earlier in 1933, and nearby, he had created another memorial for the Reichsführer ss Heinrich Himmler. This took the form of a large circle of Saxon Stones through which meandered a path (illus. 101), ringed on both sides by hundreds of stones (once engraved with suitable Fascist mottoes and the name of the donating village, for they were gathered from all over Germany). It was this pathway that Bauch invoked for Bergen-Belsen. The insensitivity (to put it mildly) of this echo of an early Germanic monument for a post-war memorial site is prob-

100 Bergen-Belsen: burial mound of massed graves from 1945.

ably lost on its visitors who do not know both sites. But the landscape and its memories need to be spoken, and it is more than curious that the Bergen-Belsen landscape cannot speak of its predecessor; it is left to the memories of landscape historians to make the connection.[9]

Even for those places where a memorial is aptly situated – such as the Pentagon Memorial after 9/11, designed by Julie Beckman and Keith Kaseman – one cannot be convinced that its landscape architecture engages with its site, even though the Pentagon *is* the site, damaged but now restored.

Despite its repertory of garden effects – curved benches, each with a victim's name, the gravel groundcover and the small pools under each of the benches and night-time lighting – there is a strange immodesty about the design. Some elements seem random, in contrast to the stern insistence on calibrating all the data – the ages of victims and years of their births and how these figures are used (illus. 102).[10] Another 9/11 memorial, Shanksville in Pennsylvania, on the other hand, engages better with the site (once the unseemly anger at the first design was adjusted, even though

101 A ring of Saxon Stones, designed by Werner Bauch in 1933 for Reichsführer SS Heinrich Himmler.

102 Julie Beckman and Keith Kaseman, Pentagon Memorial, Arlington, Virginia, 2008.

the outrage seemed beside the point). The Field of Honor, designed by Paul Murdoch, has a ceremonial gateway that leads to a walled and 'sacred' space that marks the final resting place of the passengers and crew. Its pastoral setting and the Tower of Voices, with wind chimes, do something to give the place itself a role in the memorial.

A central issue is just how, with what imagery, these horrendous tragedies are to be remembered. And why do we tend to use gardens, garden elements and landscapes as the vehicle of memorialization? And how long can human memories sustain these memorials in the years after the event? Some memorials can even be appealing because they are temporary: for the Spoleto Festival, Martha Schwartz's 'Field Work', for a nineteenth-century cotton estate in South Carolina, hung sheets of white cotton scrim on wires along the surviving slave cabins;[11] this simple intervention, beyond the performance of the sheets themselves – flapping or hanging with dew, coloured by sunlight – elicited a deep and complicated meditation on slavery, on the ships that transported them (the sheets seemed like sails, but also like ghosts to some visitors) and on white (the colour of death for many Africans); they even suggested the white canvas tents of a Civil War encampment.

Architects and landscapists have worked to find appropriate forms of memorial; not all of these involve gardens and landscapes, but the almost universal use of flowers for burials and memorials has given the garden or some idea of gardens a central role in memorial design. Jack Goody's *The Culture of Flowers* (1993)[12] sees flowers as a fundamental part of graveyards throughout the Caribbean, 'unforgettable flowers' in Ahmadabad and in cemeteries in Cambridge (Massachusetts) and Bologna, the Egyptian idea that the deceased were born again from lotus leaves, Confucian rites in Korea, the stern refusal in graveyards of fake or even potted plants, along with wreaths, or the notices that require dead plants be removed 'each Wednesday'. The irony of cut flowers is, of course, that they die; gardens planted with perennial flowers, on the contrary, can renew themselves every springtime. Though when some 9/11 memorial designs in the United States opted to plant trees for every person killed,

relatives were dismayed at the thought that even one tree, perhaps 'their' tree, might not survive. There was also, as Goody observes, a strong objection by Protestants in post-Reformation Europe and North America who found the cult of flowers 'Popish', though this form of extreme fundamentalism did not survive the provision of flowery tributes that would sustain those who mourned. If doves are more customarily used as signs of peace, Picasso's poster for the Stockholm Peace Conference in 1958 depicted a bunch of flowers passed from one hand to another (this is illustrated on the jacket of Goody's book).

Maya Lin's Vietnam Memorial, designed when she was still a student architect, certainly invoked its location: the Mall celebrates many national heroes in its park landscape, and Lin's elegant and austere design, with its two black walls descending into the ground to meet at their lowest point, is a strong landscape event among more architectural memorials of the Mall (illus. 103). People respond to the memorial in a variety of ways: tracing names, awed by the endless lists, leaving flowers even though the site is not specifically garden-like. Though its abstract form concerned people who wanted a more personal and nostalgic response, the design in fact allows a richer and perhaps more lasting response to this emotional national tragedy than the representational figures of three soldiers erected nearby a little later. And the vilification of that young designer and her subsequent success continues to dog new proposals for monuments on the Mall, like that for Dwight D. Eisenhower by Frank Gehry that has failed to pass the National

103 Maya Lin, Vietnam Memorial, Washington, DC, 1982.

Capital Planning Commission: once again, there were issues of family members objecting and how a person should be represented and in what symbolic landscape. The debate between abstraction and realism is a perpetual theme in all memorials, as it is in modern sculpture: yet many traditional gravestones incorporate an image of the dead person's head or even a photograph or statue of the deceased. Since gardens and landscapes are both 'real' and 'symbolic', they must function as a crucial way of mediating between these rival aesthetics.

Another architect, Michael Arad, joined later by a landscape architect, Peter Walker, created the 9/11 Memorial in New York that ensured that more substantial landscape elements were invoked. The pools with their falling waters drown out the adjacent noises of the urban context, and allow its visitors to retreat into their own thoughts. The lines of trees (swamp white oak and sweetgum), for which there was no local reason for being there, make sense: groves of trees were a traditional, sacred motif as long ago as ancient Greece, and they also mitigate the otherwise urban milieu.

104 The 9/11 Memorial at Ground Zero, New York.

People have objected to the 'military' lines of trees; but some careful precision, some formality, in design is essential. The sublime sense of infinite watery depth in the pools, inscriptions of names, and the occasional offering of flowers merge garden and graveyard (illus. 104).

For the design of the Invalidenpark (illus. 105) in Berlin in the 1990s, Christophe Girot faced equally tough, if different, historical memories, and his design was promoted by a determination to make this 'new Berlin' look to the future and not the past, not least because, as he noted after its

completion, 'this memory . . . [will] become fainter with time'. The site itself was layered on a parade ground from the nineteenth century, a wooded parkland designed by Peter Joseph Lenné, a memorial chapel from 1891 to commemorate the Franco–Prussian war (subsequently destroyed during the Second World War) and then, during the Communist regime, the area which the East German police used 'as a makeshift staging area for border control, one block from the Berlin Wall and the Invalidenstrasse checkpoint'.[13] The memorial's most striking feature – a 'Sinking Wall' –

may mimic the destroyed Berlin Wall, as it seems to be subsiding into the ground amid a reflecting pool, into which water flows down its granite wedge. The pool itself is based on the footprint of the nineteenth-century chapel, and its placement is set askew in the strict geometry of the streetscape, as if to register something different within the area, while the whole site itself, tilted at a barely perceptible angle, is acknowledged at the edges, where a careful, slight threshold leads visitors down into the space. Girot hides the references – the footprint of the former chapel, even the former wall itself ('the narrative', he says, 'is hidden in the abstraction of the wedge'); so does the woodland, by means of some trees from the original space, and the ginkgos around the water basin ('ancient symbols of hope and perseverance'). Kids play on the wedge, climbing it into the sky.

Memories are essentially about our recognition of absence, of loss, the voids made in the fabric of life.[14] Yet some memorials, like that in Berlin and another in Amsterdam, while not neglecting to make the ground itself sensible of its history, also strive to establish them as sites for the future; if not 'enthusiasm for the new', at least a promise of healing. In Amsterdam on 4 October 1992, an Israeli cargo plane, with a crew of three plus one passenger, crashed into an apartment building,

105 Invalidenpark, Berlin, 1992–7.

106 Bijlmer Memorial, Amsterdam: the tree that survived and 'saw it all', completed 1994–8.

killing all on board and 43 inhabitants and injuring others. As always in these circumstances, the memorial involved delicate negotiations with the bereaved and local authorities, but also with the place itself. Georges Descombes, working with the Dutch architect Herman Hertzberger, seems to have succeeded with this Bijlmer Memorial.[15] A solitary tree (illus. 106) that survived the crash ('The Tree that Saw Everything') helps to focus meditation, and children have contributed tiles from the damaged building to a mosaic base that surrounds it. The footprint of the destroyed build-

ing is outlined by a ditch in the ground (this trench, a 'negative volume', anticipates the dual pools on the site of 9/11 in New York); a faint spurt of water at its centre marks the point of impact of the plane; paths destroyed by the crash are partly highlighted 'in alternative materials' and a new walk (which traces the 'pathways of the rescuers') crosses the new green space. The different memories of that horrible event and hope for the future are drawn into a quiet and undemonstrative whole. It was largely empty when I visited it on a Sunday morning, with a few inhabitants of the

107 Kathryn Gustafson, Diana, Princess of Wales Memorial Fountain, Hyde Park, London, 2004.

nearby apartment buildings moving quickly along the paths.

An infinitely more cheerful memorial, in both its design and in the way it is used, is Kathryn Gustafson's Diana, Princess of Wales Memorial Fountain in London's Hyde Park.[16] On a sunny, even humid Saturday in June 2014, it was alive with kids splashing and wading through the bubbling waters or standing in the quieter flow (illus. 107). A fountain was called for in the competition brief, and the form of it as a necklace emerged from 3-D imaging and stonecutting technology

that modulates both the channel and how the water passes through it. That a memorial invokes a fountain, in whatever form, enlivens the scene and its visitors; the 'necklace' itself slopes gently down to a wider, more shallow pool at its base, thus allowing a quieter and reflective moment. What from the air, or in design drawings or mentally while one is on the ground appears an elegant silver necklace, gets animated as the water flows down the channels that widen and narrow; it is crossed on several occasions by 'bridges' that lead on curving paths into the central area of the 'necklace'.

The site itself is not enclosed, but open to Hyde Park and the adjacent Serpentine, so across the fountain or from within its interior ring of grass we have views of the world beyond.

To memorialize the 2011 massacre of 69 young men and women on the tiny island of Utøya in Tyrifjorden, a lake near Oslo, a memorial is situated on a mainland peninsula reaching out into the lake. The artist, Jonas Dahlberg, isolated the tip of the peninsula by crosscutting an open-water channel through the rock, turning the tip into an inaccessible island. Visitors reach the nearside rock face of this channel by means of a short tunnel, emerging onto a balcony above the water to read the names of the victims engraved on the opposite face. Dahlberg describes the sculpture as a 'symbolic wound' and the cut as a physical representation of 'sudden loss', metaphors that perhaps resonate with the horrible event, yet allow personal reflection, strengthened too by the memorial's physical and emotional distance from Utøya itself.

The Garden of Forgiveness (Hadiqat Al-Samah) in Beirut shared the same ambition with many other fine memorial projects: to memorialize, in this case, centuries of conflict and warring faiths, and to invite forgiveness after the most recent war in Lebanon had come to an end (illus. 108).[17] The site is in the historical centre of Beirut, destroyed during the sixteen-year civil war, at the conclusion of which archaeology was able to explore the 5.7-acre landscape. Old roads and house foundations were unearthed, including the footprints of different places of worship. Gustafson

Porter (the firm of Kathryn Gustafson and Neil Porter) was selected to re-envisage how this space could be created as the first public garden in Beirut and at the same time draw attention to the long history of this ancient cultural landscape from Roman times to the present day. They relied on a variety of strategies: plants were selected to represent the various regions of the country, from its mountains, clearly evidenced in the upper, green section of the site, to the Mediterranean coast, evoked by Judas trees, olive groves and citrus trees. Visitors also enter this sequence (another threshold) by passing over an oblong pool, reminiscent of the *chahar bagh* in Islamic gardens, with two crosswalks; the reminiscence of Islam is there, as is a mosque and Christian churches, but the historical formulae are not insisted on or slavishly represented; yet the plurality of this country's history is clear for all to see. As we proceed down the central *allée* from the *chahar bagh,* there are three religious buildings to our right, with a further three across the bottom of the site, and then we enter the archaeological site, where the designers echoed the typical Roman cross-streets of north–south (*cardo*) and east–west (*decumanus*); among the gardens established in the foundations are herbs used in Roman cooking, medicine and dyeing. Across the lower end of the site is a pergola that protects the bedrock on which these lower religious buildings sit; the signs of medieval streets are thrown by shadows of the pergola onto the pavement beneath, and roses ('a flower that originated in the Middle East') are beginning to climb over its structure. The palimpsestial nature of the

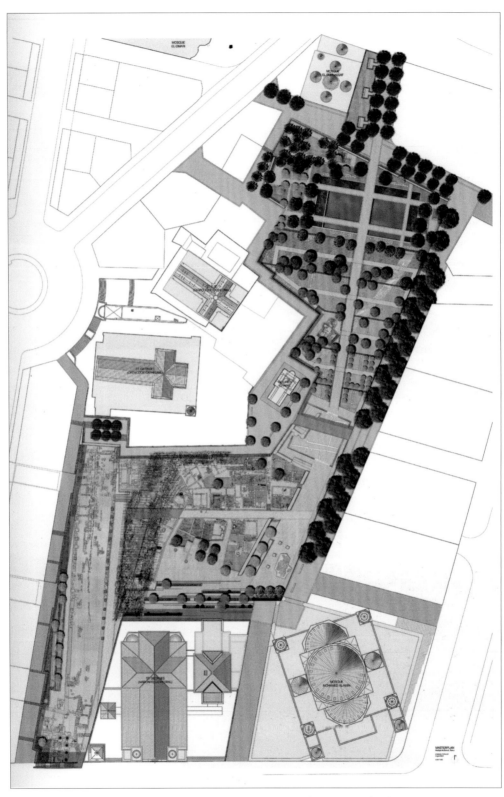

108 Ground plan by Kathryn Gustafson and Neil Porter for the
Garden of Forgiveness (Hadiqat Al-Samah), Beirut, 2000–2006.

design was based on a children's map of Lebanon made some years ago, which the designers annotated / overlaid with phrases ('ancient relics', 'geological forms', 'the tradition of garden making', and so on) that controlled how they eventually came to see how forgiveness and prosperity could remake Beirut ('metaphors for unity'). It is a powerful ambition for the design to fulfil: one can only hope that Beirut can still learn from the contemporary work as the designers did from the past (as I write, this hope seems depressingly remote).

Battlefield sites are about envisaging the lie of the land, and the armies that manoeuvred over them, but not (usually) about the manipulation of the landform by modern designers. Much literature, on-site guidance and museums can help us to recover them; but of course what we want to see is the place of encounter 'as it was'. We can read about the Battle of Waterloo in Stendhal or Byron, and there is an account of how the battleground looked in W. G. Sebald's narrative of his visit there, though it required 'a falsification of history'.[18] The Waterloo Panorama is 'housed in an immense domed rotunda' ('a circus-like structure'), where the immense painting views the whole scene 'in every direction' ('it is like being at the centre of events'). Across a cluster of life-size wax figures of horses, wounded and dying soldiers and hussars, all dressed in 'splendid uniforms . . . to all appearances authentic', Sebald gazed at a vast (110 x 12 yds) mural, painted in 1915. Yet this 'representation' barely touched his memory of the death of 'fifty thousand soldiers and ten thousand horses', and neither could he know where they were buried, for all he sees is 'silent brown soil'; nor did a recording on the battle in the Rotunda, given in Flemish, help Sebald recover any true vision of what was after all a momentous encounter between the British and the French. It was only when he closed his eyes and saw the action through the imagination of the hero of Stendhal's novel *The Charterhouse of Parma*, 'wandering the battlefield', that it seemed to come alive in his imagination.[19]

Flanders Fields was the Great War battleground where so many soldiers lost their lives across a wretched, shifting no-man's-land. Their deaths cannot always be individually remembered, since so many were unrecorded or their bodies not recovered; but the site of so much tragedy and bloodshed has called for some memorial, not least because it is still scar tissue that hurts 100 years later. The territory of Flanders Fields itself has been recorded movingly in poems, novels and films that begin to bear witness to that horror for those who fought there, as well as in memorials elsewhere, like the Shrine of Remembrance in Melbourne, where liminal courtyards conduct visitors into the inner shrine and a thin line of green granite marks the eleventh hour of the eleventh day of the eleventh month (Armistice Day).[20] But the Flanders landscape itself still needs to offer comfort to those touched by the miseries of this war and, more generally, to those scarred by other twentieth-century wars. For people living today not born before the 1914–18 conflict (increasingly a minority), the duration of that sorrow may not last unless the landscape itself is made to bear witness for lost lives and for those who once lived and farmed there.

The Portuguese firm PROAP, who have made something of a name for themselves in honouring historical sites, designed a Remembrance Park in Flanders Fields along 70 km of no-man's-land, sometimes as wide as 4 km (illus. 109).[21] The agricultural land had been erased during the war, and those battlegrounds were further obliterated by subsequent farming. But in addition, this loss was aided by those who wished to 'erase forcibly the memories of brutality and trauma', even though three million people died there. So PROAP ensured that throughout that same park it would honour both memory and oblivion. The two 'parks' were in fact coterminous: memories would be signalled by remnants of the war, and oblivion by evidence of voluntary (or deliberate) erasures of it. The trails or 'tunnels' (echoing the wartime trenches) would often overlap or intersect, converging on sacred places, marked both by signs of war and by features in the landscape. The intersecting paths required visitors to reflect on the dialectic of memory and oblivion, since we can recall and forget with equal ease. But not only two parks, but two historical moments, superimposing two calendars running parallel with each other (1914–18 and 2014–18), their compression heightened by monuments of the past like cemeteries and by contemporary events and reception areas (car parks, museums, cafés). The proposal also wanted visitors to approach the parks through gates, doorways or over thresholds, liminal points of awareness about what was about to be experienced. The thrust of

such a design would have educated those with no personal memories of the First World War, as it would also etch on the landscape signs of that history. Flanders Fields was and still is a place of deep consequence to those who fought in the to-and-fro of trench warfare (and now for their descendants), but also for those who wish to live there and cultivate the land.

Though many died on Flanders Fields, few found burial there. Cemeteries are the ultimate resting-place for many, and that many cemeteries are gardens brings physical remains and memories together. (For those who prefer cremation, their ashes also partake of whatever landscape was chosen for their scattering: 'In that rich earth a richer dust concealed', wrote one poet of the Great War.[22]) Yet modern cemetery design is generally conventional, not surprisingly when their role is essentially limited to burial itself and to inscriptions that commemorate the deceased. They take the form either of regular plots, maybe family tombs for different generations, and crypts or rows of caskets that hold ashes. The opportunity, therefore, for some fresh design is small, and many 'rural' cemeteries, which determined the design of cemeteries throughout the nineteenth century and early twentieth, have succumbed to overcrowded, urban-like complexes, such as Père-Lachaise in Paris or Laurel Hill in Philadelphia. Mount Auburn in Cambridge, Massachusetts, has managed to preserve much of its pastoral landscape, but the Woodland Cemetery in Stockholm, by Erik Gunnar Asplund and Sigurd Lewerentz, is a better example of how the forms of the landscape (hills,

109 PROAP, design for the Remembrance Park in Flanders Fields, 2009.

woodlands and groves, open vistas) complement the chapels, graves and crematorium and make it at once a modernist treasure and a recollection of local and European architectural histories. The forest graves in the burial grounds, with diminutive crosses and markers, are particularly sobering under the huge pine trees.[23]

At least two others attempts have been made to rethink conventional burial grounds:[24] one public, Igualada in Spain, the other private, the Brion Family Tomb in the Veneto (though that cemetery is open to the public). The Spanish site,

only partly completed, has been described as a 'relationship between landscape and the forgotten' (illus. 110).[25] The rugged, semi-arid land around the bed of the Riera d'Òdena has been excavated; a wide plaza-like descent is lined with gabion walls and with concrete crypts, each small cabinet space decorated with flowers; railway ties (or sleepers) are embedded randomly in the paths, which will eventually be shaded with trees; some of the walls tilt inwards as if they were the edges of the escarpments along the riverbed, and the entrance at its summit is marked by a set of masts in Corten steel, between which we descend into the excavated cemetery.

The Brion Family Tomb, designed by Carlo Scarpa, is approached through a conventional Italian *campo santo*, where there are small mausoleums similar to those that lined the walls at Igualada (Scarpa termed them 'shoe-boxes'[26]). But once entered through the overlapping circles of the Propylaeum (illus. 111), we enter a hidden world, where a Japanese-like water pavilion gazes northwards across a lawn to the Arcosolium, under which are placed the Brion sepulchres. The whole *hortus conclusus* is formed in concrete, elegantly moulded and decorated with mosaics, with a multitude of

layered slabs and steps; the outside perimeter is like a defensive city wall, alternated with buttress-like insertions, and the farm fields abut upon it. Inside, the walls block out all but the tops of surrounding trees and a distant view of the San Vito d'Altivole (Treviso). The other part of this L-shape site towards the west contains the chapel, a pool and a grove of cypresses; Scarpa's own tomb is placed exactly at the juncture of the two halves.

The composition is astonishing. The crafted concrete, the Japanese pavilion and its lily-pond and the curve of the Arcosolium are insistently modernist and abstract; yet the sepulchres, references to early Christian burial, the mosaic

110 Entrance to the Spanish cemetery, Igualada, Catalunya, 1995–6.

111 The entry (Propylaeum) to the Brion Cemetery (near Treviso, Italy), by Carlo Scarpa.

decoration reminiscent of Venice and the ambience of other cemetery spaces (even the lychgate into the west end) – all speak of other traditions. The Brion complex is one the most exciting moments of modern memorial art, and its landscape, what it excludes and what it quietly admits, is an ineluctable part of that excitement.

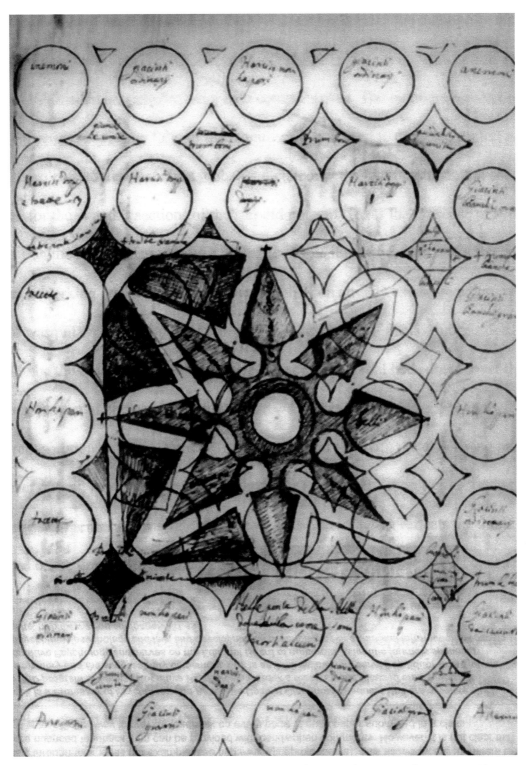

112 A mid-17th-century manuscript with designs for private gardens near the convent of San Lorenzo, Piacenza.

NINE

BOTANICAL GARDENS

Botanical gardens have a long history, and their forms are generally limited in the interests of displaying the plants that have been assembled. Certainly, there were moments when an inventive fantasy of their layout was entertained (illus. 112), but in general, and especially for purposes of scientific investigation and botanical instruction, these gardens presented their materials in succinct and discrete planting beds that were suitable both for gardeners to maintain and students to observe the plants at close quarters.

Early Renaissance botanical gardens – at Padua, Pisa, Montpellier, Leiden, Uppsala, Paris and Oxford – are well documented, and this is not the occasion on which to repeat their histories; some were the work of distinguished botanists, like Clusius (Charles de l'Ecluse) in the Netherlands and Linnaeus (Carl von Linné) in Sweden.[1] But the need for such gardens continues, and therefore some attempt has been made to find modern versions of their conventional shapes, not least as a means of encouraging participation in this type of garden beyond those principally concerned with botany and horticulture. Indeed, contemporary discussion of this type is focused less on scientific

issues and more on the formal management of them as public gardens.[2] And many of them, as discussed in the following chapter, have lent themselves also to the display of sculpture as well as plants. A more enterprising, if perhaps less seductive, joint offering came in the Montreal Botanical Garden, where 'living plant sculptures' from over twenty countries that blurred the line between the sculptural and the botanical were entered for the 2013 'mosaiculture' competition: gorillas were figured in plants, and huge monsters in flowers, not stone, vaguely alluded to the 'monster park' at Bomarzo.[3]

Some modern botanical gardens seem to privilege a nationalist agenda, in part as a means of focusing on indigenous materials: hence the Australian Garden in Melbourne or the National Botanic Garden of Wales, or the local emphasis at Oaxaca (all three are examined below). Sometimes there is also the need to see that a nation acquires its own botanical garden as an emblem of its scientific capabilities as well as national prestige, though here there is usually also a concern to reveal a distinctly modern design. The garden by Roberto Burle Marx in Maracaibo, Venezuela, though now in some disrepair, was both a work of design and, given his horticultural skill, a distinctive collection, and included the first horticultural school in Latin America. Another first botanical garden was established in Israel, a determined attempt to link the native Palestinian landscape to both the Bible and other Jewish sources; it was established by Nogah Hareuveni in the mid-1960s on the basis of his father's (Ephraim) repertory of national botany. First housed at his father's house, then linked for a while to the Hebrew University, and finally sited, with support from Ben-Gurion, at Neot Kedumim in the Judaean hills, this 'national biblical landscape reserve' was opened in 1984, and the site was a symbolic map of the country, a narrative text in its planting, associations and the naming of its segments: a Dale of the Song of Songs, a Pool of Solomon, the Menorah or Candelabrum Hill.[4]

A cluster of modern botanical gardens are worth reviewing in more detail: at Bordeaux, created by Catherine Mosbach, at Barcelona by Bet Figueras and Carlos Ferrater, at Oaxaca which started as the Jardín Etnobotánico in 1988, at Cranbourne near Melbourne by landscape architects Taylor Cullity Lethlean, and at Shanghai with various designers and planners. Other attempts to formulate a new typology have been proposed, like one for Puerto Rico by Field Operations that, while it did not get beyond the drawing-board, envisaged a new role for its urban site. Old country estates have been annexed and augmented with modern installations, like the National Botanic Garden of Wales: here we find

a layout and presentation of materials by Katherine Gustafson inside Norman Foster's huge glasshouse, also an intriguing narrative of Welsh geology, and a conventional walled garden, where new researches of botanical material are presented.

There are some general considerations for all modern botanical gardens: do they celebrate locality or a worldwide, but usually and inevitably limited, plant range? While many early Renaissance botanical gardens assumed that they could represent all the world's wonders and thereby recover the original plenitude of Eden, they soon were overwhelmed with the newly discovered riches around the globe and were forced to limit their holdings in one way or another.[5] Further, do modern botanical gardens resist the habitual layout (small, narrow beds each dedicated to one species), and do they encourage visitors to encounter – not simply groupings of material – but more sudden and unexpected discoveries? Do they invoke new materials, if not of plants themselves, but of materials with which to construct the site? How much are they attuned to the traditional role of investigation and scientific study?

Catherine Mosbach's Bordeaux design (another remaking of an industrial site, a topic that is taken up in chapter Eleven) is particularly attentive to these new options. Its narrow, elongated site, at right-angles to the Garonne River, stretches from a water garden, through artificial mounds of different plantings, into a series of – now much more conventional – oblong beds, each with their own water tank, and then finally across a lawn to the garden offices, conservatory and (de rigueur,

113 Catherine Mosbach, Bordeaux Botanical Garden: the water garden, from 2011.

one imagines, these days) a café. The water garden plays with a geometrical network of rhomboid beds on one side of the lake, and it is the most striking aspect of this project (illus. 113). The Environment Garden (illus. 114), as it is called, has eleven randomly shaped segments of artificial habitats (you can actually spot the wires within the concrete forms), and these provide various materials and topographies (grassy dunes, dry prairie and so on), and each is provided with a map of the materials collected (illus. 115). It provides a contrast to both the water garden and the 'Field of Crops' that follow, but it is far less successful or convincing than either. The follow-

ing sector gathers different related domestic plants into oblong segments (illus. 116), each one being attached to a water reservoir equipped with its programmed watering mechanism. The surrounding walls of the garden and open areas within it also play with some slightly unexpected forms – split logs stacked to make the walls, elongated boards sunk into the ground – that parallel, somewhat randomly, the length of the garden (2,000 ft long but only 230 ft wide), and some elaborate gates near the river where abstract leaves signal entry into the botanical garden.[6]

The world heritage site at Oaxaca in Mexico is sited on the grounds of a former Dominican

114 The Environment Garden (*Galerie des Milieux*) across the lake at the Bordeaux Botanical Garden.

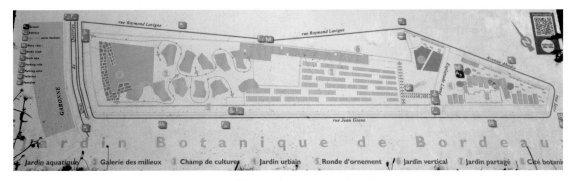

115 Plan of the Bordeaux Botanical Garden.

monastery (from 1570) of 6 acres (illus. 117). The design utilized the old drainage channels and irrigation systems, ponds and former lime-kilns, and a paved road that once brought wagons onto the property. Working with the painter Luis Zárate were an architect, Francisco Toledo, and an ethno-botanist, Alejandro de Ávila. They aim to present specimens of the Oaxaca state in both dry and wet zones, with an emphasis on both old and new plants used for medicine, and food for households and religious purposes, hence the emphasis on its eth-nobotanicity. As in many older botanical gardens

116 Oblong beds of the vegetable garden ('Field of Crops'), the Bordeaux Botanical Garden.

117 The Oaxaca ethnobotanical garden, Mexico, from 1993.

there is a library, which visitors are encouraged to use. The rich ecosystem in Oaxaca has more species of cycads, agaves, chilli peppers and maize than can be found in any other site worldwide: a garden of cycad plants, which have evolved over 230 million years, and other cacti (one barrel cactus weighs many tons and is centuries old) make this an especially localized and focused collection. It also features sculptures in wood and stone, like the one by Toledo himself: a huge chunk of Montezuma cypress 'clad in mica' over which red-dyed water drips, signalling the importance of cochineal. There is also a section of the garden devoted to a cave in the valley where archaeologists discovered very early remains of local agriculture (corn, bottle gourds).

It is modern material, Corten steel, at both Barcelona and Cranbourne, and their staggered angles and format, that make clear we are in a modern botanical garden. Barcelona was completed in 1999;[7] its entrance, consisting of four steel doors, with the initials of J[ardí] and B[otànic] and B[arcelona], are slung between blind concrete walls. Inside, the generous spaces play well with exposed concrete for paths, and the Corten-lined terraces, which unlike many Mediterranean terraced landscapes jut and bend energetically across and down the hillside; indeed, these abstract shapes

118 Barcelona Botanical Gardens, completed in 1999.

119 Barcelona Botanical Gardens.

recall, yet refuse to mimic, conventional south-ern landscapes (illus. 118). The steel walls, often tilted, are used to form nooks and acute crannies, where the plants have begun to flourish and hang over the terraces. Built materials (in the absence, at present, of rich plant growth, though they will arrive quickly in this climate) are everything and they tend to dominate the existing plants; even the palm trees seem dwarfed by the spaces and the angular, metallic forms. It is indeed the formal excitement that offers itself – the rusty-brown steel wedges, the white concrete slabs of pathways with their complex pattern of joints, the insertion of wooden walkways over the ponds (illus. 119), the

folded steel seats that look like rectangular logs on metal feet, the large steel capitals laid into the pavements that lead to the entrance that spell out the different planting zones in Catalan: Xile (Chile), Califòrnia, Sud-Africa, Meditterrània-Occidental, and so on. All the zones featured here have similar climates, characterized by long dry summers and very mild rainy winters, and this, while wide-ranging in its geographical spread, actually makes for a coherence of planting, and the garden is dedicated to researching and pro-tecting this cluster of typical materials, like the Peruvian pepper, the hemp and date palm. And the situation of this botanical garden high above the city and with views of sea, mountains and the Olympic sports facilities connects it with the world which the garden is dedicated to isolate, and to preserve its typical plantings.

The opening in 2012 of the second, final phase of the Australian Garden occupied the northern segment (21 ha) of the Royal Botanic Gardens at Cranbourne, near Melbourne, Australia (363 ha); it was designed by landscape architects Taylor Cullity Lethlean in association with the plantsman Paul Thompson.[8] This Australian Garden, the 1991 Charter for which called for scientific enquiry into Australian flora and was dedicated to the 'beauty of endemic ecologies', was created on land of the Bunurong peoples and clearly declares an Australian concern for an inclusive national identity and sense of place. While the larger area is composed essentially of natural bush with open grasslands, eucalypt forests, heathlands and wetlands, the Australian Garden is strikingly and wonderfully contrived.

It is radically and deliberately opposed to most older European models; we might be tempted to call it postmodernist (the mix of geometry, meandering lines, the scatter of different garden types), but such labelling scarcely helps to understand its significance. For it is less its form – immediate, but not as richly rewarding in the plan as when experienced on foot – than the need to involve visitors in discovering and experiencing its materials. At more conventional nineteenth-century botanical gardens, Sydney and Adelaide, for example, we can surely find the obviously indigenous trees by wandering in a pastoral, European landscape; here

at Cranbourne the design articulates the sheer otherness of its native culture, in not only several demonstration plots of local species and planting schemes or signage (notices to watch for poisonous snakes, acknowledgement of indigenous culture's use of controlled burns), but its anthology of ecological conditions that are as rich as Mosbach's Bordeaux garden was minimalist. The plan represents, but does not map, Australian landscapes; its iconic microcosms distil, or epitomize, what it is like to view different Australias in one place, and thus Cranbourne is as much an adventure for Australians as it is for foreigners. It suggests how remarkable and innovative – often metaphorical – it is, both in its formal as well as botanical materials; sculptures by Mark Stoner and Edwina Kearney in the Red Sand Garden (illus. 120) or Greg Clark's Escarpment Wall, among others, announce different geological conditions. From the Visitor Centre one gazes over the startling Red Sand Garden on a former sand mine, where the ceramic sculpture appears as a salt-encrusted landscape viewed from a plane, or suggests aboriginal art. A path to the left could take the visitor along the curving Eucalyptus Walk beside a dry river bed; to the right are crescent-shaped mounds, like sand dunes, that at their rear heave up in rust-red steel cliffscapes, below which the waterway, beginning at the dried-up lake, flows and bubbles down to the river. Around and beyond these large and dominant events are arranged a variety of smaller gardens and experiences (illus. 121): display gardens to show off visually spectacular Australian plants, suggestions for gardening in the back yard, in the

120, 121 The Australian Garden at Cranbourne, near Melbourne, photograph 2014.

city, in 'lifestyle gardens', in a 'water-saving garden', or the 'future garden'. The Gondwana Garden sets out Australia's origins – hexagonal basalt columns and rainforests, while coastal regions – sand spits and *Melaleuca linariifolia* – make a Seaside Garden. There is an Arbour Garden, a Promenade Garden and one for kids, though the schoolchildren were everywhere that morning, scribbling, drawing, running to identify the smooth-barked apple (*Angophora costata*) or the Western Australian Christmas tree (*Nuytsia floribunda*) – it was nearing Christmas after all. There was a 'Weird and Wonderful Garden' and 'Desert Discovery Camp' and two hills that afforded views over

the largely flat site, and everywhere (for a non-Australian especially) a rich palette of strange trees – peppermint, box, stringybark, ironbark, Queensland bottle tree (*Brachychiton rupestris*), or grass tree (*Xanthorrhoea*, *Kingia*) – and the rare sighting of the endangered southern brown bandicoot.

The huge botanical garden to the southwest of Shanghai, where I was only able to spend a day, is more conventional in its displays and less eager to insist on its modernity, though some Corten steel bulkwarks are juxtaposed to many elegant, layered drystone walls. Indeed much of its structure and references gesture to the past;

122 Shanghai Botanical Garden.

123 The flooded quarry at the Shanghai Botanical Garden.

the many workers wear pyramidal coolie hats as they work, which seemed at once both traditional and somewhat surprising in a modern and communist China. The surrounding territory outside the garden had several waterways, and the insertion of these into the well-watered site will eventually enable boats to enter (illus. 122). The flooded quarry, worked until 2000, begins with a stunning and somewhat scary descent inside the cliff through a Corten steel box and down

onto a floating wooden bridge or pontoon, which leads visitors across the water under the cliffs with reminiscences of old Chinese engravings of rocky mountainscapes and grottoes, and then takes them up through another twisting tunnel to the surface (illus. 123). This part of the garden was designed by a most distinguished and subtle landscape architect, Zhu Yufan, who insists that the quarry is neither a landscape nor a post-industrial reliquary, but a *garden*.[9] Its effort at sublimity certainly makes the remainder of this botanical garden somewhat conventional.

Shanghai's new botanical garden is contained within an irregular circle, and the conservatories (extremely modern structures) and offices and entry pavilion are located around its perimeter, with the flooded quarry and lakes at the centre. Meandering paths guide visitors through its sections, and a northeast hill crowned with a pagoda presides over the whole. The different segments are large and more park-like, clearly presenting, grouping and labelling (in Chinese and English) the botanical and horticultural materials; the rich accumulations of irises, for example, seem as much

suited to an extremely well-furnished and maintained public landscape as to a place to study botanical specimens (illus. 124). The rapid urbanization of Chinese culture seems to call for a Western presentation of both landscapes and elements that were not part of the Daoist or Confucian mindset,[10] and a Western visitor to the Shanghai Botanical Garden certainly feels more at home than, say, in the gardens of Suzhou itself.

Sites like those in Bordeaux, the countryside outside Shanghai, the hillside over Barcelona or in the outskirts of Melbourne were all botanical gardens created in places where their forms and

124 Iris beds at Shanghai Botanical Garden.

landscapes were made *ad nuovo*. But others have utilized sites that were either already designed or were situated within urban conurbations. Two of these – in Wales and in Puerto Rico – suggest how landscape architects have sought to laminate their own scientific and design visions onto existing territory, in the process of finding fresh ways to identify the purpose and pleasures of botanical gardens.

The site chosen for the National Botanic Garden of Wales at Middleton, Llanarthney, Carmarthenshire, was a Regency landscape created by and for Sir William Paxton, when he purchased the estate after his return from India in 1789. He built a new neoclassical mansion by Samuel Pepys Cockerell and, with the assistance of Samuel Lapidge, created a doubled-walled garden and surrounding parkland, a memorial tower for Lord Nelson on a neighbouring hill and a spectacular sequences of lakes (partly drained in 1939), complete with bathing facilities and a sailing barge. It was this somewhat derelict and overgrown landscape that I first saw in 1988, taken there by William Wilkins (who also introduced me to the derelict garden at nearby Aberglasney, see chapter Twelve); we went to explore the possibility of creating a National Botanic Garden of Wales on the site of this former estate. This has happened and is well-established, with plans to recreate the necklace of lakes (mostly silted up and wooded now) and restore what was once a considerable woodland.[11]

The Botanic Garden itself now contains a splendid glasshouse, designed by Norman Foster, a walled garden restored and flourishing, other gardens – Japanese, bee, bog and sculpture gardens –

and a generous set of the usual appurtenances: café, restaurant, second-hand bookshop, plant and gift store, an apothecary shop, science centre and library. Three elements in particular are striking and they relate to the collections, the research pursued there, and the geological topography of Wales itself.

The approach from the entry towards the Great Glasshouse is marked by a rill, or sequence of runnels, designed by the landscape architect Hal Moggridge with Tony Jellard, that winds its way down the slope, sometimes disappearing briefly underneath the pathway, and then through a series of basins that contain a geological history of the Towy Valley flood plain (illus. 125). Each segment presents one chapter of Welsh geology, with boulders and stones (sourced by Professor Dianne Edwards) and plaques that describe that particular stratum, its age and the geological components and what might have grown there (lichen on volcanic rocks from 450 million years ago, Precambrian rocks from 625 million years ago). Geological strata are, after all, the foundation of later botanical flora.

The centre of the walled garden is an elegant circle, set within four quadrants that tell the history of flowering and kitchen plants. But around the water basins, seats and paving is an unusual presentation of material that the innocent eye may not take in. The Garden is researching the DNA of Welsh flowering plants, all 1,143 of them; this information is then DNA-barcoded (analysing three examples of each species to ensure correct coding) and then eventually shared globally on the Barcode

125 The geological history of the Towy Valley at the National Botanic Garden of Wales, Llanarthney, Carmarthenshire.

of Life Database (BOLD). After a careful taxonomy is ascertained of when, where and by whom the plant was collected, a small section of a plant (leaf fragment or pollen grain) is barcoded (using genes rbcL and matK), which can be used in various ways: to understand and mitigate the effects of biodiversity loss and climate change, track pollen carried by bees, assist archaeological investigation of ancient sites, show what animals eat (collected from dung), help in the understanding of herbal medicines, and which can even be invoked for forensic testing. DNA-based science also informs the plantings within the double-walled garden, where plants from all over the world are arranged according to the Angiosperm Phylogeny Group (APG III system), rather than in other conventional systems (Tournefortian, Linnaean, and so on). The planting scheme is not readily visible to the informed botanist, let alone the average visitor; there is nothing to show that this exquisitely maintained botanical garden is unusual, though notices explain the system. A gardener, working in one of the quadrants, when asked where I might find a certain plant, expressed, jokingly (I suppose), his mild unease that further DNA discoveries might force him to engage in a wholesale movement of some plants to another sector!

126 The Great Glasshouse, designed by Norman Foster, 1995–2000, planting by Kathryn Gustafson & Partners.

If the walled garden is itself interesting by virtue of its scientific approach as well as its aesthetic appearance, the Great Glasshouse is undoubtedly the *pièce de résistance* (illus. 126). The weekday that we visited it was full of schoolchildren, their laughter and chatter filling the huge arched conservatory ('O ces voix d'enfants, chantant dans la coupole!', as Verlaine wrote). The layout of Mediterranean plants from five continents (Europe, Western Australia, California, Canary Isles, South Africa) was designed by Kathryn Gustafson & Partners. The landform directs our gaze and thus our visit, as the map at the entrance suggests it might; the paths descend into the ground and peel off from the primary circuit. They weave around the rocks and terraced planting beds, up and down ravines, past cliffs, a waterfall and pool, through a variety of micro-climates. It is a space of discovery for both

127 Field Operations, computer rendering of the research unit and related educational facilities
at the projected Puerto Rico Botanical Gardens, 2004.

the adept botanist and the curious explorer, who will find, not only plants, but the painted forms of aboriginal art lurking, as snakes and other beasts, beneath the density of foliage.[12]

An emphatically urban site, by contrast, was chosen for a reformulation of an existing university garden in the centre of Puerto Rico that dated from the late 1800s. James Corner, of Field Operations, presented the proposal to the university and then published it – luckily, as its thoughtful exploration of modern botanical gardens now survives as the only record of the project.[13] He addressed, first, the issue raised at the start of this chapter: why we still need botanical gardens, and how they might be made interesting to those with little immediate interest in botany or horticulture. Such gardens

are always a hybrid, as are cities like Puerto Rico: so, Field Operations proposed three rival schemes or 'provocations', which eventually were synthesized. This was a sophisticated version of Ian McHarg's strategy of layering different design proposals, which Corner had derived from his early training under McHarg at the University of Pennsylvania. Corner drew on three types or schemes: a botanical forest, focused on ecosystems and utilizing an already mooted 'Ecological Corridor' through the city centre; a botanical public park, adjacent to a new rail system, that would be dedicated to events in spaces (rooms, stages, platforms) shaped by the planting; and a 'botanical city', with emphasis on botanical production and sales and revitalizing a river corridor with its ability to draw in neighbouring areas of the city. It sought to merge the 'three natures' of garden, city and the 'wild'. The traditional role of botanical gardens (collecting, education, research; illus. 127) was enlarged to accommodate civic and economical benefits (spectacle, recognition of an exotic ambience). An ambitious project, unhappily stalled in 2005 (these things happen) after a change of government and when priorities at the university were altered, but one that outlines a radical and firmly urban strategy for botanical parklands that can inspire others, though its dedication to one locality, carefully observed and as carefully enhanced, will challenge those who use its ideas for making other places elsewhere.

128 'Where sheep may safely graze' at the Morris Arboretum, Philadelphia.

TEN

SCULPTURE GARDENS

Two useful aperçus on sculpture gardens, which proliferate these days, come from Robert Smithson and Ian Hamilton Finlay. Smithson noted as early as 1968 that, as outdoor museums, sculpture parks become 'a limbo of modernisms', while Finlay in 1980 argued that, in sculpture parks, 'art savages Nature for the entertainment of tourists'.[1] Smithson implies that sculpture parks which celebrate modernist works soon lose their aura and survive in a limbo that is neither heaven nor hell. Finlay is even more caustic: the use of 'art' or sculpture, he implies, is only there to please the tourists, who will not know how to appreciate 'nature', which is savaged (ruined? despised?) for their entertainment; sculpture's attack on nature also demeans the world of art as well as nature. For it is an interesting, as well as a slightly empty, claim that many American sculpture gardens bill themselves as 'Art and Nature' parks, or announce that they were created 'with the intention of combining art and nature'.[2] For all gardens and designed landscapes are precisely that.

This chapter is less concerned with Smithson's concern that the modernity of sculpture dates, or ceases to 'talk' to us. Rather, it is how sculptural items themselves 'talk' to the natural context in which they are found; how does the scenery of sculpture parks, their gardens and landscaping, enhance the insertion of sculptural items, and how does that insertion reveal the scenery? It is supposed to be an exchange of benefits. And an interesting element of that dialogue is the use of land forms *as* sculpture: designers like George Hargreaves and Kathryn Gustafson shape land by weaving and modelling the site so that we see the land itself as sculpted.[3] Thus Maya Lin's 'Wave Field' at Storm King, the topographical playfulness of the garden at Graz in Austria designed by Dieter Kienast, or the moulded forms of the Red Sand Garden at Cranbourne's Royal Botanic Garden (see previous chapter), engagingly seek to avoid the threat of 'art' savaging 'nature'.

The sudden explosion of sculpture parks by the end of the twentieth century is extraordinary: as early as 1967 Smithson himself suggested (ironically?) that the dull centre of Passaic, New Jersey ('a typical abyss or an ordinary void'), could be 'pepped up' with 'an outdoor sculpture show'.[4] By 2013, in the United States alone, over 60 such locations are listed in a variety of different contexts as a guide to 'Art Parks'. In the United Kingdom, the Yorkshire Sculpture Park was the first such creation, and unlike those in Grizedale Forest or the Forest of Dean (see below) it mixes permanent with temporary exhibits; it took its inspiration from the open-air exhibitions in London parks held between the 1940s and 1970s, and it was established on a former eighteenth-century estate, Bretton Hall, now Bretton Hall College (in this it parallels the new National Botanic Garden of Wales created in the former grounds of Middleton Hall, discussed in the previous chapter). Though it now has some indoor galleries, the eighteenth-century grounds have many landscape features – follies, a deer-house converted by James Turrell, a camellia collection and an ice-house – into which landscape works by British sculptors, notably Henry Moore and Barbara Hepworth, are now inserted.

This explosion of sculpture parks may be explained in three ways: the enlarged scope and materials of objects to be displayed; the use or reuse of neglected and unwanted land, or land that could be saved from development; and the introduction of sculpture into these new contexts as a way of luring people into them, whether forests, Yorkshire hills or museums.

Modern artists have come to use bigger and more massive materials – steel, especially, but also bronze and ceramics, for which museums cannot find sufficient room; in many cases, those materials are also apt for exposure to the elements, where time can contribute its patina to the material. Sculpture gardens have also been added to museums to expand their cultural mission and extend the institution's footprint. Other sites that have been taken up for sculpture parks are woodland and forests. Some sculpture gardens, like Socrates Sculpture Park in Long Island City, founded in 1986 by Mark di Suvero, was established first as a collective by local artists on a former industrial site, but has blossomed into a small outdoor urban space and a meeting place for artists as well as an exhibition place for distinguished visitors.

But sculpture, as Finlay's aphorism implies, can be used to lure people to respond to sites that seem uninteresting or uninviting. People who frequent botanical gardens and arboreta are presumably those with a keen interest in horticulture. But for just as many visitors, these places are simply parklands, and to encounter sculpture in them may also encourage an interest in flowers and trees that they would otherwise neglect. Hence many botanical gardens, like Wellington in New Zealand, or arboreta, like the Morris Arboretum in Philadelphia, install sculptures temporarily or permanently to provide an added interest for their botanical collections. The Morris Arboretum solicits children to explore the treetops in nets and lofty promenades, by finding a spider suspended in the branches, or by the sight of huge bugs stalking across the meadow, reminiscent of horror movies, an amusing and even ironic riff on sculpture gardens themselves. Some items are more attuned to the historical locality: on the road leading up to the Morris Arboretum 'sheep' graze on the pastoral slopes of what was once a large nineteenth-century estate (illus. 128).

But that invitation, then, to augment the function and purpose of these gardens and parklands focused primarily on botany and arboriculture allows a more subtle agenda. All sculptures are contrived and imagined (as Finlay says, they are 'art'), and to install them in natural scenery invites an intriguing dialogue between what we lazily term nature and culture. True, many such installations are made in landscapes that have themselves been designed (like the Morris Arboretum). But the insertion of sculpture encourages two different responses: either the new artifice reminds visitors that the landscapes are themselves contrived and artful, or alternatively the newly inserted artifice makes the scenery appear more 'natural' than it is. To have seen Christo's orange banners and 'gateways' throughout Central Park in the winter of 2005 was to acknowledge a clear difference between them and the landscape; equally, to have observed Christo's insertions winding along Central Park's pathways drew attention to the original contrivance of Olmsted's and Vaux's design. While botanists will surely be focused on the plants, and connoisseurs of modern art on the sculptures, there is a further relish to be discovered in the dialogue between them, a dialogue that is an essential element in modern sculpture gardens (illus. 129). We may be drawn to Christo's orange banners or children to the huge bugs lurking beneath the trees in Philadelphia, but these derive much of their effect from their situation; we recognize and ponder the essential interchange between the worlds we invent and the world from which we draw our inventions: the wind ruffles Christo's banners, or the

129 Richard Nonas, River Run/Snake in the Sun, 2001, at the Museu Nacional d'Art de Catalunya, Barcelona.

immense bugs remind us of smaller insects there. In the 500 acres of meadow and woodland at Storm King in New York State, it is the often huge and abstract gestures of the sculptures that contrast with the landscape, yet their own conspicuous artifice alerts visitors there to the subtle landscaping of William A. Rutherford, Sr. But for almost all the sculptures at Storm King, it is the scale of the works in the surrounding landscape, as much as it is the dialogue between art and nature, that is fundamental to their impact. Other work there uses the land itself to compose sculptures that relish the scale at which they work: Andy Goldsworthy's winding wall through the trees uses stones collected on site, then dips into the pond before climbing the far hillside; Maya Lin's undulating earth-folds mimic the rhythms of water.

While the guide to American art parks divides them into three sections on 'Leisure Spaces', 'Learning Spaces' and 'Collectors' Spaces', the dialogue is the same: we learn from the spaces, which we also seek for leisure and the chance to respond to a collector's taste or whims for what is displayed there.

Such a dialogue is not in fact modern, though recent sculpture parks and gardens seem to make it more prominent, not least by utilizing often extensive or designed landscapes. The Louisiana Museum of Modern Art in Copenhagen is a series of pavilions, zigzagging through a wooded landscape that stretches between two bodies of water.[5] The glass walls bring in the scenery, so that some of the sculptures seem about to walk outside (illus. 130), while others outside advance into the interior spaces; more abstract forms inhabit a garden landscape where they seem to have grown.

130 Sculpture at the Louisiana Museum of Modern Art, Copenhagen.

The earliest sculpture gardens in the modern era were established in Rome during the sixteenth century.[6] A combination of the Renaissance emulation of classical culture with the discovery of dozens of buried Roman or Hellenistic statues allowed the creation of sculpture gardens at the Villa Belvedere in the Vatican or the nearby Cesi garden, where ancient examples were displayed.[7] That the presence of these images within designed landscapes promoted a dialogue between different arts was self-evident, and it encouraged that emerging Renaissance interest in the *paragone*, or theoretical comparisons between different art forms (painting and sculpture, music and writing, and even art and the garden). Everybody saw a relationship – endlessly changing, no doubt, and subject to local and cultural conditions – between art and nature. Though a rare example, the Renaissance also saw at least one park peopled with sculptures carved from the living rock, which invites a rather different adjudication of the *paragone*: in Bomarzo, a wonderful and strange medley of figures, beasts (both mythical and zoological) and inscriptions on urns and other insertions (seats and caves) spring from the Etruscan soil.[8]

What was initiated in Renaissance Italy spread across Europe in a multitude of gardens where statues, some authentic, some modern copies, enhanced and yet stood in careful contrast to the land and a designer's manipulation of it. From Versailles, peopled with representations of mythical figures, to English gardens like Chiswick, Stowe and Rousham, sculpture played an essential role in the configuration of place-making. And in most

of these, the choice and the placement of sculptural items was apt and significant. To glorify Louis XIV as *le roi soleil*, a sculpture of Apollo was established in a pool below the château, and it represented his horses, that had driven the chariot of the sun, bathing in the waters at the end of their daily transit through the heavens; a different Apollo, now with his lyre, graced the parterre nearby. At Chiswick, in William Kent's second rendition of the exedra,[9] Roman statues occupy the niches in the hedges and gaze across the lawn at Burlington's Palladian mansion; at Stowe, four full-length classical figures in the Temple of Ancient Virtue confront the Temple of British Worthies across the River Styx, the mythical stream that separated the living from the dead; but for a diminished modern world the British are presented only as busts in niches, unlike the full-length figures of antiquity across the stream. At Rousham, a more nuanced, or even risky arrangement of statues allowed the naked figure of Venus in her Vale to be studied by a leering satyr in the surrounding vegetation. Yet the scattering of other sculptures at Rousham – a Lion Attacking a Horse, a colossal figure called Apollo or maybe Antinous – seemed more random and suggests that for smaller estates it was less a coherent narrative, as at Versailles or in the Elysian Fields at Stowe, than a simple delight in displaying copies of ancient sculpture.

Indeed by the later eighteenth century many people were objecting to the careless and meaningless proliferation of sculptures: Thomas Whately in *Observations on Modern Gardening* (1770) objected strongly to what we would call iconographical items – historical and mythological sculptures like river gods, 'heathen deities', columns 'erected only to receive quotations', and other 'puerilities' (all his terms). These he chose to term emblematical, and he found them simply 'ingenious', useful at best to 'recall absent ideas'. Recalling what was represented in statues had indeed been the proposal by Joseph Spence in his *Polymetis* (1747, with two more editions in 1755 and 1774): since he thought his contemporaries lacked sufficient knowledge of the ancient gods, he wanted to establish a parkland full of temples, in each of which one classical deity was represented as a statue, on medals and other artifacts to teach Englishmen who had forgotten their Classics. By the late eighteenth century the abundance of temples in a landscape like Stowe must have seemed not unlike Spence's proposal but without the pedagogical emphasis. Horace Walpole, for instance, thought Stowe was a confused glut of images. No doubt having read his Whately, Walpole also rebuked even earlier designers (in particular George London and Henry Wise) who had 'stocked our gardens with giants, animals, monsters, coats of arms and mottoes'.[10]

Thus a careful invocation and placement of appropriate sculptures within gardens and estates dwindled and was often lost after the eighteenth century. Mythical images or abstract personifications of the ancient deities or the seasons were replaced by statues of famous contemporaries or local worthies; these personages now graced urban plazas as well as the estates of industrial barons. Furthermore, the inability to obtain legitimate ancient sculptures meant that modern copies, as

well as representations of modern persons, occupied places where meaningful classical items had once been placed – meaningful, in that they once appealed to a culture that understood their iconographical status rather than items that referenced local, and sometimes quickly forgotten, people.

A return to sculpture in the twentieth century was a combination of a new interest in the kind of sculpture that required extensive landscapes with a marked interest in abstraction; conversely, the promotion of sculpture in garden centres found that small suburban gardens were invaded with representational items. Abstractions renewed the older dialogue between art and nature by imaging forms that suggested, sometimes obliquely and intriguingly, what was around them. It is in fact quite astonishing that in most of the sculpture gardens discussed in *Art Parks* the incidence of human forms is either eschewed entirely or highly abstracted;[11] what is offered is a repertory of items that are either absorbed in their own formality, or represent at some remove the artist's understanding of the world around them.

Occasionally, especially for their use in smaller, designed spaces, we now discover 'found objects' taken directly from the landscape and presented as sculpture – what Christopher Tunnard, having surveyed the rather dismal tradition of garden sculpture in the nineteenth century, recommended in 1938 in his *Gardens in the Modern Landscape*. Under the influence of the painter Paul Nash, who was taken with both the vestiges of ancient tumuli and with found shapes in the natural world, Tunnard proposed utilizing weird tree stumps that he juxtaposed to the artifice of land-scape design. He also advocated abstract shapes in sculpture, and was famous himself for utiliz-ing a recumbent figure by Henry Moore on the terrace of Bentley Wood, near Halland in East Sussex.[12] As Moore's images are at once repre-sentational and abstract, they jibe well with gardens that are both natural, by their reliance on plants, yet also abstract, by virtue of recomposing forms from outside the garden in a new composition. Dan Kiley also found another Moore sculpture essential to terminate the wonderfully austere alley of honey locusts at the Miller Garden in Columbus, Indiana. (That this Moore piece has now, sadly and disastrously, been sold off, will lose an essential dialogue between sculpture and site in this iconic modernist garden, which will need to adjust itself to a more subtle play of nat-ural forms in Kiley's design.)

Sculpture arrived, too, in the suburban garden, sometimes supplied via the local garden centre but equally by inventive formulations by garden own-ers. Some are mildly conventional; others, crazily personal. Bernard Lassus' exploration of the imagery among what he called *habitants-paysagistes* (those who designed their own property) drew upon girlie magazines, Hollywood cartoons (Snow White, Popeye with his can of spinach) and fables like the hare and the tortoise running their race to the end of Monsieur Charles Pecqueur's garden (see illus. 47). And if those inventions drew on a wealth of popular literature and films, nowadays domestic gardeners will rely on a far less inventive repertory of ready-made garden items, the reasons for which

often seem no more obscure than the need to show off to their neighbours. Local garden centres (and indeed the Internet) can supply an astonishing range of sculptural imagery, from classical urns and Medici Venuses to a veritable zoo of animals, along with the chic apparatus of more noble resi-dences (black jockeys in coloured uniforms holding lanterns). No wonder, then, in a move at once celebratory of ordinary garden ornament and ironic at this bourgeois pretension, Martha Schwartz brought dozens of frogs from a local garden store, painted them gold, and set them in a pool at an Atlanta Shopping Center. And for a temporary installation in Germany, she paraded painted dwarfs, gnomes, storks, windmills, pigs, flamingos and black jockeys holding lanterns, all mounted on white plinths as used in museum displays of sculptures, explaining that it was 'a democratic process of design in which people have a choice, and exercise it. Millions of dollars worth of these objects are sold every year . . . They reflect who we are and how we would like to be seen. They come to characterize a larger collective landscape.'[13]

In all of these, there was inevitably, and more often than not interestingly, a dialogue, variously thoughtful, critical, celebratory, ironical or banal, between the inserted items and the outdoor set-ting and residence that were found for them. The dialogue that transpires when we enter the realm of formal sculptural gardens and parks is more obvious, more serious, if not solemn. In the 50-acre garden of Joop van Caldenborgh's private founda-tion in a suburb of The Hague, originally designed in the early nineteenth century by Jan David Zocher, a landscape architect, are works by Moore, Sol LeWitt and Sylvie Fleury among others. Each has 'its own zone',[14] which carefully explores how that particular piece will look and how to respond to its place in the wood, on paths or on lawns, and how it 'talks' to visitors.

One is often uncertain how to understand the dialogue between the form of the item and its meaning and context, even with knowledge of how the piece had been entitled; that is perhaps part of the adventure and these provocations (illus. 131). Sculptures labelled 'Untitled' elicit a free range of response, and Donald Judd has mostly 'untitled' works at the Chinati Foundation in Marfa, Texas. Noguchi's Sculpture Garden in New York's Long Island City seems to have no titles at all, but most of van Caldenborgh's collection are entitled. Alternatively, titles seem designed to provoke: the title of Yoji Sasaki's 'The Garden of Visceral Serenity' at the Cornerstone Gardens in Sonoma, California, invites some puzzlement as to its palpable paradox, in that the striped lawn, gravel and Corten steel cabinet offer neither serenity nor much visceral response.[15] There is a veritable skill at inventing names that do play well in many gardens; Margaret Evangeline's *Gunshot Landscape* in the woodland of the Fields Sculpture Park in Omi, New York State, displays a painting of a similar woodland peppered with bullet holes; Louise Nevelson's 'Transparent Horizon' at MIT exposes through its massive steel frames an imaginary vista; and Mark di Suvero's *Ave* salutes the museum

131 Visitor contemplating Tim Lees's *The Heart of Stone* (1988), the Forest of Dean.

facade at Dallas with its dramatic gesture of red steel.

Both artists and curators devise titles as well as locations of where to site their pieces. At the Getty Museum in Los Angeles we know that artists could review a siting of their work using mock-ups of the proposed piece. Sculptors at the Storm King Art Center in New York State could both choose a location for their piece and arrange to move it after installation to a better location. Isamu Noguchi, for instance, wanted a mount immediately outside the main museum building at Storm King for his granite *Momo Taro* (illus. 132)

132 Storm King Art Center, New York, a view across the meadows past Isamu Noguchi's *Momo Taro*.

so it catches the visitors' attention as they emerge from the museum; his title, though, requires knowledge of a traditional Japanese folk hero, brought into the world from a peach, to read its form and narrate its story; nonetheless, as this is a rare interactive piece, children have the experience of climbing it and still miss the meaning.[16]

Some sculpture parks are located in forests, such as Grizedale in the English Lake District, or the Forest of Dean in Gloucestershire.[17] Here there is no landscaping nor obvious manipulation of the whole site; some organization of the immediate terrain may take place, or the artist can seize the given opportunities of the woodland. And in many examples, the materials draw on the woodland context: sculptures at Grizedale use timber and tree branches, rocks and elements from quarries, drystone walls, even the erosion that water makes in the undergrowth; some invoke shapes of organ pipes, or animals (within a landscape alive with red and roe deer); some, less plausibly, introduce painted images of Indians or revolvers shaped with moose horns. A rare insertion by Colin Rose of a steel circle, 40 ft across, isolates the landscape around it – a minimal (and maybe ironic) gesture to our need for a picturesque framing. In the Forest of Dean there is less attention to what we might discover in a wood, though we can find a large cube made from a variety of smaller squares and rectangles of timber, a massive and eroded quarried fragment, some banal representations of animals, a huge pine cone and its shell, and the reinstalled

The Iron Road by Keir Smith that uses elements at the end of railway sleepers with carved items placed between them: as Smith says, the use of a disused railway line blurs 'the boundaries between site and sculpture' (illus. 133); his carved insertions – an open book, a feather, cloud shapes – 'carry a sense of meaning but are not decodable'.[18]

As forests have often been thought of as natural cathedrals, a series of stained-glass 'windows' by Kevin Atherton (illus. 134) hang from the branches of trees in the woodland in Gloucestershire. In dense thickets an installation (difficult to find, in fact) by Ian Hamilton Finlay features tree plaques (illus. 135) that urge silence (no savaging of nature here). This move recalls the Renaissance literary tradition initiated by Ariosto,[19] where lovers' names were inscribed on living trees. Finlay also used the same motif in his own garden at Little Sparta and

133 Keir Smith, *The Iron Road*, 1985–6, installed on a disused railway line inside the Forest of Dean Sculpture Trail, Gloucestershire.

134 Kevin Atherton, *Cathedral*, 1986, the Forest of Dean Sculpture Trail, Gloucestershire.

in the private Fleur de l'Air in Provence. But he also marks or draws attention to trees by placing marble or stone bases around the trunks of trees, as he does at the Kröller-Müller Museum in the Netherlands,[20] thus making columns of trees, in the spirit of Laugier's appeal to nature as the basis of architecture.

Sculpture gardens and parks have been made on college campuses, former fairgrounds and military bases, ranches, large or enlarged former private estates, when owners have died or where maintenance is prohibitive, or where the style of parkland is uncongenial until it is inhabited by wonderfully modernist works. Remnants of picturesque bridges and a Gothic coffee house still survive in a romantic park at Celle, near Pistoia in Italy, remarkable for its size and its range of sculptural items within a very varied landscape. Here sculptors have created installations in places chosen by themselves: thus Finlay opted for an agricultural area on the fringes of Villa Celle's woods to situate what he called 'The Virgilian Wood' (1985), outside what he termed the 'Forest of the Avant-garde' where most of the modern pieces are located. Here in this olive grove, barely modified, he installed bronze baskets of olives, replicas of ancient ploughs and more labels on trees to celebrate Roman traditions of agriculture and poetry.

Celle allows a rich variety of dialogues:[21] sometimes with other sculptures, so Robert Morris's *Labyrinth* observes in the distance Alice Aycock's *The Nets of Solon*; sometimes with the land itself, as when Dani Karavan's *Line 1-2-3* directs a white line of concrete between two tree trunks and out

135 Ian Hamilton Finlay with Nicholas Sloan, *Schweigen*, 1988, one of a series of tree plaques in different languages in the Forest of Dean Sculpture Trail, Gloucestershire.

into the woodland: or when Fabrizio Corneli's metallic *Grande Estruso* seems like the skin of some monster, sloughed off and left in the undergrowth. Some pieces are directly allied with land art, in their invocation of time and the very ground itself: Richard Long's *Grass Circle,* or Alan Sonfist's *Circles of Time.* Other areas play literally with where they are sited and the materials found there. Water too, as well as the ground, can play a role in sculpture parks: thus at Celle, Marta Pan's two bright-red aluminium pieces float freely on the lake, while ponds elsewhere have solicited work like Allen Bertoldi's *Wood Duck*, which emerges from the water in front of the Nassau County Museum of Art in Roslyn Harbor on New York's Long Island.

Indeed, the 'expanded field' of sculpture, as set out by Rosalind E. Krauss,[22] has taken advantage of land artists, like Mary Miss, Michael Heizer, Alan Sonfist and Vito Acconci. Sonfist's *Endangered Species of New England* at the deCordova Sculpture Park and Museum in Lincoln, Massachusetts, offers steel images of the leaves of the sugar maple, burr oak, American chestnut and elm (illus. 136) and buries a time capsule of seeds from each species in the ground under the sculpture. A buried line and circle isolate a ring of grass in the lawn at the

Menil Collection (Heizer's *Isolated Mass/Circumflex #2*), and at the Laumeier Sculpture Park in St Louis, Missouri, site-specific sculptures honour ecological and natural environments with works by Finlay, Mary Miss, Frances Whitehead and Acconci's *Face of the Earth #3*, where a large face grins from the earth amid a circle of sunken seating.

As with other forests, the Celle woods contain surprises, like Caliban's hymn to the landscape 'full of noises' of Prospero's island. A trench descends into the earth and from that dark underground passage the visitor emerges into a luminous glass box, a veritable jar upon the hillside, to invoke Wallace Stevens's 'Anecdote of the Jar'; this is Bukichi Inoue's 'My Sky Hole'. The surrounding olive grove 'rises up' to the insertion, which (like the jar in Stevens's poem) takes dominion of the

136 Adam Sonfist, *Endangered Species of New England*, 2012, deCordova Sculpture Park and Museum, Lincoln, Massachusetts: steel representations of leaves of sugar maple, burr oak, American chestnut and American elm.

agricultural landscape, though the glass cube here does 'partake' of 'bird' and 'bush'. The Tuscan surroundings are suddenly seen afresh through the glass walls of the cube, or, if a visitor is inside, he or she discovers the whole landscape of olive groves through the lens (literally) of the sculptural glass box (illus. 137).[23]

The installation of 28 sculptures at the Getty Museum derived from a bequest to the Museum of the Fran and Ray Stark Collection of 20th-Century Sculpture.[24] Its campus had already been landscaped by the Olin Studio, with fountains, and a splendid cactus garden by Dennis McGlade, that juts out of the site towards the distant city of Los Angeles, and both seem themselves to constitute a sculptural insertion; subsequently, too, Robert Irwin designed his own and somewhat elaborate garden on the southern end of the campus, and, by the artist's own account, it also offers itself as some horticultural equivalent to the museum's collection of paintings (see chapter Seven). So the arrival of the Stark Collection required the Getty to arrange it around the already established campus, a task that the Olin Partnership (as it then was) took on, with the close cooperation of Getty curators, including Antonia Boström. (Irwin, meanwhile, has insisted that no sculpture could be placed in his garden.)

The siting of the pieces is partly revealed by the full-page illustrations in the catalogue, where they are necessarily photographed in close-up to show off the pieces themselves. The dialogue of items with their settings is better appreciated when we can not only walk around them – an essential element of sculptures – but can move towards or away from them and when the landscape, either immediate or distant, takes shape around them. Though individual items would ideally have been better scattered around the site, finding (in Boström's words) 'appropriate space and air, and establishing harmonious and relevant groupings or juxtaposition', it was agreed between the Getty and the Stark trustees that the collection would largely be focused on two locations, in a garden and on a terrace, both named after Fran and Ray Stark.

The garden greets visitors as they arrive at the train departure area that will bring them to the hilltop; here they can pause and examine, among others, the work of three British sculptures before they embark on their 'sculpture discovery tour' to the terrace, where they will find items by Hepworth, Magritte, Aristide Maillot and, again, Moore. The garden below is composed of small 'rooms' and, given that the austere blocks of Richard Meier's building above are not insistent down there, the sculptures dialogue more with the surrounding landscape. In contrast, against the blocks of Meier's building and terraces, items like Marino Marini's *Angel of the Citadel*, or the recumbent woman in Maillot's *Air* levitating over the whiteness of rising stairs, both accept where they are sited and wittily acknowledge the aptness of the titles in those locations. If the lower garden allows intriguing juxtapositions between the individual pieces, on the terrace above they tend to speak less for interaction than for solitary contemplation.

The California site is of course splendid, and many of the sculptures acquire an additional

137 Bukichi Inone, *My Sky Hole*, 1985–9, glass, in the Gori Collection, Parco di Celle, near Pistoia, Italy.

intensity by being seen against distant landscapes: Robert Adams's *Two* holds its stainless steel sheets against the immediate hillside and the distant high-rises, or George Rickey's *Three Squares Gyratory* moves in the wind over the same landscape. In what is also a fairly arid and austere California landscape, colour holds up well and encourages a sense of humour for Alexander Calder's *Shiny Top, Curly Bottom* or *Jousters,* Fernand Léger's *Walking Figure* or Roy Lichtenstein's *Three Brushstrokes.* Humour may be endemic to these items, but the invention and wit (in the old sense of intelligence) is apparent in much of the siting of sculptures. Some of the catalogue photographs capture the very local surroundings of the plantings, and while

this may change, it alerts one to the necessary closeness while confronting Maillot's *Summer* against a single tree or Joel Shapiro's bronze *Untitled* against a Natchez crape myrtle; the latter's insistence on the abstraction of his work, along with the marks of the wooden model from which he cast the bronze, are accentuated by the tree's bark and rich spread of its trunk.

The Stark Collection sculptures arrived after the Getty campus was built and laid out, though the Olin Partnership worked in both capacities. But a host of brand-new sculpture parks and museums have emerged with designs by eminent professionals, sometimes with the acquisition of pieces specifically chosen for the new site, as at the

National Gallery of Art in Washington, DC, also by the Olin Studio. While some early sculpture museums, like the Hirshhorn in Washington, DC, have small garden effects in their surrounding plazas, others have extended their spaces to include them. If the much reformulated sculpture garden at the Museum of Modern Art in New York has no opportunity to expand,[25] others have been able to do so; three in particular are interesting, because they both colonize new territory and call on exciting designers.[26]

The Olympic Sculpture Park, an extension of the Seattle Art Museum, was designed by the architects Weiss/Manfredi, with Charles Anderson, landscape architect, and opened in 2007. It occupies a former fuel depot and transfer rail station. The interest of this park is the 'landscape' into which and on which it is placed. In other sculpture parks it is largely a dialogue between the sculptural pieces and their natural or recreated territory. Here it must be said that the challenge to any sculpture (most have not yet been installed) is formidable as the parkland itself performs mightily. It joins the city to the waterfront with a 40-ft grade change; dramatic, zigzag green platforms leap over railroads and a highway to reach the waterfront of Elliott Bay on Puget Sound (illus. 138). The new walkway along the water incorporates a 'restored' beach, in effect a reinvented curve of boulders, debris and logs, while the planting, higher up, and in the Neukom Vivarium glasshouse and Simulated Forest Ecology, is native to the Pacific Northwest; a 60-ft forest log is installed in a concrete tub, a gesture reminiscent of Tunnard's fondness for 'found

objects'; it would be stronger if it were allowed to compete with the sculptures and not 'packaged' inside the tub. The descending lawns where the sculptures – some permanent, others temporary – will be installed also compete with the high concrete panels that line the pathways to the shore and with views over the Sound.[27] Some big pieces do their best to enlarge the parkland – yet I suspect that even the familiar pieces of Alexander Calder's large, red *Eagle* or Richard Serra's lesser known steel *Wake* have to work hard to compete with the terrain. *Wake* is a formidable and wondrous grouping of russet-coloured steel plates, and it makes an impact in its own enclave at the top of the park, more impressive than the weak exhibition pavilion further along the top, from which the zigzag descends. Fortunately, as Serra explains in a video on this sculpture, the 'subject of this piece is not its image and it is not the steel. It is you. Your experience in walking through becomes the content.'

In October 2003 the Nasher Sculpture Center garden, designed by Peter Walker, was inaugurated (see illus. 94). The building is by Renzo Piano, and it was he who approached Walker to collaborate on the site of two city blocks of a parking lot in the Dallas Arts District. In interviews with Jane Amidon, published three years later,[28] Walker explored how he responded to this 'type' of a garden by drawing on his past experience – his insistence on revealing both 'nature' and 'design', which in this case also needed respect for the sculptural art that would people the garden, on 'exploiting the horizontal' that had driven many of his previous designs, and his love of minimalist art, including land art. The garden had to provide a stage for sculptures (which would change, as they rotated from the Nasher collection), so a physical design was required that didn't compete with the sculpture and yet provided sufficient 'nature' to dialogue with whatever was placed there. It became more simple as the design evolved: walls blocked sound from outside, fountains added their garden sounds, the walkways were lined with live oaks, for Walker wanted a public space to suggest the original intimacy of the Nashers' private estate; the garden also had to respond to rhythms of Piano's building at the west and, at the east, its descent via stairs to an interior auditorium. The spaces were designed, first, by thinking of the different sizes of modern sculpture, including their impact on visitors – a Richard Serra 'wall' versus George Segal's human figures – and then devising

locations that curators could use for changing exhibitions (it was decided that no more than 30 pieces would be shown at any one time). As big pieces would have to be brought into the garden and large machinery would be used to deliver them, there was little point in devising 'garden rooms' to set off the sculptures; they themselves had to 'form the spaces' of display. It is classical (Walker would say 'universal'), not fussy or picturesque in its details, with a limited tree palette of live oaks, cedar elms and close-clipped holly; simple, yet concealing a considerable 'armature' for the mechanical technology.

How you devise places for the exterior display of sculpture also preoccupied the Minneapolis Sculpture Garden, as it expanded under a trio of landscape architects. Dedicated in 1988, it epitomized the development of a major collection,

138 Weiss/Manfredi Architects, the reinvented shore on Puget Sound, Washington State, 2007.

paralleled and challenged by ideas in landscape architecture. The location is a former armoury site with adjacent, much-frequented ground that became known as Armory Gardens. In 1913 it was an exhibition site for a convention of the Society of American Florists and Ornamental Horti-culturalists. Meanwhile the Walker Art Center, which had opened in 1927 across the road from the armoury, was demolished and its green space was occasionally used for displays of sculpture. In 1971 a new museum building by Edward Larrabee Barnes replaced the old; this included terraces for the display of sculpture; but with increasing pressure on space the Center joined with the Minneapolis Park and Recreation Board to make the site of the former armoury into a permanent sculpture garden.

The Barnes project, designed jointly with landscape architect Peter Rothschild, had four enclosures and broad *allées*, with primly shorn evergreen walls providing a neutral background for all sorts of sculptures (illus. 139). In its turn the axis of the Barnes garden was continued into an open naturalistic field where Claes Oldenburg's *Spoonbridge and Cherry* fountain was placed. Barnes also designed the conservatory that extends down the western edge of this garden; it provides a climate both for horticultural opportunities otherwise unavailable during Minnesota winters and for sculptural viewing (including Frank Gehry's *Standing Glass Fish,* 1986). The design of the horticulture was entrusted to landscape architects Barbara Stauffacher Solomon and Michael Van Valkenburgh. In 1991 the latter also designed the

'arbor' and flower garden beyond the field with the Oldenburg; its irregular spaces nonetheless echo the quartered precision of Barnes's initial layout. Now a further landscape by Michel Desvigne has been designed for the sloping hillside behind a new museum extension by Herzog & de Meuron: a grid of paths penetrates a woodland of Minnesota birches and bluestem, which the French landscaper has referenced as a nineteenth-century designed 'nature' meeting the Jeffersonian grid.

Altogether the Walker (and walkers) will have very different spatial experiences of sculpture within a range of different landscape gardens and land-scapes: the Barnes version was of early European gardens, with *allées* and geometrical enclosures; the conservatory's interior sequence of experimental renderings of plants, earth and rocks contrasts in turn with the Oldenburg-dominated irregular meadowscape, and then with the flower garden and arbor, and now with the Desvigne woodland of Minnesota birches and bluestem. Artifice and 'natures' now collaborate to deliver a 'succession of surprises' to visitors and fresh zones for sculpture's own performances. It is a dialogue where Finlay's idea of the savaging of nature by art may call a truce.

139 Aerial view of the 1988 Minneapolis Sculpture Garden at the Walker Art Center, Minneapolis.

140 Michel Desvignes, Passage des Étangs Gobert, Versailles, 2013.

ELEVEN

DROSSCAPES

'All world's glory is but dross unclean.'
EDMUND SPENSER, 1585

'The theme of reconversion of great spaces with
functions or occupations that time and
circumstances have made obsolete is precious and
profoundly current.'
PROAP, *Landscape Architecture*

Many of the places explored in other chapters
actually deal with what is here called 'drosscapes', since more and more 'space' for making
gardens and parks is found on landfills and other
obsolete industrial infrastructure. What distinguishes the approach of this chapter is that we see
in the making of place both the reformulation of
redundant or waste sites and at the same time
evidence of their earlier existence.

The term was coined by Alan Berger in his
book *Drosscape: Wasting Land in Urban America*
(2006). It is a sobering as well as a paradoxical
book, not least because his stunning photographs
of these wasted lands make them attractive – the
(mostly) aerial views lend these sites the beauty of

a new sublimity. His text is largely devoted to
describing and naming (in a series of acronyms) a
cluster of truly dysfunctional places, which gives little sense of how they might be transformed; among
others there are LINS (landscape of infrastructure),
LOCOS (landscapes of contamination) and even
LODS (landscapes of dwelling, that is, suburban
sprawl). A further book is promised that will address
this; all Berger does is suggest a 'strategy to pro-
ductively integrate' such sites, asking the designer
'to search for, identify, and educate the stakeholder
or group most likely to realize the need for change'
(p. 239). Berger takes his title from a sonnet by
the Elizabethan poet Edmund Spenser ('all world's
glory is but dross unclean'); that Spenser was preoccupied with gardens and landscapes throughout
The Faerie Queene suggests the glory or gold that
could lurk beneath the uncleaned dross of today's
landscapes.[1]

There are three, obviously related, aspects of
drosscapes: what once had been there, the process by which they are cleaned up, and how we
learn to see that process; for it is not simply a
question of not finding any dross to observe,
but – from a landscape-architecture perspective

– seeing how well it has been *re*worked. To see *how* dross has been cleaned is an essential part of our response to it and of our judgement of its success: an invisible design is not very engaging. Thus the High Line in New York, by now an extraordinarily famous (indeed overcrowded) example of drosscape, is a reworked elevated railway line that highlights remnants of the rail line, the rich planting throughout by Piet Oudolf and the skill with which the new design makes itself visible: this self-consciousness comes not just in planting that could not be found on any abandoned railway line or the benches throughout its length, but with the subtle *faux* concrete rail lines (interspersed with actual remnants) that curl up at the pathways when they meet the planted beds (see illus. 69).

A landscape designer like Martha Schwartz is particularly active and 'vocal' in ensuring that we notice what she terms the 'curating' of the 'urban environment'.[2] She brings her own flair to curating sometimes by the use of patterns and colour, fragrant disruptions of form yet happily invoked in conventional green spaces, joining her new to what was old or derelict. Like many designers, she has been drawn to the devastated Ruhr region in Germany: for her *Power Lines*, she salutes the electricity lines that cross the land by planting lines of corn directly below them on the ground, then establishes a radical cross-access of bright red plastic bales that lead up the hill to a statue of Otto von Bismarck, the Iron Chancellor who first unified Germany. The design embraces metaphor (red is the 'colour' of power, but Bismarck too

was powerful) and recycling, which is after all what is happening to the Ruhr. And every year, with the farm operator, the agricultural land will be harvested, the hay re-baled, the ground re-ploughed and re-seeded; what was in the first instance a temporary exhibition continues to re-animate the land on which Bismarck benignly gazes, which the power lines still traverse.

The success of Duisburg-Nord Park, also in the Ruhr, is that we view what was once there through the lens of the now; or maybe, through the lens of the old we grasp the potential for what can happen today. This does not always happen: Central Park was established on a wasteland of squatters, debris and marauding goats, and nothing of that remains to be seen, except in old photographs. Parc André Citroën in Paris was in fact built on the cleared headquarters of the Citroën factory; the park is interesting in itself, but nothing except its name suggests what was once there (excepting a forlorn bust of Monsieur Citroën). By contrast at Parc de Bercy in the east of the city, there are (just) sufficient remainders of the former Dépôt des Vins to make a visitor, if attuned to the history of the site and quick to spot some telltale signs, capable of seeing both the transformation and what has been transformed.[3]

It helps to look dross in the face, as Berger's photographs do so well, and see what it is and what, perhaps, we want to see retained as a memory of it. When I first arrived in America, I was dismayed by the so-called 'Bad Lands', the New Jersey that the train passes through after leaving New York City for Washington, DC; further south,

I was dismayed again to see how frequently American buildings could simply be abandoned only for the same thing to be erected on the next lot. While I guess I have got used to acknowledging that there was more abundant space in America than in England (though for how long?), I now find the 'Bad Lands' poetic, because I have learned to look at them with fresh eyes: the wetlands, the channels winding through forests of phragmites, the water fowl wading along the marshes, the rusting bridges permanently open, telephone and electrical masts soaring above the water, many shrubs and the occasional determined tree, random tracks that seem to lead nowhere, the elevated expressway and the occasional building which announces that it processes clean linen for hotels miles away. It is a land of drosscape that I'd hate to see 'improved', partly because it speaks so clearly of how such a cultural landscape has emerged. We need some reminders of what we are eager to remedy, especially when they have a beauty of their own. So I like the huge cooling towers of electricity plants in the

UK, for one of which Brenda Colvin has provided a new landscape (see chapter Seven), the three white domes of the Early Warning System on the North York Moors, the whirling arms of modern wind turbines, or the sight of pylons striding evenly over the land ('the statement of their steel / Contradicts nature's softer architecture'[4]). One of the earliest attempts to accept and yet rework a redundant site was a gas works in Seattle; it could of course have been demolished, but Rich Haag saw its poetry, around which he created a park by capping the toxic earth with a green sward where people could play; though the soil is still leaching toxins and the gas works are now fenced and inaccessible, they are, though much diminished, a modernist folly in the landscape.

The image here of Gas Works Park (illus. 141) implies that the way we look at 'bad places'[5] – through a camera lens, for example, though erstwhile with a tinted Claude glass – can change our attitudes towards them. Berger's camera (a 'CONTAX 645 with Fuji Velvia film') makes his subjects

141 Gas Works Park, Seattle, 1971–88.

appealing, while at the same time making us realize that they are worth taking seriously. Another earlier response to drosscapes, also with an Instamatic ('What rationalists call a camera'[6]), was by Robert Smithson, touring the entropic realm of Passaic in New Jersey: his images are mundane – gushing waste pipes, sandboxes, a pumping derrick, a wood and steel bridge, a concrete plant – which having photographed he then labels as 'monuments', 'ruins in reverse', hints of new constructions that might eventually be built. He refuses 'crass anthropomorphic' glosses on the sexual possibilities of pipes spurting water into the river, but sees a 'unitary' chaos, a fascinating and appealing place without a rational past or without the 'big' events of history. His voyage to and through Passaic responded to its physical conditions as well as his relish for a new aesthetic. One commentator calls his monuments 'lethargic', deriving the word from the mythic river Lethe in Hades that caused drinkers to forget; out of which cultural forgetfulness Smithson draws inspiration. He was not a landscape architect; but those that are can ask the same question – 'Is it impossible', asks Bernard Lassus, 'to rediscover and/or invent a landscape from the one that is blemished, over-exploited, and not easy to interpret?'[7]

The decay of old infrastructures is not a contemporary phenomenon, nor is it confined to the United States, on which Berger focuses. Modern society worldwide is increasingly confronted with the need to replace and transform airports, railway marshalling yards, landfills, defunct mills, old reservoirs, harbour facilities, piers. Parc de la Villette in Paris took over the abattoirs, yet all you see now of the original site are the magnificent iron pavilions and the house of the abattoir manager, to which a chunk of one of Bernard Tschumi's red follies is attached like a limpet. These are what the German landscape architect Peter Latz terms 'dealing with bad places'; yet, as his iconic parkland for Duisburg-Nord implies, this 'dealing' can take various forms.

This touches on the distinction that I made in *A World of Gardens*, which seems useful to both designers themselves and the societies for which they cater – a distinction between the prose and the poetry of landscape architecture. Many spaces today need 'cleaning', and designers can play a fundamental role in achieving that, as Berger indicates; but the topic needs also to be taken to a more conceptual, metaphorical or rhetorical level in which non-designers can learn to understand place-making, which is what Smithson offered us in writing about Passaic. Put simply, landscape architects have to provide, on the one hand, good 'prose' – places that are useful, convenient, equipped with some necessary items like pathways, steps (accessibility ramps), seats, facilities like toilets, places where kids can play safely and grown-ups stroll peaceably. The poetry of place (a term sometimes used by designers like Paolo Bürgi or Martha Schwartz, among others) will push designs beyond, yet not neglect, the merely utilitarian and practical; they enlarge our vision, stimulate our thoughts beyond the immediate surroundings, usher us physically and imaginatively into places that surprise us, or make us realize that previous place-making had not quite done anything like this.[8] The 'cleaning' of drosscapes should achieve that rare excitement that comes from doing something well *and* beautifully, like Duisburg-Nord, the High Line or like Brooklyn Bridge Park, which creates a new beauty out of what previously were seen as wastelands. Some 'gardens on paper' may also prove to be 'poetic', perhaps too visionary to win approval or funding (see chapter Thirteen).

One person's poetry can be, of course, another person's poison; tastes change, and change in different social situations. But the idea that a design be perceived not only as a design, but as one that makes a place useful and/or 'poetic', needs to be tested: a comparison of three recent park designs in France can help.[9] All three either took over former railway yards or contributed to transport infrastructure, and all are firmly dedicated to the practicalities of their users. Jardins d'Eole serves an area with many North African immigrants, providing outdoor space, vegetable gardens, basketball courts, walls to be covered with graffiti (removed ever so often for new images); places to 'hang out', but also small grass areas where people enjoy a solitary snooze. Parc Clichy-Batignolles is more genteel, with straight walks, seating and benches separated by berms, planted with trees, to provide variety in a flat place, shrubs and flowers, including some in sunken waterbeds; it also provides a skateboard area down one side of the park with an area for watching the action. Both sites accept the elongated areas of railway marshalling yards; Eole quite emphatically by stretching

a raised walkway along its length with views to the west over the existing railways at the gares de l'Est and du Nord and over a gravel area within the park; this echoes how railway lines are laid out, but also suggests (faintly) a desert geography for the immigrants that will slowly allow plants to root themselves to make their own 'garden'. Parc Clichy-Batignolles has some intricate paving that emphasizes the elongated site and will eventually take the eye towards Renzo Piano's Palace of Justice, but otherwise makes little effort to do more than make a pleasant interlude in an otherwise banal neighbourhood. The 'Passage du Jardin des Etangs Gobert' at Versailles (illus. 140) won a prize from the 'Trophées de la Mobilité', that (avoiding the bureaucratic jargon) awards contributions to transport infrastructure: this design addressed the large and heavily used station at Versailles-Chantiers. A wasteland (*friche*) in an empty reservoir (*étang*) that once served the fountains at the château was transformed into an open space edged with thousands of new and varied trees that line the pedestrian walkway around it. It found for suburbia 'a new nature' and 'a territory free of representation'.[10] The nearby Versailles gardens are of course full of representations. It is both a 'waiting-room' for those taking a train, a place to stroll and circulate with pushchairs, and a pleasant route through the new park, down stairs along new baseball courts and then into the *quartier* Saint-Louis. The mayor of Versailles affirms that, despite the improvements, 'nature has preserved all of her rights' (a key notion when *droits* or civil rights became an assured feature of the

French Revolution). Desvigne's design responds, then, as does much of his work, to random spaces, leftovers in the modern city:[11] here it caters to the needs of railway users who live in the town and also retrieves a historical relict of the chateau of Versailles, while at the same time making the design both attractive and – especially when the trees grow – more visible: in the centre of the *prairie* is a meandering bench in the form of a slice of a tree-trunk bole designed by the artist Inessa Hansch. Whether you can read this metaphor is moot, but it certainly asks visitors to observe that within the recovered wasteland somebody has been at work. It is also a deliberate artwork, whereas its treescape and the worlds of the other two parks are far more sotto voce, depending as much upon how their users recognize any aesthetic dimension in them.

Another response to railway dereliction – a result probably of using more diesel traffic and more frequent air travel – is the Natur-Park Schöneberger Südgelände, south of the Tempelhof Airport in Berlin. The term itself notes the opposition or dialogue between 'nature' and the arts of park-making; it also implies a poetry that comes from that exchange. The exchanges were political and social as well as ecological, the result of much debate about how the area should be treated during and after the Cold War; the success of this debate on the ground is clear, even if the rival factions may still be divided. The place itself mingles, on the one hand, ecological zeal to bring visitors into a area of rusting industry, spontaneous growth of forest and seeds once brought by freight trains from all over Europe with, on the other, landscape designers and artists who invest in it – graffiti artists, those who repaint the locomotive and repoint the brickwork of the turntable, the construction and maintenance of the belvedere, and tree-house. The walkways, or *begehbare Skulptur* ('walkable sculpture'), proposed by the art collective Odious, alert visitors to this dialogue – the steel walkways protect you from compacting the soil or damaging plant communities, but the rough gravel and crushed stone elsewhere remind you of the texture of railway structures. 'In the lightness of the design there is a depth and complexity' (illus. 142).[12] Old railtracks survive in the straight lines of the new paths which are interrupted by trees that grow in them. The entry into the park makes the liminal moment explicit: across a manicured lawn and through an opening in a bright yellow wall, visitors enter the new forest; the entrance contrasts with plants thriving on the disused railtrack on top of the wall and with a derelict water tower, which once fed the steam locomotives, glimpsed over the trees. Inscribed on the yellow wall are words of a German geographer, Karl Ganser, *die Kunst ist der nächste Nachbar der Wildnis* ('art is the nearest neighbour of wilderness').

Latz + Partner provided a supreme example of the dialogue of poetry and prose at the Duisburg-Nord Landscape Park in the German Ruhr, and it is justly famous (illus. 143, 144).[13] The park has grown up around and within a derelict steel mill and foundry, the destruction of which the designers refused to contemplate; that it would be enormously expensive was less the concern than

142 Natur-Park Schöneberger Südgelände, Berlin, opened 2000.

would be the loss of a powerful and sublime piece of modern infrastructure. Instead, they reused much of the surviving fabric for active recreation – climbing walls, scuba-diving, jogging, cycling trails and a children's playground – provided an amphitheatre for drama and concerts (its arena comprised of huge steel plates from the old foundry), floodlit the chimneys and cooling towers at night with work by the British light artist Jonathan Park, and reserved the rest of the site for parkland and for gardens established within the former ore bunkers; for one of the walled enclosures, the designers copied a box garden from their own house at Ampertshausen. Duisburg-Nord is a wonderful infusion of trees and planting into what was a toxic terrain: scents of blossoms mingle with the still palpable aroma of rust and coal, fragments of machinery become sculptural moments, water irises bloom in the River Emscher (previously hidden in a culvert), plants crowd into the ruins

143, 144 Duisburg-Nord Landscape Park, designed by Latz + Partner, 1990–2002.

and under the overhead walkways. What were abandoned, dark satanic mills renew our modern sense of sublimity.

The same vision has informed other places by Latz + Partner in Saarbrücken, Turin and Israel:[14] a refusal to erase what could be reformulated, and layering derelict or contaminated sites with new garden ideas. Nonetheless, echoes of garden-making traditions do not mimic any one mode – no picturesque, no Baroque formats. So at Saarbrücken Harbour, which was virtually destroyed in the Second World War, a sunken garden is placed between the River Saar and the filled-up coal-harbour basin, which Latz did not want to open up (illus. 145). The garden incorporates a cluster of readily understood garden items: a modern pavilion, a sunken water theatre (Latz sees this as a gesture to both the Mausoleum of Augustus in Rome and the botanical garden at Padua), a grove of trees, a series of small squared gardens, avenues of poplar trees either side of the autobahn that jumps over the garden and the river and under which Latz places a water basin like a mirror; there is also a brand new water-gate, a ruined folly-like fragment of a curved brick facade, through which water from the park is pumped and descends from different levels into the lake; the cascading noise cancels some of the surrounding traffic on the

bridge above and purifies and oxygenates the water. Lines of trees through the park recall the former tracks for trains and cranes, and like any number of older gardens organize new site-lines into the adjacent urban landscape. Elsewhere, the onsite debris has been structured into forms that guide one through the gardens, a new 'rubble aesthetic' where collage affirms both ruptures and continuity.[15]

In contrast to the weave and intricacy of gardens at Saarbrücken Harbour, the garden element at Parco Dora, Turin, is more austere and conventional. Yet the rectangular flowerbeds, park benches and trees (as yet small) are not only overwhelmed by remains of the former factory but are given a fresh vitality by that contest. And when shrubs climb up the 30 steel pillars that

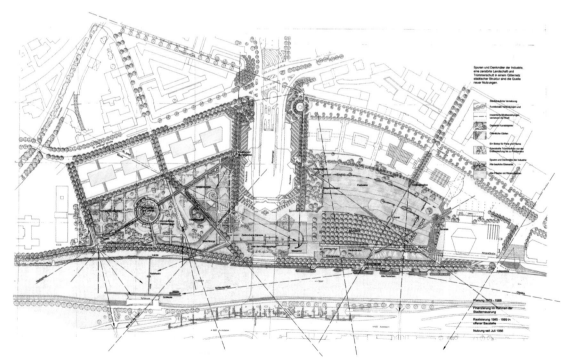

145 The design for Saarbrücken Harbour Island, Germany, 1985–9, where an autobahn cuts through the park.

146 Parco Dora, Turin, Italy, designed by Latz + Partner, from 2004.

once held the roof, when the trees make a canopy that mimics the adjacent roof of the former office building ('a technical canopy', says Latz), when a water garden has been made within the concrete foundations of the Vitali iron foundry, and when the concrete lid over the river running through the site has been lifted and the unnatural culvert revealed, it will seem, in Peter Latz's words, 'futuristic' (illus. 146). There is much new housing close-

by (first built for the 2006 Winter Olympics), so the space will be more intensively used, with skateboard ramps and other municipal activities for recreation and leisure; but a long, elevated walkway between the towers, to some of which access can be made, will provide a 'completely different view of the site in the future'.

A huge 'earthwork', 85 metres high, in the flat lands near Tel Aviv is the result of the accumulation

147 Plan for Hiriya Mountain, Tel Aviv, from 2004. The central oasis on the mountaintop, lush with tropical planting and maintained by a stormwater management system.

of household and commercial waste over half a century, an Israeli 'Mount Trashmore'. Hiriya Mountain occupies land of a little Arab town of that name, abandoned by its inhabitants after the war of independence in 1948. The flocks of birds – vultures and seagulls (a real hazard to Ben Gurion Airport) – the smells of methane and from rotting material, polluted water leach-ing into neighbouring rivers: it was on every account a disaster zone. In 2000 nearly three dozen distinguished artists were invited to come up with suggestions for the site: land art, muse-ums, research parks and all sorts of utopian and bizarre projects for the country's 'navel' (as it had come to be called). Eventually an interna-tional competition was launched by the Beracha

Foundation, which was won by Latz + Partner in 2004.

Their proposal was to keep the mountain as a centrepiece of Ayalon Park: but retaining its conspicuous silhouette and steep sides involved much understanding of its stability and the chemistry of what might be going on inside it, for its identity is precisely that of being something created by humans *as* a landscape. And this landscape would draw on a cluster of archetypal forms: a *wadi*, terraces to surround the mountain and sustain the cliffs (which Latz wanted retained rather than flattened, as engineers had proposed), an inner oasis or hollowed-out segment created by the original access routes of lorries delivering trash, and more terraces with gardens and secret gardens that lead to a belvedere with views of Tel Aviv. It required immense technological skills to deal with methane, accumulated rainwater and cleaned water from a recycling plant, planting for both agriculture on and around the base terraces and surrounding the oasis above. But the design also promised a poetry of place – not just the planting, the sunken oasis, the high belvedere with its canopy 'shaped like a paraglider', or the night-time lighting to mark the descent after dark, but a clear-sighted *idea* of both a past that could not be ignored and a future that respected its transformation (illus. 147).

Ballast Point Park, on one of the many promontories that jut into Sydney Harbour, was created by landscape architects McGregor Coxall and was opened in 2009;[16] it is but one of many landscapes marking these headlands: the same firm did the BP Park across the bay, and Peter Walker did another, also visible from it. But Ballast Point Park is somewhat different, in its celebration of defunct infrastructure and in creating an enormously successful community park for the neighbouring and upwardly mobile area of Balmain, from which the parkland is reached down the hill. Where once oil had been delivered, made into grease and shipped out by lorry, and the delivering ships reloaded with ballast, the site had become a derelict and toxic wasteland of storage and containment tanks. Only three oblong and horizontal containers now survive, but the tanks are memorialized in both an invented outline of a former tank, inscribed with a line from the Australian poet Les Murray, and lower down by a series of circular, Corten steel rings in grass that mark the former tanks (illus. 148). Downwards towards the ocean, visitors are led through a wondrous landscape of new and old concrete walls, some of which have been sliced to make stairs or to gain entry from a walkway onto the ring of grass circles; there are steel walkways alongside the water or through vast cliffs of gabion blocks made from local brick and stone rubble (into one of which a security helmet has been enclosed). Areas of grass have been recovered by uncovering infill around the rocks; terraces and an amphitheatre are sculpted out of the cliff; seats and gravel mark overlooks or the site where an even earlier villa was excavated (some of the discovered artifacts are displayed in a case). As we left along the upper belvedere, neighbours were enjoying an evening barbecue.

148 Ballast Point Park, Birchgrove, Sydney, Australia, 2009.

Just as other 'bad places' have become sites of reinvention, so industrial sites become urban housing – Hammarby Sjöstad in Stockholm has 9,000 housing units and commercial space and water-treatment basins – while garbage dumps, given the current demand and requirement for better recycling, have become a big opportunity for designers to respond: Metabolon landfill in North Rhine-Westphalia caps its mound in bright orange,

visible for miles, its sides black rather than grassed. Moerenuma Park in Higashi-ku, Sapporo, Japan, was originally a garbage landfill site before being designed by Isamu Noguchi; opened partly in 1998 and with a grand opening in 2005, it consists of nine sectors – a Forest of Cherry Trees with seven play areas for children, a beach, a play mountain, a music shell, a sea fountain, water plaza and Mount Moere.[17] I also particularly like Mount

Trashmore, a public park in Virginia Beach, where rather than heads of famous presidents as carved on the face of Mount Rushmore, there are mountain and lake trails, a host of activities and entertainments and a 24,000-sq.-ft (2,200 sq. metre) skate park that features an extensive street course including an above-ground, 7-ft-deep (2.1 m) bowl.

Nor are all sites that require or call for dross-cleaning those that are considered toxic, redundant or dangerous. Different kinds of threat, cultural and even artistic, have been encountered and compensated for: in New York both Bryant Park and Jacob Javits Plaza responded, respectively, to the threats of an unwelcoming park in the middle of downtown Manhattan (see chapter Six) and to the unnerving steel sculpture of Richard Serra's *Tilted Arc* in Lower Manhattan. This loomed over city workers in their lunch breaks outside City Hall, so it was removed and replaced with a garden insertion by Martha Schwartz – a cheery dialogue between a purple ground surface and green benches that encircled small grass mounds (the benches were copied from the long benches on the Mall in Central Park, but here weave their way around the mounds and across the open plaza). Not a threat, though people talking on the benches had the strange sense of talking to people slightly behind them on the circular seats. But it too was replaced with a new plaza, by Michael Van Valkenburgh, which gave more emphasis to garden materials, regular benches and scattered stools, and a clear way through to the adjacent federal building.

Rural as well as urban landscapes, as Berger's photography showed, require thought and care. Vulnerable coastal lines have to be saved from excess vehicular traffic and pedestrians that wear away the dune ecology – which Nádia Schilling did in Portugal for the first stage of the restoration project at Arribas, where wooden pathways, platforms and steps directed visitors and at the same time taught them to appreciate the complex landform. Fields threatened by new housing in the German Ruhr can be 'saved' by an ingenious redesign, from which inhabitants learned to appreciate the adjacent agriculture. The local farmer, with advice from a designer like Paolo Bürgi, found he could enhance his fields with imaginative ploughing and planting, and make routine, prosaic work appealing with visible forms and bands of field flowers that caught the attention of the new suburban inhabitants (illus. 149, 150).

Countrysides left barren and uninviting, with the scars of abandoned quarries, can be brought into both agricultural usage and even garden-like parks: one in Hammonton, New Jersey, close to Philadelphia, was a former clay quarry filled with illegally dumped household waste and used for unauthorized off-road vehicle use, while the land around it had been the scene of a murder and an attempted invasion by a motorcycle gang. First it was destined for housing developments; when the deal fell through its present owner, with proposals from Martha Schwartz, turned it around into a place that incorporates an arboretum, a park and a garden. Schwartz terms the Winslow

149, 150 New field designs for the Ruhr.

Farms Conservancy 'a large-scale agricultural project' that reclaims the place for ecology, admits a variety of programmes (dog training, organic farm, artist's retreat), and allows the landscape a strongly aesthetic dimension. Its visual forms reclaim not only the abused land with elements of garden art, like Bürgi's fields in the Ruhr, but earthworks, avenues of rotund cedars, contrasted field crops, circles within the woods, mown clearings marked with lines of trees. The reclamation is therefore palpably that – a cleaned drosscape, where we see both what has been refigured and the legibility of the new figures.

151 The garden of the Paleis Het Loo, Apeldoorn, showing in the background the restored Dutch garden, and in the foreground the shadow of the tree on the lawn of the later 'English' area.

TWELVE

REINVENTED GARDENS

Kathryn Gustafson's rehabilitation of Crystal Palace Park in London in 2005 tried, as its designers argued, to recover a 'lost place' after considerable neglect.[1] They essentially accepted Joseph Paxton's plan, despite the loss in 1936 of the glass palace itself and insufficient funding for the whole project. They chose to re-emphasize only certain parts of the original design: his grand terraces, the long axis down into areas of calculated informality, where reformulated water edges and paths could lead through a revitalized picturesque landscape into Paxton's original Geological Time Trail. That nineteenth-century educational narrative and the deliberate element of exploration and discovery were at the heart of the rehabilitation – researching older plant materials (re-treating a rhododendron dell), finding the ferns that 'matched the dinosaur age', and seasonal planting that helped to emphasize the dimensions of deep time. The designers also wished to provide 'some decree of awareness about the subject matter', thus asserting, not only the educational object of Paxton, but a dominant aspect of eighteenth-century picturesque, arguably central to any landscape design that does not want to escape, under the radar, our

recognition of it *as a design*. A recognition of the centrality of design is especially central to the recreation or reinvention of gardens.

Given the inevitable vulnerability, or even total loss, of gardens, for even with excellent maintenance plants grow and then die, while hard space can also decay, it is understandable that people want to recover them, especially famous ones that didn't make it through time's depredations or fashions of cultural taste. It is a fact, too, that it is not just *old* gardens that need this attention: Dan Kiley's NationsBank Plaza in Tampa, Florida, is sorely in need of conservation; Geoffrey Jellicoe's cathedral precinct at Exeter – a processional way with subtle variations in step width and height – is threatened with 'modernization'. In 2014 the Frick Collection art museum in New York proposed, to accommodate its enlargement, eliminating a Russell Page garden there, of which there are few comparable examples, rather than any attempt to recreate it. While more recent designs may enable something more like an 'authentic' reconstruction, there are still problems with their conservation.[2]

At issue here is what does one do, or want to do, or feel that it is necessary to do, to 'recover' a decayed or 'lost' garden? There is a triad of rein-ventions: first, the rehabilitation of a specific landscape, one arguably famous or unusual, that has decayed and yet needs to be brought again to light; second, the creation *ad nuovo* of a garden in a 'style' that we want to recognize as 'Japanese', 'Elizabethan', 'Chinese' or 'Italian'. But in those two approaches a third option can be possible: the rethinking of older gardens, whether locally spe-cific or stylistically generalized, that can honour their origins (cultural and formal elements) as well as make them recognizably new. This is the most challenging of the three, negotiating how to permit a site to resume a new life and accept its modernity, along with the impossible if not absurd task of making an original site 'authentic' – absurd, in that no modern person, even a historical expert, can really grasp today how a former garden would have been 'read' originally. We may accept that *materials* could be 'authentic', traditional Chinese items like rockwork, galleries, zigzag bridges and inscriptions; we could even try and 'bring back Olmsted's planting'. But beyond that, it is a ques-tion of whether modern visitors respond to how a site was originally viewed, to how it would have been received by its contemporaries: would we know an Olmsted plant nowadays when it was reintroduced as being original? We might just recover a garden's original *forms*, but today we see those very forms differently; any authenticity tends to be our own.[3]

A modern reconstitution will bear the traces of its contemporary refashioning: thus the geog-rapher David Lowenthal noted that even 'A granary reconstructed with Roman technology and properly aged materials nonetheless looks wrong, because its specificities destroy our flexible image of the past. The reconstruction fixes or freezes a particular image, *short circuiting the imag-ination*.'[4] It is useful to recall the story 'Pierre Menard, Author of the Quixote' by Jorge Luis Borges, where Menard chooses to write out Cervantes's *Don Quixote* word for word exactly as originally written; the modern text is the same as its original, but how it is now read will be dif-ferent; the interaction with a seventeenth-century novel by a modern reader will be different from that by original readers of the Spanish book.[5] Of course, if chance has it that a reader today uses Menard's version and mistakes it for the original, s/he is still reading *Don Quixote* as a modern reader. In a reinvented garden, we should be able to appreciate both an original text or style and its contemporary handling or visitation.

Total reformulations of lost gardens are rare because they are expensive. In 1988 the Dutch government decided to recover the garden of the Paleis Het Loo to mark the tercentenary of the invitation to William of Orange and Queen Mary to assume the English and Scottish thrones fol-lowing the banishment of James II. The palace itself was contemporary with the original garden, created for William after his departure (he never saw the garden in his lifetime). But during the nineteenth century, as happened to many older geometrical designs, the garden site was buried under a naturalistic 'English' landscape. But in this instance, the original Dutch garden had not only been recorded in many engravings and careful verbal descriptions, but – once excavation took place – many bits of the original layout were discovered below the nineteenth-century grade. Thus it was possible to make the whole garden anew (illus. 151), with one exception: a corner of the 'English' garden contained a tree much beloved by the Dutch queen, set in a grassy area that was not included in the reinvention. The recreation was an astonishing and costly recovery, and it did look remarkably 'authentic', if a touch 'brand new' and clean (I was a member briefly of one of the committees that advised on the work, so maybe I'm biased). Given that few Dutch gardens of that period survived in the Netherlands, it was good to see what one might have looked like. Yet the surviving fragment of 'English' garden at one side and at a higher grade clearly made the restored Dutch one precisely that (restored). Thus it lent itself to uncritical as well as expert appraisal.

A similar recovery at Kenilworth Castle was far less successful (illus. 152).[6] The garden was famous for receiving Queen Elizabeth in 1575, and its lavish design and display for the royal visit were described in a long letter by Robert Laneham (Langham) the year afterwards; but nothing now remained on the site. An early attempt to re-vision the original garden was a big disappointment. So

152 The restored garden at Kenilworth Castle, 2009.

after considerable research into sixteenth-century gardens and planting, though there was little useful archaeology (just the footprints of an aviary, remains of a terrace and a fountain base), the garden was completely 'restored' and opened in May 2009. Now all visitors bring into it their own fabric of assumptions and beliefs, so it can presumably please those who enjoy the video (but not the garden?) where costumed actors and one purporting to be Queen Elizabeth parade the grounds; they can forget that the wild birds in the restored aviary are not original (it is now illegal, anyway, to cage them) and, while the obelisks and fountains may be plausible, the planting is imaginary and wholly speculative (Laneham said nothing about plants except that they had a 'sweet scent'). In short, the scale, materials and structures are anachronistic, but could perhaps please those who want a timeless, instant 'history'.

A restoration that seems to have managed a judicious compromise, even more than Het Loo, took place at Aberglasney in Carmarthenshire, Wales. I was myself at the very initiation of this garden restoration: in February 1988, with William Wilkins, I visited this sadly neglected site to find what seemed to me, in front of the ruined shell of the house, a very early cloister garden that echoed both another British seventeenth-century garden at Moor Park and memories of *cryptoportici* in Italy that Englishmen could have seen. It was an astonishing find, and I am said to have exclaimed on site to Wilkins, 'This is one you have to restore!' ('you' being the newly established Welsh Garden History Society, of which he was then president).

With a colleague at Lampeter I then wrote a brief essay on the place to explain what we thought had been there in the sixteenth and seventeenth centuries;[7] thereafter, I could only watch from afar as it was slowly recovered and re-established. It was in June 2014, in pouring rain, that I got to see it once more.

Whether what we see there now in the 'renewed' version can be in any way 'authentic' is doubtful. But it is an unusual place, which has made a clear acknowledgement that, as with so many gardens, this is a palimpsest with visible evidence of a multi-layered past of alterations and additions. When in 1608–9 Aberglasney became the home of the Rudd family, the property was described as having 'seven messuages, seven gardens, and seven orchards', which gives some sense of the alterations that have occurred over 400 years. It was perhaps Bishop Rudd of St David's who built the cloister.

But that feature (illus. 153) is central to the site, for it dominates the surrounding gardens, and the material of its stonework, steps and decorative pavements have been carefully recovered and restored. It is possible that the western end (directly opposite the house) was made first to provide views from its upper terrace, and that the lateral arcades and terraces were added later. The open terrace above the cloister arcade allows a view of the pond below and the countryside westwards towards Grongar Hill, made famous by the poet and painter John Dyer, who lived in the house in the early eighteenth century, and whose poem 'The Country Walk' (1726) seems to gesture

153 Aberglasney cloister, from 1995; photograph 2014.

towards the house (the 'dome' of his poem derives from the Latin *domus* or house), while his other conventional landscape topoi could allude to the garden itself. Between house and cloister is a modern gesture to a convincing late sixteenth- or early seventeenth-century simple grass parterre; the rectangular pond beyond has been restored; in the walled garden to the south is a recreated and very plausible confection of early garden forms and materials (illus. 154); there is a Victorian arboretum, a vine house and dog kennels also to the south of the cloister. Much of the history of the site remains uncertain, and that indeed actually helps visitors to appreciate what they see: an accomplished restoration of the garden's central and most crucial feature – along with a ruined sixteenth-century gatehouse and a tunnel of ancient yew – becomes the centrepiece of a handsome modern garden that intimates an ancient garden without proposing a facsimile of it. Aberglasney makes no attempt to recreate a sixteenth- or seventeenth-century garden (indeed it would be impossible to do so on the basis of what we have discovered about the place).

Besides recreating a known site at some key moment of its history and the history of garden design, another mode addresses a generic version of a supposedly well-known foreign style. Today we have dozens of 'Japanese' and, to a lesser extent, 'Chinese' gardens that are created outside those countries, though many were constructed under the supervision of Japanese or Chinese experts.[8] The 'Garden of Awakening Orchids' (*Lan Su Yuan*) in Portland, Oregon, the 'Garden of the Reclaimed Moon' in Berlin, the Chinese garden created by Zou Gongwu at Snug Harbor on Staten Island, based on a famous Suzhou garden, or the Astor Memorial Court in the Metropolitan Museum of Art in New York – all were the efforts of Chinese workers and craftsmen using materials from China and with instructions from Suzhou or Beijing. Yet our entry into each of them is marked by our self-conscious acknowledgement that they are foreign to that place. The Metropolitan Museum's is something of an oddity, for the courtyard is actually as

154 Aberglasney, the southern garden.

155 Shofuso ('Pine Breeze Villa') Japanese House and garden, Fairmount Park, Philadelphia, 1957.

much an exhibit as the paintings, sculpture and furniture in the surrounding galleries; but we are still aware of crossing a cultural as well as a physical boundary.

So too is the Shofuso ('Pine Breeze Villa') Japanese House and Garden, designed by Junzo Yoshimura, first exhibited at the Museum of Modern Art in 1954 before being removed to the Centennial Fairmount Park in Philadelphia and reopened in 1957 (illus. 155).[9] (This was in fact the third Japanese structure in the park since 1876.) A new entry was designed by Isao Okura and a larger garden established by Tansai Sano (who had made only a pond for the house when

displayed in New York); the garden work was later passed to an American who had worked in Kyoto. Just how is it Japanese? Partly because it is mostly surrounded by a high wall, we cross the new threshold into a different culture, which we know, in various ways, how to read: shoes are removed before entering the seventeenth-century-style house, there are the miniature stone pagoda and Misaki-style lanterns, a tea pavilion for aficionados, and koi swim to meet visitors at the edge of the pond. Some of the rocks and planting are convincing in their grouping – or at least what we'd not find in an American garden unless it deliberately imitates Japanese garden ideas.[10]

156 The monochromatic palette of the Japanese Garden at the Montreal Botanical Garden, 2006.

Yet what visitors, if not Japanese experts, *expect* of Japanese gardens plays a greater role than any attempt at authenticity by the designers. This was vividly demonstrated by events at the Japanese Garden within the Montreal Botanical Garden (illus. 156).[11] Designed by a noted Japanese designer, Ken Nakajima (1914–2000), it has over twenty years undergone some radical changes that erased or suppressed his personal vision to bring it into conformity (sic) with some general, even clichéd, notion of a Japanese garden: austere, monochromatic, Zen-inspired. Nakajima was indeed inspired by traditional garden art, but sought to make it new: for there was, as he remarked, always 'a particular relationship between an [individual artist] and nature, not a set of rigid rules'. Yet in the afterlife of this garden's construction, its client moved it insidiously towards the conventional, lookalike Zen garden, where colours were removed, where it was augmented with bamboo and moss and the ubiquitous lantern, and interpretative panels steered the visitors back to what it was felt they expected. What 'sells' is what visitors think they want in a Japanese garden.

Perhaps things can be reinvented differently *inside* Japan or China – after all, Japanese gardens away from home have to be 'Japanese' gardens, but 'in Japan, it would only be a garden.' A famous Chinese poem tells of peach blossom discovered in a garden in southern China down a secret tunnel; this inspired the city of Changde, Hunan Province, to recreate the poem; so maybe this deliberate and reverse garden ekphrasis – making visible now what was previously only written – needs to be received differently. But other contemporary Chinese designers have tried to utilize past traditions in new ways inside China. The firm Turenscape made a new parkland along the Huangpu riverfront for the 2010 Shanghai Expo: while designed specifically to become an enjoyable public space after the Expo, it also aimed to improve flood control and improve the

quality of the highly polluted river. The narrow 14 acres of Houtan Park took deliberately what Turenscape's designers called an 'ecologic' approach, with water filtration and reconstructed wetlands, therefore modern, yet at the same time reusing industrial structures and materials.[12] But it also relied on three primary elements of traditional Chinese garden design – water, rocks and terraces (illus. 157) – which might re-introduce urban citizens to the seasonal rhythms and traditions of Chinese agriculture. Furthermore, it did not eschew some of the cherished motifs of traditional Chinese gardening: borrowed views, hiding the hand of man (moss covers many of the water-purifying elements in the park) and an intricate, even dense, spatial experience.

It is a different matter when a garden is designed and implemented by a Japanese American in a

157 Turenscape, Houtan Park, 2009.

158 Isamu Noguchi, the garden at UNESCO, Paris, 1956–8.

location that is essentially 'outside' any national culture: the UNESCO garden in Paris by Isamu Noguchi (illus. 158). It has the feel of a Japanese garden even if we do not know its designer was a Japanese American, and we can register that it embraces various Japanese formal elements and cultural references: the use of stones, calligraphy, the 'stepping stones', perhaps the fortified bases ('cusps') and walls of Japanese castles, or the long walkway that cuts across the garden that is derived from stages used in Noh theatre. Yet, as Marc Treib insists in his book on the garden,[13] it is a modern garden: the cubic central lantern, the concrete seats on the Delegates' Terrace (more cubes

and 'tweaked' forms), and the interweaving of curves of water, grass mound and pebble floors are as much a homage to Hans Arp as to Kyoto. Though it does not 'refuse' an historical style, it extends its forms and, of course on this particular site, its uses.

Strongly national or period garden styles seem to tempt people to remake them, and in the process even rethink them, deliberately or because they are conditioned by those who finance and use them, even if native craftsmen are involved. A classic example of such remaking is Villandry in France. In 1914 Dr Joachim Carvallo and his American wife purchased a twelfth-century castle in the Indre-et-Loire that had been enlarged in the Renaissance and augmented in a later layout (canals, basins, terraces) and again in the nineteenth century with lawns and a park in the 'English' style. They turned a hectare on the south into a garden of love, inspired by their visions of a French Renaissance, and then between 1914 and 1918 an ornamental *potager* to its west. A belvedere allows views over them and from that elevation the astonishing anthology of garden forms can be appreciated: inventive, elaborate, an adorable fantasy of exotic forms in the compartments, also a garden that requires intensive maintenance. Many of its individual elements are lovingly researched; the *potager* drew on illustrations of sixteenth-century gardens in Du Cerceau's *Les Plus Excellents Bastiments de France* for arbours, fountains, vegetated tunnels, vegetables and flowers in nine *plates-bandes* of intricate geometrical design, and (in the love garden) box and coloured flowers evoke different loves – tender, impassioned,

fickle, tragic; a Maltese cross, and the arms of Languedoc and the Basque country are laid into their patterns. While it is clearly nostalgic for the courtly love (*amour courtois*) of the troubadours, it is also a fervent, indeed almost surrealistic and so modern, elaboration of fantasy, without any precedence in sixteenth-century garden design.

Can recreations have a flavour of irony? Irony that the dead past could still be reanimated? Irony expected in an audience, but cheated by the success of reanimation? Irony that is surprised when new cultural fashions have not totally eliminated previous garden forms? Achille Duchêne's humorous drawing of 1932 (illus. 159) is entitled *Before the Storm*: but what storm? Modern figures are rolling up parterres like carpets, a border with miniature box pyramids is being folded away, a dog is running away past a discarded heap of pillar tops (pyramids and balls), and a somewhat elderly man is carefully carrying a topiaried pyramid of yew right out of the garden and the drawing's frame;

159 Achille Duchêne, *Before the Storm*, humorous drawing, 1932.

the dimly sketched garden behind this activity is regular, its far distance between the woodland edges shrouded in falling rain.

The humour is subtle, and suggests Duchêne's relish for fashioning a learned revision of early French gardens, largely those by André Le Nôtre or deemed to be by him or gardens created in his style; but the revision is sustained and energized by his vision of the new.[14] What the sketch also seems to represent is less concern for the details of flowery parterres and forms, that is, the local decoration, than a feel for extent and space in French landscapes. Vaux-le-Vicomte today is largely the result in 1901 and 1924 of the work by Henri and Achille Duchêne in the layout and embroidery, such as they are, of the parterres, though it is not how seventeenth-century engravings show them. But the somewhat diminished modern foreground actually draws out the power and perspectival effects of the long view that are at the heart of this wonderful space and our understanding of it. A seventeenth-century visitor might want a more detailed foreground before he accessed the larger space, but I think that these days we miss that far less when we can take in the longer view.

But the masterpiece of the Duchênes' work is Courances (illus. 160), re-designed prior to 1914 by Achille for its owner, Ernest de Ganay, a great and important historian of French gardens. It is still magnificent, simple, even austere, probably less fussy than its original parterres and missing the fountain at the far end of the vista. It draws out the poetry of its waters (moat and lake), the lawns and gravelled *allées*, and the clarity and depth

of the main axis stretching between woodlands into the distance. Duchême was not interested in generating a historical *effect*, but in responding to the immediate call of specific places. The modernity of all this at Courances is unexpectedly echoed by an Anglo-Japanese garden created (though not by Duchêne) in the 1920s and hidden within the park; both gardens are cunningly eloquent of older styles yet proud of their own.

But of course we know that Courances is in France, whereas the Duchêne designs for the parterre at Blenheim or those for millionaires in California, though they may recall the seventeenth-century style, do not elicit any useful associations for those places; Sir John Vanbrugh's Blenheim maybe deserves a Baroque supplement for a historic building that can also complement Lancelot Brown's classic parkland; Duchêne certainly uses with great effect the contrast between the immediate garden and the extended landscape and between the garden's geometry and the large expanse of water beyond it. The Duchêne style is indeed a 'style', historically grounded; but then Achille's vision was about a need not just to maintain French garden design, but to envisage developments that were still based on 'our inherited national characteristics'. There were rarely copycat designs; it was less that he 'revived' the 'precisely laid-out, mathematical "garden of reason"', as Mary Hawthorne writes, than his shrewd understanding of the spatial excitement of French gardens; his work is thus sadly misrepresented when it is photographed from above, simply to show off the 'mathematical garden of reason'; the seventeenth century had a far deeper

160 Courances, France.

and more theoretic idea of mathematics. Achille Duchêne's 1935 book, entitled significantly *Les Jardins de l'avenir* (of the future), anticipated a decline in resources for private place-making and foresaw an expansion of place-making to large parks, which some of his restored gardens have, in some sort, become. His collection of drawings for the future suggests his instinct for innovation, wit and even irony; the designs can be exciting, but the nationalist fervour of some of his commentators (like *anglomanie* in England or in lovers of England) is a touch disturbing.

A less copyist and scholarly attitude towards French garden art came from Achille's younger contemporary Albert Ferdinand Duprat, between 1925 and 1935. His astonishing garden at La Roche Courbon following a restoration appeal by Pierre Loti drew loosely on a seventeenth-century painting of the then abandoned garden, and may look like an old design, surrounded as it is with regular garden forms of pyramid and spheres. But its regular lake, or *miroir d'eau,* is almost too intimate and the huge architectural grotto that looks towards the château too grand to be anything but an inspired riff on traditions of French garden-making.

Another skilful designer, one also focused on his native landscape, was Pietro Porcinai. He took the historical traditions of Italian private villa gardens, specifically the use of garden compartments, emphasized many of their local elements – the *limonaia*, farm buildings – but added his own repertory of modern living and less elaborate forms (see chapter Two). But another modern reinvention came from outside Italy, the result in part of the English nostalgia for life in Tuscany. Cecil Pinsent, a friend and partner of Geoffrey Scott, author of *The Architecture of Humanism* (1914), worked on at least four gardens there during the early twentieth century: Villa La Foce, Villa Le Balze, Villa I Tatti and the Villa Medici, all of which would strike visitors, if not 'authentic', as strangely equipped to convey the essence of a Tuscan villa and garden.[15]

161 Cecil Pinsent, Villa Le Balze, Fiesole, 1922.

The buildings themselves are old, if augmented over the years, but the gardens are original and modern in subtle ways. Villa Le Balze (designed in 1912, now owned by Georgetown University) is tucked into a narrow platform with *giardini segreti* on both sides of the villa that look down towards Florence; a narrow space behind the house has obelisks and urns on a divided staircase, with niches, busts and extensive pebblework (illus. 161). It is the exaggerated inwardness of the whole garden, despite the 'windows' that open out of the first garden towards the valley, that strikes one as modern. It speaks of Tuscan-ness, but its accent is self-conscious, playful, beautiful, even somewhat implausible.

But Villa La Foce is Pinsent's masterpiece (illus. 162). Its elements and forms are again seemingly endemic, very Tuscan; but its tone, its accent, is very new, less a question of vocabulary than of syntax, a series of gradual and linked movements. It gives the impression of timelessness – in the words of Geoffrey Scott 'past things contemporary with present [ones]'. But it is, nonetheless, a contemporary achievement: in the words of the poet in T. S. Eliot's 'East Coker', 'every attempt / Is a wholly new start', a 'raid' on what has already been achieved in order to articulate something fresh. As Olin's drawings and annotations of Villa La Foce make clear, Pinsent is 'a modern designer'; his travertine stonework is machine-cut and plays with 'classic Rococo shapes', but looks 'more like Bob Venturi than the eighteenth century'! It is the garden's equivalent to the surrounding landscape, for its first owner, Antonio Origo, transformed

162 Cecil Pinsent, Villa La Foce, Tuscany, from 1924.

the bare clay hills – the *crete senesi* – into a productive, even georgic landscape. Yet like the land, the garden and its plantings have matured into a unique place, with its own authenticity.

Outside their country of origin, garden forms and styles may tend towards caricature. In the nineteenth century the British in India strove to fabricate convincing memories of gardens and parklands back home, and they worked hard to do so, even if the locals found them a touch bizarre and the topography and plant materials were not suitable. Even indigenous rulers in India were tempted to make similar 'English' gardens.[16] English and Scots gardeners travelled throughout Europe to help install versions of the 'English' style, from Thomas Blaikie in France, to William Gould or Charles Cameron for Catherine the Great in Russia, where clients were often inspired and then supported by treatises that promoted the 'English' style; this local *anglomanie* can be curious. Another 'reverse migration' can be found outside Prospect, Tennessee, where an American college professor, 'driven by a relentless passion' in the words of *The Tennessean Life* (11 November 2001), is turning a rural farmland of 200 acres into an English garden: a fragment of a neo-Roman peristyle, once part of a local courthouse, gazes across an irregular lake; other views ('Pope's Surprise') call in the country not his own; urns and a Palladian arch, a cascade, a 'Greek' statue, a *patte-d'oie* (reminiscent perhaps of Chiswick), and a rustic stone bridge with three arches. But a Pavilion of American Music overlooks the Arnold Schoenberg Terrace and leads to an Aaron Copland lawn within woodlands (there is also a Cole Porter Meadow, Richard Rodgers and Oscar Hammerstein Meadows and a Charles Ives Pond) which tie this intriguing and visual eccentricity of *anglomanie* into an auditory native culture.

There is also what might be called a 'neo-historical garden' (a term suggested by Bianca Maria Rinaldi) that is aware of a site's history or of an early garden programme or device, but finds a totally modern way of rendering it. Such has been the experience on two occasions of Bernard Lassus: for a new *bosquet* at Versailles and a new vision of the Tuileries Gardens. Both projects were carefully designed, but never got to be built. They are, in short, gardens on paper: the Tuileries is better taken up in my final chapter, but the Versailles proposal is more relevant and useful here.

The *bosquets* of Versailles have been reformulated on several occasions over the years (most famously by Hubert Robert for the Fontaine d'Apollon). The latest – that of the Théâtre d'Eau – was the occasion of a *concours* in 2012. The unsuccessful project by Lassus for that competition provides a useful gloss on the theme of reinventing gardens interestingly (illus. 163). Relying on the original meaning of theatre, Lassus wanted a theatrical *mise en scène* where the 'action' would be discovered gradually as visitors walked down the *allées* through the *bosquet*: these were formed first by the tall hedges of the *bosquet* walls, then by lines of trees, and finally by rows of artificial, pyramidal trees (*lisières taillées*) formed of steel and perforated in the shapes of leaves, and lit from below, with the lights changing as visitors moved down the *allée* toward the fountain itself. The new fountain at centre stage was contained between two glass plates, 2–3 centimetres apart and 5 metres high, and the water programmed to present different and changing scenographies that played themselves out on the glass walls, between which the jets were forced. The five panels of the water theatre, 2.5 metres wide, were set as if within wings or coulisses as in a theatre, and (like royal visitors to Versailles in the seventeenth century) could be observed from both the audience (*salle*) and from back stage (*estrade* or *scène*).

Thus Lassus resumes a seventeenth-century water theatre, but in modern terms, faithful equally to Louis XIV and to our own delights in play; the changing lights inside the artificial trees are particularly theatrical. Fountain technology is routine these days (as is recirculating water), but his own characteristic strategy was to manipulate materials

163 Bernard Lassus, project for a redesign of the Théâtre d'Eau at Versailles, 2011.

– the various forms of trees down the *allées*, and the various forms that the water would take (to be seen from both sides of the stage) as it was thrust between the glass plates. But like so many modern proposals for garden types these days, stymied by costs, rival aesthetic notions (gardens and garden patrons being still very conservative), and the fierce rivalries among competing designers (all French designs of more than half a hectare are subject to competitions like this), Lassus' ingenious vision of taking one segment of Versailles into the twenty-first century while honouring its location has stayed on the drawing-board. And that is where we go for the final chapter.

VILLE DE SAINTES
L'HOSTELLERIE SAINT- JULIEN
Jardin de Bernard Palissy

Le Jardin délectable

Prendre une source pour la faire
dilater
à mon plaisir par toutes les parties
de mon jardin

marquer la quadrature

quatre parties égales

une grande allée

des cabinets

un verger

Echelle 1/100

Atelier Bernard LASSUS

164 Bernard Lassus, proposal for Le Jardin délectable of Bernard Palissy, 2001.

THIRTEEN

GARDENS ON PAPER

'Design is of things not yet appearing; being but the pictures of ideas only.'

JOHN EVELYN[1]

In 2013 the A+D Museum in Los Angeles exhibited images of buildings, landscapes and transportation schemes that never made it past the drawing board; renderings, models, blueprints and computer sketches envisioned a brave new world, more fabulous than anything LA had ever seen: an interior landscape in a huge rotunda for the city's airport by Pereira & Luckman, with palm trees and gardens, new proposals for Hancock Park and for an Arts Park (by Frank Gehry), and a 'Green Carpet' by SITE for Pershing Square. The exhibits were published the same year, also on paper, as *Never Built Los Angeles* (New York, 2013), edited by the curators, Greg Goldin and Sam Lubell. Whether these were questions of 'If only . . .', or 'just dreaming', or 'things to make whenever there were funds', the idea was not entirely new. Some very early predecessors included the Garden of Venus in the *Hypnerotomachia Poliphili* (1499) and Bernard Palissy's 'Le Jardin

délectable', described in his *Recette véritable* (1563).[2] The first was a literary fantasy, though invoking contemporary garden forms; Palissy's utopian garden was described elaborately to glorify God's handiwork by making a three-dimensional, built version of Psalm 124 (Palissy was a Huguenot, dedicated to the availability of the Bible in the vernacular); yet it was also a scheme that he must have deemed possible. The garden that is described in his book relied on his skill as a ceramicist (of which we have some evidence), gardener and grotto-maker to create nine cabinets, four of which were made by firing their interiors as in a kiln, the others by weaving tree trunks into arbours.

It was this imagined garden that Bernard Lassus, winning a national competition in 1990, wished to recreate in celebration of the 400th anniversary of Palissy's death (illus. 164). In the town of Saintes, where Palissy had lived, the park was to be public, an apt landscape equivalent of the Huguenot faith in the people's access to biblical texts. Like the contemporary Théâtre d'Eau at Versailles (see chapter Twelve), the Palissy park was also a reinvention, a way of translating his text into tangible form: Lassus took the tripartite original – a sequence of hillside, parterre with cabinets and meadow – but combined the meadow with the hillside, created versions of the nine cabinets and the important sequence of water that Palissy describes, enclosed it and made pathways for access through the park. It was as visionary as Palissy's, but so far has failed to find sufficient funds for what would, I imagine, be a technical challenge. So it remains, tantalizingly, on paper.

As both these Lassus projects make clear, many of today's designers find themselves with exciting designs that do not succeed in competitions. More and more sites that are up for redevelopment or replanning are required to hold competitions; in France, for example, a *concours* is required for any site larger than half a hectare. Lassus was *invited* to design the small Jardin Damia by the Direction des Parcs Jardins et Espaces Verts de la Ville de Paris (see chapter Six) without having to enter a competition, but for Versailles there was an invited competition, and a national *concours* for the Palissy park; for a redesign of the Tuileries Garden Lassus was, with others, consulted. He won that for the town of Saintes and another for a new airport at Notre-Dames-des-Landes, where an ugly workers' strike still holds up the airport construction; but he did not succeed in designing the Tuileries.

Though it remains one of his most exciting and thoughtful projects, it is still on paper, though handsomely recorded, with some commentaries, in a privately printed volume in 1991.[3] The project addressed not only a crucial question for that site, namely, how to reinvent an old and famous garden that had seen a series of inventions over the centuries. But how could a once aristocratic park, opened after the French Revolution and thereafter a site of enormous popular gathering and entertainment, bang in the middle of a Paris that every visitor knows – between the Louvre, the Arc de Triomphe and the Champs-Elysées – maintain its prominence, its historical significance and become a public park for today?

In answering those questions, Lassus invoked what he called 'inventive analysis', a method that would explore what was there and had been there, and then let those analyses invent a contemporary creation. He recognized, as any historian would, that the space had enjoyed a series of reinterpretations by societies which used it differently at each moment of its history. This multiplicity had to be made, he argued, 'poetically tangible, and to be followed to the present'. His solution was to create a palimpsest on the site with five layers of different gardens: the central axis, at its current level or grade, returned the Tuileries to how it had been for André Le Nôtre; to its north, at lower levels, were a garden of André Mollet (20 cm below grade) and that of the Medici (80 cm below grade). To the south, towards the river, were a nineteenth-century garden (50 cm higher) and, higher still (170 cm), two pools that Lassus himself designed alongside the Seine. Yet each segment had to be approached differently: for the Le Nôtrean and nineteenth-century areas Lassus could plan a restoration; but for the Mollet and for the Medici, they needed a rehabilitation and re-invention respectively. The pools were new, but

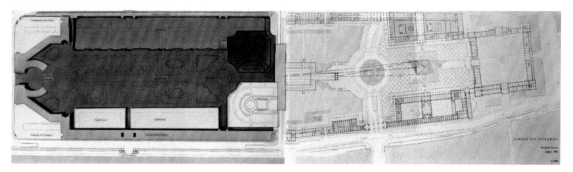

165 Bernard Lassus, a new Tuileries Garden, with a diagram showing the displacement of the axis as it pivots on the round pond at the start of the Le Nôtrean parterre, 1990.

clearly inspired by traditions of French gardens. What this scheme would have achieved was a combination of reinvention and restoration, based on whatever was known about materials and designs of those periods (illus. 165). What actually got to be installed was a mediocre mish-mash of French garden forms with no historical resonance.

But a new Tuileries Garden had also, for Lassus, to be related to the larger, modern city: the Pyramid by I. M. Pei in the Louvre courtyard had not been aligned with either the Arc de Triomphe du Carrousel at the end of the original gardens, nor yet the further arch on the Place Charles de Gaulle. But the creation of the enormous Grande Arche de la Défense on the western hill beyond the Seine suggested a long urban axis from it, through the Arc de Triomphe to the Carrousel arch; but for the axis to reach into the Louvre required a light displacement, which Lassus perspectively engineered. It pivots with a slight displacement of the axis at the point where the circular pond at the end of the Le Nôtrean segment comes in line with the Pei pyramid in the Louvre. This is helped also by the asymmetry of the lateral

parterres, with the lower levels of the Medici and Mollet pulling the eye slightly in the direction of the Rue de Rivoli (illus. 166). The new garden would thus have situated itself, and gained more significance, within the larger urban landscape.

As the projects presented for the Palissy memorial, the Tuileries and the Versailles theatre make clear (see illus. 163), these days we have to talk about 'gardens in a computer' rather than 'gardens on paper'. Some designers still work with pen and pencil on paper, but their offices usually convert these into digital versions to be manipulated as discussions evolve within the firm or with a client once the project succeeds in a competition. Gardens on paper (as I shall continue to call them, to avoid cluttering the text with alternatives) are there for many reasons. They can be ways of working out a problem, just as writers will work through different formulations to reach what they want to say, some of which drafts have a life of their own. They can simply be dreams, 'pictures of ideas only', in Evelyn's words, that may have no foreseeable chance of being built. But more frequently, gardens on paper are simply the results of unsuccessful competition entries. It is true that, for obvious human reasons, the proclamation of failures is not a high priority for designers; yet those that do publish unsuccessful projects have the chance to show both the range of their projects and, more interestingly, how creative solutions can slip between the cracks of municipal inertia, financial shortfalls or being 'too visionary' – a proposal that is unable to win sufficient approval. For whatever reason, it can often be that the best ideas never get built: the architect Oscar Niemeyer said that the favourite among his Algerian designs (a 'revolutionary' mosque in Algiers) was unbuilt.

An architect colleague tells me that what he calls 'dream projects' in architecture are quite rare, apart from projects done for self-promotion and speculative work, which some of the *Never Built Los Angeles* exhibits entailed. Neither Frank Lloyd Wright nor Le Corbusier did any, though Ludwig

Mies van der Rohe drew his House for an Architect when he was unemployed after leaving the Bauhaus, and Erich Mendelsohn famously sketched visionary projects during the Great War. Louis Kahn produced a drawing called 'The Making of a Room', which is not a garden, but does show a landscape outside; his annotations talk of 'natural light' and of a 'Great American Poet' asking an architect 'What slice of the sun does your building have?' The room is a 'place of the mind', a term that can also describe gardens on paper.[4]

Landscape architects do dream on paper. Isamu Noguchi proposed a work to be seen from the moon – a nose, eyes, open mouth and forehead sculptured in desert sand, which might be one example of a dream, an idea only, imagined before humans could view the earth from the moon's surface.[5] That landscape architects may do this

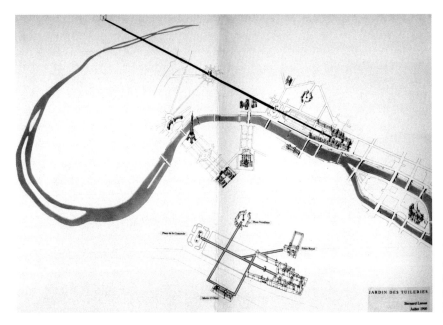

166 Bernard Lassus, diagram showing the axis from the Arche de la Défense to the Louvre.

more frequently than architects seems plausible: their work always seems to be lower on the list of human desires and social needs than buildings, yet the need to articulate an idea can trump the chance of realizing it. Equally, if you accept Emerson's notion that fields, streams, woods and caves are the structure of our consciousness, then it may seem natural for the landscape architect to invest far more time on speculative designs. Landscape architects have also tended to dream, since they have a long tradition of learning from the past, either in mythology, verbal descriptions, or paintings of gardens and the natural world, all of which have to be pondered and dreamed before they can be reformulated in designs. Landscape architects may learn by dreaming on paper or on a computer by doodling fragmentary or dismembered bits of projects, sketching pieces for bigger designs, by simulating built work (the activity of many design students), or as marketing tools for professionals. To what extent such paper gardens are dreams depends in large part on the impetus as well as their reception. Paper designs can be used to argue for a point of view, when the projection itself is still unbuilt, or when a paper 'war' between rival images can doom or finesse a project.[6] Humphry Repton used gardens in the pages of his Red Books as part marketing, part thinking aloud for clients who needed to be persuaded of his proposals; yet sometimes these Red Books were not acted on, and his watercolours were left for display in the client's sitting-room.[7] This still happens.

Hannover in Germany organized a project to create a dozen new gardens throughout the city,

for which twelve designers were invited to submit proposals; these were exhibited at the Sprengel Museum in the spring of 2002 and published 'on paper' in a volume, *Kunst Garten Kunst*, with four commentaries on experimentation in garden-making. The designers saw very different possibilities in their selected sites – some small and self-contained, some inserted into a complex urban development; both responded to the competing needs of a modern city: leisure and convenience, stimulation and relaxation, juxtapositions of pedestrians and vehicles, opportunities for fantasy or pragmatic necessities, the role of history versus contemporary circumstance. One of the most intriguing proposals sought to respond to that complex agenda: Paolo Bürgi's 'vision and re-vision' of a former historical site, a late seventeenth-century garden devised for Franz von Platen, but now virtually subsumed and largely lost in the modern city. His proposal was to insert within a modern parkland a reminiscence of Baroque garden art in the form of a theatre, appropriate since the Platen garden had been linked to the still surviving Herrenhausen Gardens outside the city by a long avenue, and Herrenhausen had, and still enjoys, its outdoor theatre. On the site of the original Platen palace, Bürgi devised a theatre of hedges 10 metres high that imitated the wings and perspective sightlines of a stage, where visitors could experience different views through its labyrinthine corridors and *enfilades* (illus. 167). Throughout the remainder of the site, axial lines of poplars and magnolias would outline compartments of the former palace gardens, and eventually,

167 Paolo Bürgi, project for the theatre at the Von-Alten-Garten, Hannover, 2003.

over the next twenty years, the park would acquire sports facilities and modern plantings within those historical memories. Meanwhile the areas designated by the tree lines were annotated metaphorically by being understood as a musical composition – movements through the park of prelude, theme, variations and intermezzo, comparable to the exploration and experience of music that might have entertained audiences in a seventeenth- or eighteenth-century theatre.

Some parks do get built, as a result of garden schemes, but in the process lose something of the initial vision or dream: such was the case for Ian Hamilton Finlay's Stockwood Park in Luton. In 1985–6 Finlay and Gary Hincks published, in a limited edition, *Six Proposals for the Improvement of Stockwood Park Nurseries in the Borough of Luton*. A cardboard folder contained loose engravings, each captioned and on different coloured paper; on the inside of the back cover of the folder were descriptions of the six proposals, eight 'Detached Sentences on Public Space' and a colophon. The engravings took images from Claude Lorrain's *Liber veritatis* of 1649, and inserted into their

redrawn landscapes a variety of Finlay's own proposals: an engraved tree plaque, a pair of silver
birches growing from 'a double tree-column
base', a woodland herm of Aphrodite, a 'group
of stones suggestive of a flock', a half-buried and
'seemingly enormous' Corinthian capital, and a
curving wall with inscribed words from Ovid's
Metamorphoses (illus. 168). When the park was
built, all the Finlay additions to the Claudean
sceneries were used, but they 'lost' the direct association with the Claudean pastoral, notably the
staffage (nymphs, river gods) that had on paper
lent Luton a *color romanus*. It was a typical and
strategic move on Finlay's part, hinting at associations in a modern parkland on paper without
imposing the parallels that visitors need to discover for themselves, or by viewing the original
proposals.[8]

Gardens on paper, then, afford an exciting
opportunity to play with *ideas* of gardens; and in
effect all garden types are playing with those ideas,
though in the cases discussed in the previous twelve
chapters they were mostly realized and so their
ideas are locked into a palpable 'here' and 'now'.
But some were not so successful, like schemes
from the Portuguese firm PROAP, who bravely
published their own book of 'lost competitions'.[9]
The introduction by one of its directors, João
Nunes, sees them as important moments of cooperation, intensive training for less experienced
designers through absorption in the proposed site
and its demands on designers, and by dialogues
with the communities that asked for the projects.
He argues that PROAP's designs are themselves 'a
solution', working at a 'level of great purity'; rather
than competitions to be 'revisited in a nostalgic and

168 Ian Hamilton Finlay
and Gary Hincks, 'Caprice
with a Wall and Wall-
Plaques . . .', from *Six
Proposals for the Improvement of Stockwood Park
Nurseries in the Borough
of Luton* (1985–6).

self-celebratory way, but a recognition of the quality of a permanent modernity'.

One such unsuccessful project for Flanders Fields was used in chapter Eight on memorials, and a new vision of Berlin's Tempelhof airport could have been used in 'Drosscapes', but is more useful here. An airfield is essentially composed of runways (in this case parallel) within a large oval of grass; this was also a historic site, created first by Nazi engineers and then, during the Cold War, the base to which supplies could be flown during the Soviet blockage of Berlin. So in two senses it was a void, an empty space and a vacuum in European politics, both ideological and civic. PROAP's proposal addressed how such a public space could encourage a 'diversity of functions of a temporary character'; in short, a space with that rarest of urban characteristics, reversibility. Their scheme (illus. 169) retained the footprints of the parallel runways, brought in and blurred the surrounding urban edges with woodlands, a water-purification system and the enlargement of a Muslim cemetery, to create a sufficient density around the fragmented central void. This was filled, within the oval and between the runways, with a host of different forms of water, both functional and decorative: opportunities for fishing, bathing and watersports; also vegetation (hills, woodland, clearings, riparian edges, greenhouses and arboretum). It was receptive to and wanted to welcome the life and culture of the surrounding urban world, assigning areas for the development of an International Garden and Architectural Exhibition and encouraging a gradual development of the new park over time.

The Flanders Fields proposal (see illus. 109), notes PROAP, was apparently too complex to respond to a project that required only a 'simple park network' (whatever that might be); the winning proposal tried 'to draw a clear line where one had never existed' and situated along that line a 'dense program of events and invocations'. PROAP's proposal was for a far less watertight scheme, and one that allowed visitors a richer and less programmed, because more abstract, parkland with discoveries scattered at points of 'temporal compression'. The Berlin scheme, they argue themselves, was 'impaired by an excessive intervention', possibly misinterpreting the preliminary programme; yet PROAP argued that the transformation of the space itself should be understood as 'an exceptional programmatic opportunity', a dynamic process capable from the start of following different paths, different phases and with different speeds of execution.

The results of a few competitions have enjoyed a life on paper when a selection of the competing designs was published and could be discussed; when a winning design did get built (Parc de la Villette would be a key example), or when, despite a successful outcome, nothing appears to have happened, as a result perhaps of shortage of funds or other uncertainties about the project (Downsview, Toronto), a publication of all or some of the rival designs allows the scrutiny and review of the 'urban park in flux'. There have been collections on Downsview Park with commentary by its editor, Julia Czerniak, along with eight other contributors, some scattered presentations of

169 PROAP's proposal for the development of Tempelhof Airfield, Berlin, 2010. Proposed insertions were A1 public art, A2 water square, A3 public walk, A4 public woodland; B1 formal gardens and water jets, B2 meanders, B3 bathing, B4 cool water streams, B5 fishing lake, B6 central lake, B7 purification meanders, B8 watersports, B9 botanical water garden; C1 square with temporary Garden Exhibition, C2 urban compartments, with Garden and Architecture space, C3 riparian woodland, C4 greenhouses, C5 wooded hills, C6 Muslim Cemetery, C7 large central clearing, C8 arboretum, C9 experimental forestry plots, C10 woodland edges, C11 sport zones.

unsuccessful designs for Duisburg-Nord, and a goodly number of books on Parc de la Villette, like *L'Invention du parc*, the first of many discussions of what promised to be a groundbreaking attempt to rethink modern parklands, including a book by Bernard Tschumi himself.[10]

Downsview Park, Toronto provides a fascinating insight into how a former airfield of 320 acres could be absorbed into the suburban life of the city that surrounds it;[11] Czerniak and her contributors are even-handed in their appraisal of the five interdisciplinary schemes that were judged in 2000 (a short list from 179 submissions). They address, variously, how a 'new landscape' could emerge, how former ecologies of flora and fauna could be reinstated, how the site could be made into a forest (a 'Tree City'), or into a reorganized topography of earthworks, ridges and pathways (a 'synthetic landscape'), or a parkland where the contemporary and the wild could cohabit ('The Digital and the Coyote'). What is striking is both how the considerable extent of the site could be hospitable to a variety of uses and experiences, and how the enormity of making a successful landscape necessitated that the park evolve over many years ('one that will take time to fully unfold': the brief required the development of the park to take place over five to fifteen years).

Many of the 'provocative ideas' used traditional forms – ridges, berms, pathways and circulation routes – and generally there were fewer provocations for the prospective users of the park, who are Photoshopped into images in conventional ways. What was newer was the invocation of 'frameworks', whether infrastructure or participatory process, rather than prescriptive programmes. But the most striking aspect of these cutting-edge designs involved what Czerniak called 'graphically stunning and rigorous' proposals, 'densely filled with diagrams, perspectives, photographs, sections, plans, and details'. It was indeed, for both the five proposals and the volume itself, geared clearly for professionals, eager to talk to each other, with considerable designer-speak ('a precisely engineered matrix') and even somewhat arcane language; it was far less concerned to address those who might use it (humans, not animals!); above all, it was not clear how the elaborate hypotheses, axioms and the strikingly metaphorical languages would be translated into built form, and how the park would 'perform' – for itself certainly, but for its visitors too. On the other hand, there was an admirable effort by all designers to make it palpable that the park was 'designed' and not a 'remnant of wilderness' but 'thoroughly and unapologetically artificial', which would certainly help its appreciation by a larger and non-professional public. The richness of some of the flora and fauna (illus. 170) would have delighted those visitors who, whether or not they thought they were accessing 'wilderness', found that they could discover their own sense of nature both for itself and for its human visitors; a truly complex cultural event.

The book on Downsview Park acknowledged Parc de la Villette as a comparable international competition, with shared insistence on frameworks as opposed to form, but in the later case

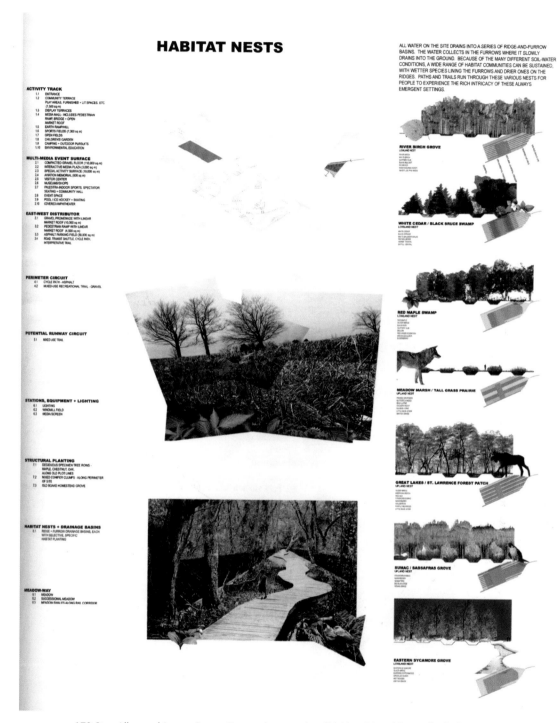

HABITAT NESTS

ALL WATER ON THE SITE DRAINS INTO A SERIES OF RIDGE-AND-FURROW BASINS. THE WATER COLLECTS IN THE FURROWS WHERE IT SLOWLY DRAINS INTO THE GROUND. BECAUSE OF THE MANY DIFFERENT SOIL-WATER CONDITIONS, A WIDE RANGE OF HABITAT COMMUNITIES CAN BE SUSTAINED, WITH WETTER SPECIES LINING THE FURROWS AND DRIER ONES ON THE RIDGES. PATHS AND TRAILS RUN THROUGH THESE VARIOUS NESTS FOR PEOPLE TO EXPERIENCE THE RICH INTRICACY OF THESE ALWAYS EMERGENT SETTINGS.

ACTIVITY TRACK

MULTI-MEDIA EVENT SURFACE

EAST-WEST DISTRIBUTOR

PERIMETER CIRCUIT

POTENTIAL RUNWAY CIRCUIT

STATIONS, EQUIPMENT + LIGHTING

STRUCTURAL PLANTING

HABITAT NESTS + DRAINAGE BASINS

MEADOW-WAY

RIVER BIRCH GROVE
LOWLAND NEST

WHITE CEDAR / BLACK SPRUCE SWAMP
LOWLAND NEST

RED MAPLE SWAMP
LOWLAND NEST

MEADOW MARSH / TALL GRASS PRAIRIE
UPLAND NEST

GREAT LAKES / ST. LAWRENCE FOREST PATCH
UPLAND NEST

SUMAC / SASSAFRAS GROVE
UPLAND NEST

EASTERN SYCAMORE GROVE
LOWLAND NEST

170 Stan Allen and James Corner Downsview panel on 'Habitat Nests', listing both the various artificial insertions and the arrival of plants and animals over 15 years.

espousing and 'indulging' more in 'the complexity of contemporary ecological thinking'. It is hard to compare paper gardens with built ones, but a comparison of Parc de la Villette with what any of the five Downsview proposals would look like when realized suggests that landscape architects, embedded within a cluster of other specialists (artists, engineers, ecologists, graphic designers, architects – but not, as far as I could see, psychologists) can produce intriguing proposals. The emphasis on a landscape's temporality and materiality and the difficult task of addressing 'biological and human diversity' would have made an interesting and tellingly modern park. One also senses that, in the case both of Parc de la Villette and any realized Downsview Park, the theory and the 'smart technology' underpinning it would be less visible than the space itself. So too, as with any garden, would be the sense that it was evolving, a process, a place that a visitor would need to frequent over five or fifteen years.

A rival vision of parkland and its Gardenesque potential, strikingly different from the successful design by Latz + Partner for Duisburg-Nord (see chapter Five), was that by Bernard Lassus, who tried to make immediately clear to visitors that the contemporary landscape place emerged from a long temporal evolution and process. Again the invention and its effect were to underline its artificiality rather than its naturalness. As with so many gardens that recall the past in fact or via mythology and metaphor, he wanted to recognize the River Emscher, which gives the character to this whole area, as having a yesterday and a

'day before yesterday' as well as a future. The heavily polluted river would be cleansed and channelled through yesterday's industrial segment, returned to a meandering path through a 'countryside of time past' with cattle and windmills, and, in the most visionary aspect of the scheme, a future section where the metamorphosis of water would be presented: gardens and laboratories that addressed purification systems of contaminated water as well as soil, gardens that registered sounds and smells and local fauna, all open to public visitation. Around this reconstructed and reinvented park landscape, where water was to be the signature of its recovery, would be located residential areas, recognitions of cultural and industrial patrimony, and a range of contemporary activities (football pitches, fishing, a motorbike racing track and a museum of old cars).

Some 'paper' ideas are utopian visions that envisage the future by recalling what had been created in the past. This notion was long ago prefigured by a late Ming scholar, Liu Shilong, who in the sixteenth century wrote an essay on 'The Garden that is Not Around' (sometimes translated as 'The Garden that Never Existed'). Recognizing that so many gardens had disappeared and survived only in literary descriptions, he wondered why gardens had to exist at all: why not skip the preliminary state of actual existence and jump into the final state of literary existence which, after all, is the common fate of many gardens? 'Only gardens on paper can be relied upon', he wrote, for, in 'an actual construction, [their] extent and arrangement are limited'. In his imaginary garden, there was a conspectus of Chinese garden marvels and human hopes: 'Inside my garden, my body is always free from illness, my heart is always free from worries.' It is a garden to be 'appreciated at the desks' of those who read about it.[12] This seems an uncanny anticipation of modern books, replete with imagery of projected gardens that celebrate the perfect and the unsuccessful; yet they may be thought of as successful in that they did not have to suffer the indignity of being realized, unfunded or lost to decay. They are best read at our desks, or in books to be remaindered or sold on eBay, even as built gardens slowly disappear.

CONCLUSION

Beyond this baker's dozen of types of garden and landscape discussed in previous chapters, we could well think of others: children's gardens, zoological gardens, hospital and therapeutic gardens, roof gardens, mobile gardens on boats or yards in trailer parks; even gardens (or landscapes) invoked metaphorically, for, as Aristotle says, 'metaphor consists in giving the thing a name that belongs to something else', which we do when a book is entitled *A Child's Garden of Verses,* or when we talk of a 'landscape of fear' in an Ebola outbreak. But the idea of any type presupposes some idea of place, which thus allows its making, be it utopian or, at times, dystopian.

Place, writes Małgorzata Szafranska, is many things: it is a pause in movement ('a stepping stone along the way through the world'), an intentional object ('it gives the natural world in which it appears a new dimension'), it is fixed and anchored in space, a sign of where the garden or park is to be found ('genius loci').[1] Yves Bonnefoy, focusing on the modern possibilities of *lieu,* insists that making a place effects a space where

our attention can be fixed through the effort of thinking:

> place is not simply an intellectual perspective, it is an emotional experience. Truly, it is reality itself, as existence proves, since experience encounters the world first from the place of the heart, and brings me to the notion of nature, for example, only through a secondary effort of thought.[2]

So Karl Kullmann argues that gardens 'in effect [make] the most permanent communion we can make with a piece of the world'.[3]

My three original points of reference announced in the Introduction were: the role of types; the contribution of gardens (broadly understood) to the larger world of places like parks; then, third, a worry about modern versus contemporary which relates, as I now see it, to how much today's (contemporary) work can elicit a future. It is a two-way process, whereby the past is canvassed to construct a future, using the present

171 Kathryn Gustafson, four *jardins* at Les Jardins de l'Imaginaire, completed in 1995; the entry path with the thread of Ariadne in the trees.

as its mediator: hence Ricoeur's remark, quoted in chapter Two, on the need in a world of global movement to learn 'how to become modern and return to the sources, how to revive an old dominant civilization and take part in a universal civilization'.

Antony Vidler's preamble to his essay on types observes that 'typology [is] the agent of architectural regeneration in an era of dispirited functionalism and willful eclecticism';[4] he insists on the '*capacity* of rules and elements according to the program *inductively* defined' (my italics). So we find in the world around us places to make for the ideas we have; Vidler asks us to look at that world *first* and then perhaps fit it to a pre-existing idea, or improvise on that theme. This implies that new programmes are understood and seized by understanding what the site needs rather than by imposing a type upon a site. This double heritage (maybe challenge or debate, *paragone)* between attending to the new *and* our need also to position ourselves in relation to permanent ideas underlines the new sense of typology (nor do 'permanent ideas' mean simply conventional ones, but those that continue to address fundamental human concerns). It privileges our sense of the future, but realizes that without a sense of what precedes it, 'nothing dates like the future'.

This dialogue implies how a taxonomy of types will regenerate both gardens and landscape architecture. For, in the first place, it is the garden type that pervades and invigorates landscape architecture, however *un*garden-like it may be: 'the appeal of the garden [is] the fundamental form of land-scape architecture'.[5] And landscape architecture itself has morphed in modern times into a host of different makings of place. Some sense of this expanding potential may be glimpsed in the varied works of Kathryn Gustafson, but specifically in her design of Les Jardins de l'Imaginaire for the town of Terrasson in the Périgord:[6] we must notice both the plural in *jardins* and the role that imagination plays there. She conflates a variety of garden elements into a public park (illus. 171–4). First, there is maze with Ariadne's thread winding through the tree tops, a rose garden, a garden of elements, a water garden, a sacred wood, a tunnel of trees and a green theatre, a conservatory, a topiary garden, a canal or long trough of fountains, and a play of axes and perspectives. Each segment is distinct (even numbered and linked to a plan), yet they merge with each other, and converse with each other, as we move up and down the former agricultural hillside. Each *jardin* is characterized by some prominent device or programme (thus making sense of Obrist's catalogue of garden types – see illus. 2), but collectively they provide a conspectus or anthology of garden elements, any one of which could be applied to, or improvised for, a public park or other garden type.

The exchange or blurring of types has been a feature of modern place-making. While Alexander Pope deemed sartorial propriety apt for people in the eighteenth century, today's 'styles' of dress sort with subjects erratically and democratically, and thus also with gardens, where we recognize how this diversity is necessary. And so in making places, sculpture invades botanical gardens; festival gardens

172 Kathryn Gustafson, Le Théâtre de Verdure, benches in the amphitheatre.

invoke both domestic or suburban themes and try out ideas that haven't taken hold elsewhere; vernacular gardens relish invention and are proud of their own taste; commercial headquarters have invaded academic campuses; while pocket parks move upwards vertically or lengthwise on linear trails. What are called drosscapes have infected 'bad places' with a repertory of elements and programmes that suit or 'sort' with the making of places as various as public parks, museums, industrial or derelict wastelands and infrastructure, abused urban pockets and riverscapes. We relish

174 Kathryn Gustafson, under the arbour in the Rose Garden.

both the discovery of the new and a recognition that it performs in ways that are familiar, if now improvised.

Les Jardins de l'Imaginaire is a public place (albeit you need to pay to enter; but it is not connected to any mansion). Also visitors are guided through the garden which means that, alas, we cannot explore it on our own and at our own speed: so we experience these *jardins* respectively and in imagination. This in its turn involves a dialogue of taxonomies that must also involve, beside the past and the future, beside type and its improvisations, the role of both the designer and

173 *left*: Kathryn Gustafson, Les Jardins de l'Eau and Le Chemin des Fontaines.

the visitor or 'consumer'. That is a somewhat distasteful word, but we lack a word that celebrates our need for and our enjoyment in spaces outside buildings, for we surely do 'consume' parks and gardens, as we consume with pleasure other things in the world, such as food, travel, company, ideas, solitude; nor does 'consumption' mean we exhaust what we consume. And the complexity of modern place-making also ensures that we do not consume gardens easily. So how people learn to understand what is provided for them is crucial to the making of place, in the spirit of John Dewey's *Art as Experience* (1958), where emphasis shifted from the achievement of the material object (garden) to how it is experienced by the viewer (visitor / user / consumer). This is where such a public park as Les Jardins de l'Imaginaire plays a role: its scenario of different gardens instructs its visitors how they might respond to each segment and thus expand their understanding of larger landscapes.

REFERENCES

INTRODUCTION: TYPOLOGIES AND OUR IMPROVISATIONS

1 I was reminded of this useful term by Robert Williams's review essay on Brown's work, 'Making Places: Garden Mastery and English Brown', *Journal of Garden History*, III/4 (1983), pp. 382–5. However, the recent use of the phrase 'place-making' by Will Self, in an acerbic and satirical piece on real estate marketing, gives me pause: see Will Self, *London Review of Books* (18 July 2013), p. 34.

2 See 'De la relation du terrain aux genres de jardins', in Jean-Marie Morel, *Théorie des Jardins*, 2nd edn (1802), pp. 115ff. A later French attempt to make such classifications was by Edouard André, *L'Art des Jardins: Traité général de la composition des parcs et jardins* (1879), chap. 6.

3 Leberecht Migge, *Die Gartenkultur des 20. Jahrhunderts*, trans. and ed. David H. Haney (Washington, DC, 2013), pp. 184–8. See also Haney's introduction, pp. 16–20, from which I quote.

4 As analysed in Anthony Vidler, 'The Production of Types', *Oppositions*, VIII (1987); and in Anthony Vidler, *The Writing of the Walls: Architectural Theory in the Late Enlightenment* (Princeton, NJ, 1987), pp. 154ff.

5 Michael Leslie and John Dixon Hunt, eds, *A Cultural History of Gardens*, 6 vols (London, 2013) has a chapter on 'Types of Gardens' in each of the volumes for that cultural period. I am grateful to those authors for their detailed typologies; that on modern gardens is by Peter Jacobs, and his typology has been most useful in devising my own chapters here.

6 This point is made by Raffaella Fabiani-Giannetto in 'Types of Gardens', in *A Cultural History of Gardens*, ed. Leslie and Hunt, vol. III, p. 43.

7 The Internet, too, yields many organizations that can help individuals make gardens: the Garden Industry Manufacturer's Association and Horticultural Trades Association, or the Federation of Garden & Leisure Manufacturers in the UK.

8 Bernard Lassus, *Jardins imaginaires: Les habitants-paysagistes* (Paris, 1977). Lassus examines popular gardens made by their owners.

9 These are the two examples offered by Bernard St-Denis in 'Just What is a Garden?', *Studies in the History of Gardens and Designed Landscapes* (SHGDL), XXVII (2007), pp. 61–76, upon whose enquiry I draw here in what follows.

10 Richard L. Hindle, 'Stanley Hart White and the Question of "What is Modern?"', SHGDL, XXXIII/3 (2013), p. 175.

11 Thomas C. Cooper, ed., *The Roots of My Obsession: Thirty Great Gardeners Reveal Why They Garden* (Portland, OR, 2012), p. 81.

12 Yve-Alain Bois, 'A Picturesque Stroll around

"Clara-Clara"', *October*, XXIX (1984) addresses this issue, but see specifically remarks on pp. 36, 44, 61.

13 Marshall Berman, *All That is Solid Melts into Air: The Experience of Modernity* (New York, 1982). Berman's following comment on modernism 'as a struggle' is on p. 6.

14 Christopher Tunnard identified 'architectural plants' in *Gardens in the Modern Landscape* (1938), a term he borrowed from M. Correvon; earlier William Robinson had used the same term in *Parks, Promenades, and Gardens of Paris* (London, 1869), when describing the planting of parks there.

15 Bernard Lassus, *The Landscape Approach* (Philadelphia, PA, 1998), p. 116.

16 I am grateful here for the discussion of this topic by David Leatherbarrow, *The Roots of Architectural Invention: Site, Enclosure, Materials* (Cambridge, 1993), pp. 1–6, from whom I quote in this and the following paragraph, with my own italics.

17 Marc Treib, ed., *Modern Landscape Architecture: A Critical Review* (Cambridge, MA, 1993), pp. 36–67; the axioms are listed on pp. 53–5. His *Noguchi in Paris: The UNESCO Garden* (San Francisco, CA, 2003) takes it for granted that this is modern, which his own design of both books endorses, which tends to confuse the arts of book-making and garden-making. See also his 'Postulating a Post-modernist Landscape', in *Settings and Stray Paths: Writings on Landscapes and Gardens* (London, 2005), pp. 206–19. For an incisive, short explanation of gardens in the modern mode see Peter Walker, 'Classicism, Modernism, and Minimalism in the Landscape', in *Minimalist Gardens* (Washington, DC, 1997), pp. 17–23.

18 His book was published in 1939 and again, with additions and deletions, in 1948. For a review of this important book see my Introduction to the reprint of the 1948 edition: Christopher Tunnard, *Gardens in the Modern Landscape* (Philadelphia, PA, 2014).

19 Tunnard also wrote on 'Modern Gardens for Modern Houses: Reflections on Current Trends in Landscape Design', in the *Bulletin* of the Garden Club in September 1941, where he saw gardens as 'stages', with 'every occupant a player'.

20 This French period is surveyed in Dorothée Imbert, *The Modernist Garden in France* (New Haven, CT, 1993). And a useful portfolio of photographic plates from the later 1937 International Exposition in Paris contains 48 photographic places of other modernists like the Belgian René Pechère or the Englishman Oliver Hill; see Jacques Gréber, *Jardins modernes* (Paris, 1937).

21 Most of these designers are discussed and illustrated in Treib's 'axioms' in the book he edited, and they are generally well known. Porcinai has come into more prominence recently with a book on him by Milena Matteini, *Pietro Porcinai e l'arte del paesaggio* (Milan, 1991), and the collection of essays on his work, edited by Luigi Latini and Mariapia Cunico, *Pietro Porcinai. Il progetto del paesaggio nel XX secolo* (Venice, 2012). Cramer is the subject of Udo Weilacher, *Visionary Gardens: Modern Landscapes by Ernst Cramer* (Basel, 2001).

22 For these types, which are not taken up here, see John Dixon Hunt, *A World of Gardens* (London, 2012), chaps 15, 8, 16.

23 David Leatherbarrow has argued for the antecedents of such modernist landscape architecture as Tschumi's Parc de La Villette – see Mark Cousins et al., eds, 'Is Landscape *Architecture?*', in *Architectural Studies*, 2 (Beijing, 2012), pp. 34–6; so too did Elizabeth Kathryn Meyer, 'The Public Park as Avant-garde (Landscape) Architecture: A Comparative Interpretation of

Two Parisian Parks, Parc de la Villette (1983–1990) and Parc des Buttes-Chaumont (1864–1867)', *Landscape Journal*, x/1 (1991), pp. 16–26.

1 DOMESTIC AND GARDENERS' GARDENS

1 Dennis McGlade and Laurie Olin, 'Planting', in *A Cultural History of Gardens*, vol. VI, ed. Michael Leslie and John Dixon Hunt (London, 2013).

2 Garrett Eckbo, *The Art of Home Landscaping* (New York, 1956) has a section on 'Case Studies', 'carefully selected to illustrate typical problems'.

3 Quoted in an article in the *New York Times* (23 May 2014) about Crispin Odey who caused a fuss, in what the *Guardian* described as a 'fowl extravagance', by erecting a large neoclassical temple for his chickens in the West of England; see Rosemary Verey and Katherine Lambert, *Secret Gardens: Revealed by their Owners* (Boston, MA, 1994).

4 Published, suitably, by the Center for American Places, Christoper Grampp's *From Yard to Garden: The Domestication of America's Home Grounds* (Chicago, IL, 2008) traces the various paths to gardendom, with particular focus on California, where the author is a landscape architect; Candida Lycett Green and Christopher Sykes, *The Front Garden* (London, 1981) and Mary Riley Smith, *The Front Garden* (Boston, MA, 1991) celebrate the garden that presents itself to the public.

5 Peter Latz, 'The Idea of Making Time Visible', *Topos*, XXXIII (December 2000), p. 85.

6 This is illustrated in my *A World of Gardens* (London, 2012), fig. 56.

7 The writer is Jacopo Bonfadio, who at almost the same time as Bartolomeo Taegio and in identical words, identified this humanistic art of gardening: see the introduction to Bartolomeo Taegio, *La Villa*, ed. and trans. Thomas E. Beck (Philadelphia, PA, 2011), pp. 58ff.

8 Penelope Hobhouse describes her 'obsession' with garden-making in 'A Garden of Happiness', in *The Roots of My Obsession: Thirty Great Gardeners Reveal Why They Garden*, ed. Thomas C. Cooper (Portland, OR, 2012), pp. 81–4. Hadspen, with its garden, has now been sold.

9 A selection of Halprin's private gardens were catalogued in *Studies in the History of Gardens and Designed Landscapes* (*SHGDL*), XXVII/4 (2007), pp. 257–355; for his public work, see Alison Bick Hirsch, *City Choreographer* (Minneapolis, MN, 2014). See also Barbara Baker, *Contemporary Designers' Own Gardens* (London, 2013), which looks at Jacques Wirtz, Patrick Blanc and Adriaan Geuze among others. On Peter Latz's own garden and his uses of it elsewhere see Sanda Iliescu, 'The Garden as Collage: Rupture and Continuity in the Landscape Projects of Peter and Anneliese Latz', *SHGDL*, XXVII/2, pp. 149–82.

10 See chaps 2 and 7 for these. I am indebted to my former student Mary Barensfeld, and to her article on this garden in *dwell* (April 2014), pp. 50–52ff.

11 A hilarious but very astute essay on relations between a professional landscape architect and his clients is James C. Rose, 'Gardens Are Born', in *Gardens Make Me Laugh* (Baltimore, MD, 1990), pp. 33–50.

12 *Le jardin en movement* (1994) appeals to a *friche*, or a terrain that has ceased to be tended, that is left to nature's own devices, though (ambiguously) also being tended by a gardener to a much lesser extent than usual. See *Planetary Gardens: The Landscape Architecture of Gilles Clément*, ed. Alessandro Rocca (Basel, 2007), where I quote Clément's remark from p. 210; images of the Défence project are on pp. 247–57, and those of

his own property on pp. 208–23. Some divergent views of his work, which has progressed from the garden of movement to the ideas that the whole planet is a garden, can be registered in Danielle Dagenais, 'The Garden of Movement: Ecological Rhetoric in Support of Gardening Practice', SHGDL, XXIV (2004), pp. 313–40; and in the riposte to it by Louisa Jones, 'Gilles Clément Revisited: Biology, Art and Ecology: A Reply to Danielle Dagenais', SHGDL, XXV (2005), pp. 249–52. The movement of his ideas is well presented in his 2011 inaugural lecture at the Collège de France, *Jardins, paysage et génie naturel* (Paris, 2012).

13 Sir Roy Strong, *Garden Party: Collected Writings, 1979–1999* (London, 2000), p. 18. He thus joins with Bernard St-Denis who would extend the idea of the garden in 'What is a Garden?', SHGDL, XXVII (2007), pp. 61–76. See Derek Jarman, *Derek Jarman's Garden* (London, 1996), from which I quote in the text, and the article on the Prospect Cottage garden by Michael Charlesworth, SHGDL, XXXV/2, pp. 172–82. Jarman's film 'The Last of England' (1987), though referring to the painting by Ford Madox Brown and not to the plenitudes of Sissinghurst, suggests something of Jarman's affinity, however different, to Clément.

14 In addition to Richardson there are a few short articles on the garden: Noel Kingsbury, 'Symbolic Intention', *House and Garden* (February 2008), pp. 124–9; Chris Young, 'The Virtues of a Valley', *The Garden* (October 2010), pp. 682–7. I also quote occasionally from Forbes's unpublished essays on the garden.

15 It always makes me shudder when garden critics say a design is intellectual; one hopes it is not a put-down, but it often is. To that labelling, we may oppose Forbes's quotation (unidentified) that 'the ultimate barbarity is the plain reading'.

16 'The truest poetry is the most feigning':

Touchstone in William Shakespeare's *As You Like It*. Forbes himself prefers 'fabled' space.

17 I leave Finlay here, as I have written about him at length in *Nature Over Again: The Garden Art of Ian Hamilton Finlay* (London, 2008).

18 Charles Jencks, *The Garden of Cosmic Speculation* (London, 2003). I have also tried to explain my understanding of it in *Historical Ground: The Role of History in Contemporary Landscape Architecture* (London, 2014), pp. 117–20.

19 On The Laskett there is a host of wonderful documentation, which absolves me of this need: Strong has written both *The Laskett: The Story of a Garden* (New York, 2003) and *Remaking a Garden: The Laskett Transformed* (London, 2014), which documents the individual segments, their growth and transformations. The Laskett is also supported by an archive in many volumes – sketches, drafts, snapshots of its creations, correspondence and invoices – at present located in the house, but eventually to be housed in the Bodleian Library: no other modern garden that I know of has such a rich and rare collection on its formation, maintenance and meanings.

20 Arnaud Maurières et al., *Jardiniers de Paradis* (Paris, 2000).

2 MASTERS' GARDENS

1 See chap. 3 for the professional designers who exhibited in nine of the gardens; these included Martha Schwartz, West 8, Gross.Max, SLA and EMBT.

2 I take this list from Günther Vogt's own projects between 2000 and 2012 in *Miniature and Panorama*, which, with his other book with Alice Foxley, *Distance and Engagement: Walking, Thinking and Making Landscape* (Zurich, 2012 and 2010 respectively), are volumes that, for me, constitute one of the most exciting expositions of a landscape architect's work.

3 Paul Ricoeur, *History and Truth* (Evanston, IL, 1961), p. 277. The hint there that we might have, for landscape architecture, a 'universal civilization' surely implied less a neglect of locality than a concern for its importance.

4 A claim made in the Thames & Hudson catalogue for Roberto Silva's *New Brazilian Gardens: The Legacy of Roberto Burle Marx* (London, 2014).

5 See the fine book by Michael Spens, *The Complete Landscape Designs and Gardens of Geoffrey Jellicoe* (London, 1994), which is illustrated with many of Jellicoe's own drawings and sketches; see also Spens, *Gardens of the Mind: The Genius of Geoffrey Jellicoe* (Woodbridge, 1992) and the essays in Sheila Harvey, ed., *Geoffrey Jellicoe* (London, 1998), with a chronology of his works and a bibliography. In Geoffrey Jellicoe, *The Studies of a Landscape Designer over 80 Years* (Woodbridge, 1993), vol. 1, there is an extensive essay, 'Soundings', on Jellicoe's own understanding of modernist art and architecture. See Geoffrey Jellicoe, *The Guelph Lectures in Landscape Design* (Guelph, ON, 1983).

6 Geoffrey Jellicoe's book with Susan Jellicoe, *Modern Private Gardens* (London, 1968), explores a veritable anthology of contemporary designers in Europe, Scandinavia, Japan, the USA and South America. This might also be compared with Peter Shepheard, *Modern Gardens* (London, 1954), which stretches the anthology further, with the inclusions, among others, of Jean Canneel-Claes, André and Paul Vera, Thomas Church, Richard Neutra and C. Th. Sørensen.

7 I first heard him explain these ideas in a lecture at MOMA in 1988, later published in Stuart Wrede and William Howard Adams, eds, *Denatured Visions: Landscape and Culture in the Twentieth Century* (New York, 1991). It became a leitmotif of his later career, that might be contrasted with Gilles Clément's visionary planetary garden or compared with Alasdair

Forbes's dedication of his landscape to a pantheon of classical deities mediated by Hillman's psychology (see chap. 1).

8 Lawrence Halprin, *A Life Spent Changing Places* (Philadelphia, PA, 2011). The volume contains a foreword by Laurie Olin, but a more substantial and lengthier account of Halprin's life is Laurie Olin, 'An American Original: On the Landscape Architecture Career of Lawrence Halprin', *SHGDL*, XXXII/2 (2012), pp. 139–63.

9 Roberto Burle Marx's own garden, the Sitio, 45 miles from Rio de Janeiro, is discussed and illustrated in Sima Eliovson, *The Gardens of Roberto Burle Marx* (New York, 1991), pp. 81–96; see also Gilles Clément, 'Burle Marx et la conception contemporaine du jardin', in *Dans les Jardins de Roberto Burle Marx*, ed. Jacques Leenhardt (Arles, 1994), pp. 85–94.

10 I am much indebted here to Anita Berrizbeitia, *Roberto Burle Marx in Caracas* (Philadelphia, PA, 2005). A more detailed discussion of this occurs in chap. 5.

11 Maria Rosa Russo, *L'architettura del paesaggio in Brasile dopo Burle Marx* (Rome, 2004), contains six pages of English text.

12 See Ines Romitti, *Pietro Porcinai. L'identità dei giardini fiesolani – Il paessaggio come 'immenso giardino'* (Florence, 2011), and note 21 in the Introduction, where contributors try to situate his work, somewhat unconvincingly, in a European, American and even Japanese context, which privileges forms over locality and local significances. This volume includes essays on Jellicoe, Halprin and C. Th. Sørensen.

13 Kathryn Gustafson and Jane Amidon, *Moving Horizons: The Landscape Architecture of Kathryn Gustafson and Partners* (Basel, 2005) discusses the Lurie garden on pp. 184ff (where the analysis seems, for once in this volume, too distant from our experience of the site, too concerned with designer-speak), but see www.luriegarden.

org; for Perigord pp. 142ff; and my Conclusion to this volume.

14 James Corner was quoted in the *New York Times* on 20 September 2014; Pope's phrase, to call in the country, has a perfect fit in the urban context.

15 As discussed by the designer in *The Landscape Approach of Bernard Lassus* (Philadelphia, PA, 1998), pp. 164–7, and discussed at more length in John Dixon Hunt, *Historical Ground: The Role of History in Contemporary Landscape Architecture* (London, 2014), pp. 20–22. For Descombes see ibid., pp. 108–9; for Bürgi, ibid., pp. 136–7.

16 See Paolo Bürgi's discussion of them in *Topos/ European Landscape Magazine*, XLII (2003), pp. 37–47; and in Michael Rohde and Rainer Schomann, *Historic Gardens Today* (Leipzig, 2003), pp. 66–71.

17 An anthology of PROAP's work is chronicled both in *PROAP: Landscape Architecture* (Lisbon, 2010) and in *Concursos Perdidos: Lost Competitions* (2011), with texts in both Portuguese and English.

18 Specifically *Miniature and Panorama,* pp. 314–19, but other examples throughout their work insist on the same poetry. The idea that different scents and smells from Zurich would emanate from drain covers in Tokyo, and vice versa, is one such poetic gesture.

19 Discussions of how landscape architects acquired their title are collected in an issue on 'Landscape Architecture' in *SHGDL,* XXXIV/3 (2014).

20 However, arrangements differ in other countries: in Sweden a National Society of Landscape Architects (LAR) was founded in 1973, absorbing earlier groupings of FST in 1921 (Society of Swedish Garden Designers) and FSTL in 1967 (Gardens and Landscape Architects). The term is not a protected title in Sweden, as anyone can practise as a landscape architect; but LAR membership requires proper education and is

also something that clients appreciate. No licence is required in France (unlike for architects, though there is some pressure to make it so), but you do have to be trained at one of the national schools at Versailles, Lille, Blois, Angers or Bordeaux, after which (at those schools only) you are granted the title of Paysagiste D.P.L.G., Diplômé Par Le Gouvernement (either the Ministry of Culture or Agriculture) in the French Federation of Landscape Architecture. In Germany the first professional organizations were founded in 1887 as the Association of German Garden Artists (Verein Deutscher Gartenkünstler) and in 1913–14 as the Federation of German Garden Architects (Bund Deutscher Garden-Architekten). In Switzerland, the professional organization Bund Schweizer Gartengestalter (BSG), was founded in 1925, later changing its name (for the French) to Fédération Suisse des Architectes-Paysagistes, but landscape architects may practise without belonging. Talk about local cheeses!

21 Henry Hubbard, *Landscape Architecture* , XXII/3 (April 1932), editorial, p. 218.

22 I am indebted to my graduate student Costis Alexakis, whose dissertation on Manning will be submitted to the University of Pennsylvania in 2015. Manning's attention to a wide range of landscape work marks him as an important, but neglected, forerunner of later 'masters'.

23 The focus on infrastructural design is mapped in such books as *Landscape Infrastructure: Case studies by SWA* (Basel, 2011), and in two books produced and edited by the Landscape Architecture Europe foundation (LAE), *On Site* and *Fieldwork* (Basel, 2009 and 2006, respectively).

3 GARDEN FESTIVALS AND EXHIBITION GARDENS

1 This is discussed in chap. 16 of John Dixon Hunt, *A World of Gardens*, pp. 208ff. See also John E. Findling, ed., *Historical Dictionary of World's Fairs and Expositions* (New York, 1990).

2 See Andrew C. Theokas, *Grounds for Review: The Garden Festival in Urban Planning and Design* (Liverpool, 2005); also U. Poblotzki, 'Garden Shows: Between Art and Business', *Topos*, XXXIII (December 2000).

3 I am indebted here to, and quote from, Peter Jacobs's essay 'When is a Garden not a Garden?', *Landscape Journal* (October 2003), which explored the Métis Gardens in their fourth year.

4 A splendid example of these summer retreats would be the gardens of Les Quatre Vents, chronicled by Francis H. Cabot in *The Greater Perfection* (New York, 2001).

5 A rather acerbic piece by Robin Lane Fox in the *Financial Times* in the Weekend Section, headlined his review of the Westonbirt International Festival of the Garden with 'Great Idea, Pity about the Results' (14 September 2002), p. 13.

6 On the Métis Festival see Lesley Johnstone, ed., *Hybrids: Reshaping the Contemporary Garden in Métis* (Vancouver, 2007), pp. 6, 8. Page references in the text are to Métis exhibits in this volume. See also the volume edited by Hubert Beringer, *Chambres Vertes / Garden Rooms*, a record of the first 2000 exhibition there.

7 Tim Richardson's lively book *Avant-gardeners: 50 Visionaries of the Contemporary Landscape* (London, 2008) looks at many of these garden ideas; see his text on pp. 151–2 and many images drawn from festival exhibits.

8 Edmund Husserl, *Logical Investigations*, trans. J. N. Finlay (New York, 1979), p. 267.

9 See the new introduction to the reprint of Christopher Tunnard, *Gardens in the Modern Landscape* [1948] (Philadelphia, PA, 2014), pp. xiv, 68.

10 Alexander Reford, in *Hybrids*, pp. 6, 8.

11 I allude here to the interesting essay by Anita Berrizbeitia, 'Design: On the (Continuing) Uses of the Arbitrary', in *A Cultural History of Gardens*, vol. VI: *In the Modern Age* (London, 2013), pp. 13–36, though she does not address garden festivals. In semantic terms, the arbitrary is at once freedom of will and a dedication to difficulty.

12 Johnstone, ed., *Hybrids*, pp. 41, 120. See also Richardson, *Avant-gardeners*, p. 222.

13 Other publications also claim that garden festivals or exhibitions can stimulate professional designers, like the subtitle of Denise Markonish, ed., *Badlands: New Horizons in Landscape* (North Adams, MA, 2008).

14 See Karl Kullmann, 'De/framed Visions: Reading Two Collections of Gardens at the Xi'an International Horticultural Exposition', SHGDL, XXXII/3 (2013), pp. 82ff, where he takes on a much wider agenda than I need to do here. His axonometric diagrams of all the gardens are in his article, and with his permission I re-used them in *Historical Ground: The Role of History in Contemporary Landscape Architecture* (London, 2014). See also his 'Small Worlds: Vast landscapes Brought to Scale', *Landscape Architecture Magazine* (August 2010). I am grateful to Karl Kullmann for help with this section and his kindly supply of images.

15 These ideas are taken up in chap. 13.

16 Louisa Jones, *Reinventing the Garden: Chaumont – Global Inspirations from the Loire* (London, 2003). I am grateful to this elaborate survey of the Chaumont gardens, references to which are included in my text: she takes up six themes besides global inspirations – 'what plants can do', outdoor art, issues of time and change, wit and whimsy, and the 'landscape question'.

17 Anne Cauquelin, *Petit Traité du jardin ordinaire* (Paris, 2005), p. 120.

4 VERNACULAR GARDENS

1 Margaret Willes, *The Gardens of the British Working Class* (New Haven, CT, 2014) has a good and lively historical survey of the topic. She is particularly good on the inventiveness of working-class gardeners during the twentieth century and the competitions that rewarded their best endeavours.

2 See John Dixon Hunt and Joachim Wolschke-Bulmahn, eds, *The Vernacular Garden* (Washington, DC, 1993), a collection of symposium lectures that tackled some of the various approaches to the topic and, in its introduction, argued for its necessity.

3 A interesting review of alternative approaches in historical scholarship, which has affinities with how we might expand landscape enquiries, is Jacques Revel and Lynn Hunt, eds, *Histories: French Constructions of the Past* (New York, 1995).

4 Micheline Nilsen, *The Working Man's Green Space: Allotment Gardens in England, France, and Germany, 1870–1919* (Charlottesville, VA, and London, 2014); Béatrice Cabedoce and Philippe Pierson, eds, *Cent ans d'histoire des jardins ouvriers, 1896–1996* (Grâne, 1996); O. Cena, *Les Jardins de la sociale* (Paris, 1992). For Australia, mainly, see Claire Nettle, *Community Gardening as Social Action* (London, 2014).

5 Mark Francis, 'Some Different Meanings Attached to a City Park and Community Gardens', *Landscape Journal*, VI/2 (1987), pp. 101–12.

6 See Brad Temkin, *Private Places* (Chicago, IL, 2005), who photographs small and intimate spaces with their accumulated oddities of found sculpture, domestic and garden equipment and the excitements of improvised colour and materials.

7 An issue of the *Geographical Review*, XCIV/3 (2004), was devoted to dwelling and uses in vernacular gardens in many cultures and for immigrants from foreign cultures in new lands. A useful bibliography is on pp. 278–83 of the introductory essay. A small book on shared community garden plots is Anne Kraft et al., *Jardiniers du bitume: Des liens fleurrissent dans les jardins partagés* (Paris, 2011).

8 Bernard Lassus, *Jardins imaginaires* (Paris, 1977) is now out of print, but offers not only an astonishing collection of imagery but some of Lassus' early theoretical understanding of how design can proceed in landscapes other than these. The Snow White narrative conceived by Monsieur Pecqueur is discussed and illustrated on pp. 168–85, and his own career is recounted on pp. 188–9. Lassus also assembled a large collection of images of these *habitants-paysagistes* not included in the volume, two of which are used here.

9 Quoted by Washington in a letter of February 1784 to the Marquis de Lafayette, so the biblical reference in the month of February makes the remark as much symbolic as real.

10 See, just to start with, Mara Gittleman, Lenny Librizzi and Edie Stone, *Community Garden Survey, New York City, Results 2009/2010* (New York, 2010), CUNY Mapping Service for the Center for Urban Research (www.oasisnyc.net), and Laura J. Lawson, *City Bountiful: A Century of Community Gardening in America* (Oakland, CA, 2005).

11 Diana Balmori and Margaret Morton, *Transitory Gardens, Uprooted Lives* (New Haven, CT, 1993), with quotations from pp. 1, 3–4.

12 I am grateful to my student at Penn State University Nastaran Tebyanian for this example and her photographs of the site.

13 Further, David Tracey, *Guerilla Gardening: A Manifesto* (Gabriola Island, BC, 2007).

14 Margaret Willes has a chapter (pp. 90–120) on the love of flowers, as well as eatables, among working-class gardeners); this too has a long tradition.

15 The *New York Times* (7 July 2014) devoted four pages of its main section to Detroit, where urban farming features; other considerations of urban farming for Detroit and Chicago are taken up in articles in *siteLINES*, VI/2 (2011), published by the Foundation for Landscape Studies. Margaret Willes, in her conclusion, also looks to British examples of urban farming, like the Incredible Edible project (2008) and other larger-scale community enterprises.

16 Quoted in the *Guardian Weekly* (20 June 2014), citing the Japanese farmer Masanobu Fukuoka.

17 Peter Aeschbacher and Michael Rios, 'Claiming Public Space: The Case for Proactive, Democratic Design', *Expanding Architecture Design as Activism*, ed. Bryan Bell and Katie Wakeford (New York, 2008), pp. 83–91. I am most grateful to Peter Aeschbacher for discussing this place-making with me and for the use of his photographs and sketches.

18 Ken Smith, *Landscape Architecture* (New York, 2009); this was later named the Bedford Stuyvesant Community Garden, 95 Malcolm X Blvd. A friend visited it in June 2014 and reported on its current, excellent state, and was told of the loss of the panels.

5 PARKS

1 Charles Jencks, interviewed in the Italian magazine, *D Repubblica* (6 April 2013).

2 Galen Cranz, *The Politics of Park Design* (Cambridge, MA, 1982) gives a useful history of 'urban parks in America'; on modern park-making, see Alan Tate, *Great City Parks* (London, 2001); Julia Czerniak and George Hargreaves, eds, *Large Parks* (New York, 2007); Martin Knuijt, Hans Ophuis and Peter van Saane, eds, *Modern Park Design* (Bussum, 1993 and 1995). Essays that explore what its subtitle states as 'From Economics to the Intangible' are in David Harmon and Allen D. Putney, eds, *The Full Value of Parks* (Lanham, MD, 2003).

3 Some of these can be followed by references in the Index: otherwise for the Turenscape park see Mary Padua, 'Industrial Strength: At a Former Shipyard, A Park Design Breaks with Convention to Honor China's Recent Past', *Landscape Architecture Magazine*, XCIII/6 (2003); Timothy J. Gilfoyle, *Millennium Park: Creating a Chicago Landmark* (Chicago, IL, 2006); for Walter Hood, http://wjhooddesign.com; for Evergreen, http://ebw.evergreen.ca/about/site; on Hannover see chap. 12; for Essen, http://whc.unesco.org; for a preview of the Queen Elizabeth Park, see *The Pennsylvania Gazette* (published by the University of Pennsylvania), November/December 2012.

4 I have discussed most of these in an essay, 'Reinventing the Parisian Park', in *Tradition and Innovation in French Garden Art*, ed. John Dixon Hunt and Michel Conan (Philadelphia, PA, 2002).

5 Czerniak and Hargreaves, *Large Parks*, pp. 211 (John Beardsley), 29 (cited by Czerniak). Adriaan Geuze made the remark in the context of a symposium: see his 'Moving Beyond Darwin', in *Modern Park Design*, p. 38.

6 This is taken up in chap. 11 on 'Drosscapes', as the site is a former military airfield.

7 *New York Times*, arts section (13 April 2010). The huge cost that has to be raised privately underscores John Beardsley's discussion of private/public park-making in Czerniak and Hargreaves, *Large Parks*, pp. 199–214.

8 James Grayson Truelove, ed., *Ten Landscapes: Mario Schjetnan* (Gloucester, MA, 2002), pp. 60–73.

9 Envisioning what would eventually become Central Park, A. J. Downing advocated at least 500 acres for a public park.

10 'The Battle of Brooklyn Bridge Park' was narrated in the *New York Times* (3 August 2014). I quote from this article here, including the man who wanted a nature, albeit artificial. I also benefited from reading an interview by Michael Van Valkenburgh in the *New York Times* (25 July 2014) and from the essay on the park by Ethan Carr in Anita Berrizbeitia, ed., *Reconstructing Urban Landscapes* (New Haven, CT, 2009), pp. 235–53.

11 See also chap. 8 on 'Memorials', where Four Freedoms might also have found a place; it seemed more useful to explore it here for what it contributes to park practice and thinking.

12 Gideon Fink Shapiro, 'A Park for Roosevelt, 40 Years Later', *domus*, 966 (February 2013), p. vi. To that extent it might serve as an example for chap. 11 on 'Reinvented Gardens', except there was nothing here before to be reinvented. What is perhaps 'reinvented' is a site elsewhere, Kahn's Salk Institute courtyard (1959–65) in California, for which chap. 7 on campuses is more apt. The new park by Kahn, being a former professor at the University of Pennsylvania, was reviewed in a lengthy article by Samuel Hughes in the University *Gazette* (March/April 2013), pp. 37–49, to which I am indebted. The Kahn quotation is from this article.

13 There is, though, an excellent essay on the Maidan by Simon Winchester.

14 Czerniak and Hargreaves, *Large Parks*, p. 204, fig. 4.

15 David R. Coffin, 'The *lex hortorum* and Access to Gardens of Latium During the Renaissance', first published in the *Journal of Garden History* and then included in a collection of his essays in *Magnificent Buildings, Splendid Gardens*, ed. Vanessa Bezemer Sellers (Princeton, NJ, 2008).

Every section of the new Brooklyn Bridge Park has notices explaining what and what not to do.

16 See Heath Schenker, *Melodramatic Landscapes: Urban Parks in the Nineteenth Century* (Charlottesville, VA, 2009). Nineteenth-century parks are discussed in Edouard André, *L'Art des Jardins: Traité géneral de la composition des parcs et jardins* (Paris, 1879), and H.W.S. Cleveland, *Landscape Architecture* (1873), with a new edition and introduction by Daniel J. Nadenicek and Lance M. Neckar (Amherst, MA, 2002).

17 See Peter Reed, ed., *Groundswell: Constructing the Contemporary Landscape* (New York, 2005), for computer visions of the projected park, pp. 156–61. Two are also illustrated in John Dixon Hunt, *A World of Gardens* (London, 2012), fig. 137.

18 See Udo Weilacher, *In Gardens: Profiles of Contemporary European Landscape Architecture* (Basel, 2005), pp. 164–8. Over twenty years ago Peter Walker wrote enthusiastically on *The Urban Public Spaces in Barcelona* for a publication issued by Harvard University Graduate School of Design on the Prince of Wales Prize on Urban Design in 1990. I quote from both authors.

19 Charles Jencks had already worked with his wife, Maggie Keswick, on their own Garden of Cosmic Speculation in Scotland, and on two landforms for the Scottish National Gallery and the Artland Park, both in Edinburgh, so he had ample experience of elaborating landscapes to explore contemporary theories of the universe. The exposition of this design is in Charles Jencks, *The Universe in the Landscape: Landforms* (London, 2014), pp. 63–85. I am also indebted to Federico de Molfetta and to his essay 'Beyond the Portello: Or a Walk on the Artificial Topography of Time', SHGDL, XXXIV (2014).

6 SMALL PARKS: POCKETS, LINEAR AND VERTICAL

1 The Jardin Atlantique was designed by Christine and Michel Pena: see their *Pour une troisième nature* (Paris, 2010).

2 See also Larry Ford, *The Spaces Between Buildings* (Baltimore, MD, 2000), in which pp. 83–138 are devoted to 'Lawns, Trees and Gardens in the City'.

3 A wide-ranging article on subway entrances and plazas, *New York Times* (4 December 2011).

4 See John Dixon Hunt, *The Venetian City Garden: Place, Typology, and Perception* (Basel, 2009), pp. 26–36.

5 I am indebted here to Rachel E. Iannacone, 'Open Space for the Underclass: New York's Small Parks (1880–1915)', University of Pennsylvania PhD thesis, 2005. A huge topic, less explored than that of big parks, but an obvious precursor of modern small parks.

6 Jane Amidon, *Moving Horizons: The Landscape Architecture of Kathryn Gustafson and Partners* (Basel, 2005), pp. 52 and 82ff respectively.

7 See the brochure *Canal Park*, published in 2014 by the Philadelphia-based design firm Land Collective.

8 Karl Kullmann's article, 'Thin Parks/Thick Edges: Towards a Linear Park Typology for (Post)infrastructural Sites', *Journal of Landscape Architecture (JoLa)*, VI/2 (2011), pp. 70–81. Linear constructions have not been without their adversaries – who wants more mini-boulevards? But see Ken Smith, 'Linear Landscapes: Corridors, Conduits, Strips, Edges, and Segues', *Harvard Design Magazine* (Winter/Spring 1999), p. 77.

9 A familiar plea of landscape architects like Olmsted. See also Heath Schenker, *Melodramatic Landscapes: Urban Parks in the Nineteenth Century* (Charlottesville, VA, 2009).

10 See West8 projects, www.west8.nl/projects/ infrastructure/sagera linear park.

11 Diana Balmori, 'From Green Corridor to Thick Edge: The Linear Park', in *A Landscape Manifesto* (New Haven, CT, 2010), pp. 30–48, here p. 30.

12 Amita Sinha, 'Slow Landscapes of Elevated Linear Parks: The Bloomingdale Trail in Chicago', *SHGDL*, XXXIV/2 (2014). Her article, from which quotations are drawn, explores a variety of different responses by students in her design workshop at the University of Illinois in Urbana-Champaign in 2011, and an exhibition of their proposals at the Chicago Architectural Club, www.bloomingdaletrail.org; Balmori, 'From Green Corridor to Thick Edge', offers a more abstract survey of linear trail problems.

13 A further meditation on this type is Kullmann's 'Green-networks: Integrating Alternative Circulation Systems into Post-industrial Cities', *Journal of Urban Design*, XVIII/1 (2013), pp. 36–58. See also Kullmann, 'Thin Parks/ Thick Edges'.

14 Jason Kentner, ed., *Stoss Landscape Urbanism*, in *Source Books in Landscape Architecture*, vol. XII (Columbus, OH, 2013).

15 Patrick Blanc, *The Vertical Garden*, preface by Jean Nouvel, 2nd edn (New York, 2014).

7 CAMPUSES

1 The main history of American campus planning is by Paul Venable Turner, *Campus: An American Planning Tradition* (Cambridge, MA, 1984). But see also the shorter essay, with his own sketches (one of which is used here), by Laurie Olin, 'Exceptional Grounds: The Landscapes of Institutions', *siteLINES*, VIII/2 (2013). Many academic institutions have published their own campus histories – of particular interest is Peter Fergusson, James F. O'Gorman and John Rhodes, *The Landscape and Architecture of*

Wellesley College (Wellesley, MA, 2000), which brings the story up to date with the masterplan by Michael Van Valkenburgh. The literature on modern and future campus design is considerable, though little of it focuses substantially on the question of 'gardens' or 'parks'.

2 In what follows I am much indebted to a friend, Ray Gastil, who has been exploring and teaching new ideas for 'campus urbanism'; I draw upon his suggestions and perspectives. See also *Campus and the City: Urban Design for the Knowledge Society*, ed. Kerstin Hoeger and Kees Christiaanse (Zurich, 2007). Another extensive design and implementation of the Novartis Campus Park in Basel, commissioned from Vogt Landscape Architects in 2006, is set out in Alice Foxley, *Distance and Engagement: Walking, Thinking and Making Landscape* (Baden, 2010), pp. 135–227.

3 William S. Saunders, ed., *Designed Ecologies: The Landscape Architecture of Kongjian Yu*, (Basel, 2012), pp. 50–55, with essays by Peter Walker and John Beardsley among others.

4 I am indebted to colleagues at the Architectural Archives of the University of Pennsylvania, which holds the Kahn archives, and to David B. Brownlee and David G. De Long, *Louis I. Kahn: In the Realm of Architecture* (New York, 1991).

5 See rival judgments on Irwin's garden by David Marshall, 'Gardens and the Death of Art', *SHGDL*, XXIV (2004), pp. 215–28; and Lawrence Weschler, 'When Fountainheads Collide', *New Yorker* (8 December 1997).

6 See Teresa Andresen, ed., *From the National Stadium to the Gulbenkian Garden* (Lisbon, 2003), particularly pp. 98–113 and (only in Portuguese) *Fundação Calouste Gulbenkian O Jardim* (2006).

7 For sketches of Ohio State's Wexner Center for the Visual Arts, see Laurie Olin, *Transforming the Common Place: Selections from Laurie Olin's Sketchbooks* (Cambridge, MA, 1996) and *OLIN: Placemaking* (New York, 2008).

8 The campus idea is also espoused now by conference centres, whether in the form of plaza, garden and even park; urban conference venues want visitors to 'experience the city they are visiting' and to be 'integrated with the community': see Martha C. White, 'Fresh Air for Conventions', *New York Times* (27 August 2014), section B7, where the site of former 1968 World's Fair, HemisFair Park, in San Antonio, Texas, is being turned into a convention centre within a park.

9 Article on Shenzen Stock Exchange in 'Inside Outside', *Lotus*, 150 (2012), pp. 28ff.

10 The excellent monograph by Trish Gibson, *Brenda Colvin: A Career in Landscape* (London, 2011), should send us back to Brenda Colvin, *Land and Landscape: Evolution, Design and Control* (London, 1947, revd edn 1970), which is dedicated to Geoffrey and Susan Jellicoe who, together with Sylvia Crow and Colvin, were the other supreme UK designers in the second half of the century. I have benefited much from Gibson's chapter on 'Industry in the Landscape'.

11 See Dan Kiley and Jane Amidon, *Dan Kiley: The Complete Works of America's Master Landscape Architect* (Boston, MA, 1999), pp. 36–9.

12 Louise A. Mozingo, *Pastoral Capitalism: A History of Suburban Corporate Landscapes* (Cambridge, MA, 2011), distinguishes between the corporate campus, the office park and the corporate landscape.

13 I owe this account to Emily T. Cooperman who wrote the successful National Historic Landmark Nomination. The site is also discussed and illustrated in Mozingo's book, ibid.

14 *Peter Walker: Minimalist Gardens* (Washington, DC, 1997), which includes his essay, ground plans, brief descriptions and photographs of sites and, just sometimes, people using them, which for all their formal elegance is what makes his designs so human.

15 These are set out in Kathryn Gustafson and Jane

Amidon, *Moving Horizons: The Landscape Architecture of Kathryn Gustafson and Partners* (Basel, 2005), pp. 56–71, to which I am indebted. The arguments are helped by the presentation of Gustafson's designs in Amidon's book: pages are divided between small, descriptive entries at the top of the page, images to which they refer, and a commentary in large type that utilizes in Amidon's commentary Gustafson's own understanding of how she approached the work and how she envisaged its significance beyond simply formal means.

16 Peter Walker 'Classicism, Modernism, and Minimalism . . .', in *Minimalist Gardens*, p. 18.

17 Peter Reed, ed., *Groundswell: Constructing the Contemporary, Landscape* (New York, 2005), pp. 144–7. Satire can have the privilege of celebrating what it also protests.

18 This is discussed and illustrated in essays in English in Andrea Koenecke, Udo Weilacher and Joachim Wolschke-Bulmahn, eds, *Die Kunst, Landschaft neu zu erfinden* (Munich, 2010).

8 MEMORIAL GARDENS

1 Erika Doss, *Memorial Mania: Public Feeling in America* (Chicago, IL, 2010). Her example is from p. 7. The literature is large; Edward W. Said, 'Invention, Memory, and Place', *Critical Inquiry*, XXVI/2 (2000), pp. 175–92; Robert S. Nelson and Margaret Olin, eds, *Monuments and Memory, Made and Unmade* (Chicago, IL, 2003); especially Jas Elsner, 'Iconoclasm and the Preservation of Memory'. An issue on 'Memorial Gardens and Landscapes' was published in *Garden History*, XLII (2014) supplement 1. I have also discussed this topic, with some overlaps of material, in a section of *Historical Ground: The Role of History in Contemporary Landscape Architecture* (London, 2014), pp. 63–77.

2 Alan Blinder, 'A Monument's Mysteries Include Whether It Can Draw Tourists', *New York Times* (18 September 2013).

3 Introduction to Nelson and Olin, *Monuments and Memory*, p. 2.

4 Pierre Nora, *Realms of Memory: Rethinking the French Past*, trans. Arthur Goldhammer, 3 vols (New York, 1996–8), I/1. A succinct account of 'Les Lieux de mémoire' is given in Nora's essay 'Between Memory and History: Les Lieux de mémoire', *Representations*, XXVI (1989), pp. 7–24.

5 I have myself also resisted a total debunking of nostalgia in the editorial introduction ('What is Wrong with Nostalgia Anyway?') for the issue on 'Nostalgia' in the journal *Change Over Time*, III/2 (2013).

6 I am grateful to Julian Bonder for showing me their 'conceptual approach', and for some images, and to Ron Henderson who was involved in crafting the proposal; the scheme did not 'go through real development & funding, so it stayed a concept' (Bonder, interview by Henderson). See also Julian Bonder, 'On Memory, Trauma, Public Space, Monuments and Memorials', *Places*, XXI/1 (2009), pp. 62–9.

7 See James E. Young, *The Texture of Memory: Holocaust Memorials and Meaning* (New Haven, CT, 1993). I am grateful for his permission to use this image.

8 I quote from the *Bergen-Belsen Historical Site and Memorial* guidebook (Celle, 2011). But I am also indebted to my colleague Professor Joachim Wolschke-Bulmahn who took me there and helped me to see the site; also Professor Wolschke-Bulmahn's essay 'Meine Stationen auf dem Weg zur Auseinandersetzung mit der "Landschaft" der Gedenkstätte Bergen-Belsen', in *Neugestaltung der Gedenkstätte Bergen-Belsen* (Celle, 2007).

9 There is no mention of that earlier 'inspiration' for the Bergen-Belsen meandering path in the guidebook cited in the previous note; my source

is Joachim Wolschke-Bulmahn's essay 'The Landscape Design of the Bergen-Belsen Concentration Camp Memorial', in *Places of Commemoration: Search for Identity and Landscape Design*, ed. J. Wolschke-Bulmahn (Washington, DC, 2001), pp. 269–300.

10 For a lengthy assessment of the Pentagon memorial, not in the end very affirmative, see Victoria Carchidi, 'Struggling with Terror: The Pentagon Memorial', *SHGDL*, XXX/3, pp. 193–207; and Witold Rybczynski, 'The Pentagon Memorial', *Slate* (24 September 2008), www.slate.com. Cardichi was a student of mine when she drafted this paper and her death soon afterwards makes that essay her own memorial.

11 Tim Richardson, *The Vanguard Landscapes and Gardens of Martha Schwartz* (London, 2004), pp. 152–3. Also essays in Rebecca Krinke, ed., *Contemporary Landscapes of Contemplation* (London, 2005), especially John Beardsley's article, 'Filling a Void: Creating Contemporary Spaces for Contemplation'.

12 This insistence on flowers as accompaniments to cemeteries and memorials is taken up by various authors in *Places of Commemoration*, ed. Wolschke-Bulmahn.

13 This and other information from Peter Reed, ed., *Groundswell: Constructing the Contemporary Landscape* (New York, 2005), pp. 70–73; and Udo Weilacher, *In Gardens: Profiles of Contemporary European Landscape Architecture* (Basel, 2005), pp. 58ff. Quotations by Girot are in 'Traces Into the Future', in *Zeitgeist Berlin Invalidenpark* (Berlin, 2006). I am also grateful to Aislynn Herbst who researched this site for me.

14 See Jeffrey Karl Ochsner, 'A Space of Loss: The Vietnam Veterans Memorial', *Journal of Architectural Education*, L/3 (1997), pp. 156–71.

15 People in Amsterdam did not want 'a traditional memorial' (Weilacher, *In Gardens*, p. 43). That

sentiment has been echoed elsewhere in Jenny Holzer's 'anti-monument' at Nordhorn on the German/Dutch border, on the site of a much earlier and controversial memorial to those killed in earlier wars; Holzer used another single, apple tree to mark the centre of a 'black garden'. She discusses this design in 'The Black Garden: Der Garten als Anti-Memorial', *Kunstforum International*, CXLV (1999), p. 89.

16 Kathryn Gustafson and Jane Amidon, *Moving Horizons: The Landscape Architecture of Kathryn Gustafson and Partners* (Basel, 2005), pp. 112ff.

17 The design is set out briefly in Reed, *Groundswell*, and quotations from this are used in my text. Other considerations of this site are taken up by Raffaella Fabiani Giannetto in the nostalgia issue of *Change Over Time* (Spring 2013) and in Neil Porter, 'Past, Present, and Future: Designing Areas Across Many Lands and Cultures', *Topos*, LXXX (2012), pp. 61–5.

18 W. G. Sebald, *The Rings of Saturn*, trans. Michael Hulse (New York, 1998), pp. 124–6.

19 Other battlefields, like Gettysburg, have been reworked by the U.S. National Park Service and are rife with information about the events and their geography within the battlefield, and there is a cyclorama of the battle from 1883 in the National Military Park Visitor Center, somewhat more satisfying than Sebald's encounter at Waterloo.

20 SueAnne Ware and Julian Raxworthy, *Sunburnt: Landscape Architecture in Australia* (Amsterdam, 2010), pp. 58ff: Australians worry that a central feature of one courtyard, a transplanted olive tree, imposes 'Eurocentric notions of plant symbolism' on an indigenous land, p. 59.

21 Again, this unrealized project is apt for discussion in chap. 13 (where is it is briefly recapitulated), but its relevance here is more potent. This is published in PROAP's *Concursos Perdidos: Lost Competitions* (Lisbon, 2011), in Portuguese and

English, pp. 26–9. Diagrams of the extent of the battlefields, the strip of no-man's-land and PROAP's hypothetical location of dozens of cemeteries, their suggestion for gates, paths and 'sacred places' is given on pp. 35 and 27.

22 Rupert Brooke, 'The Soldier', in *The Collected Poems* (London, 1946), p. 150.

23 See Caroline Constant, *The Woodland Cemetery: Toward a Spiritual Landscape* (Stockholm, 1994); and Marc Treib, 'Woodland Cemetery: A Dialogue of Design and Meaning', *Landscape Architecture*, LXXVI/2 (1986), pp. 11–123.

24 Some fresh ideas, mainly of Europe's war memorials, are discussed in Michael A. Stern, 'The National Cemetery System: Politics, Place and Contemporary Cemetery Design', in *Places of Commemoration*, ed. Wolschke-Bulmahn; also Ahenk Yilmaz, 'Memorialization on War-broken Ground: Gallipoli War Cemeteries and Memorials Designed by Sir John James Burnet', *JSAH*, LXXIII (2014), pp. 328–46.

25 Reed, *Groundswell*, p. 110.

26 This tomb is presented with some stunning photographs by Guido Guidi in *Carlo Scarpa Architect: Intervening with History*, and discussed in essays (Montreal and New York, 1999).

9 BOTANICAL GARDENS

1 I have explored these early gardens and given references to them in chap. 8 of *A World of Gardens* (London, 2012). An issue on both historical and projected modern botanical gardens was published in *Studies in the History of Gardens and Designed Landscapes* (*SHGDL*), XXV/2 (2005).

2 Botanical gardens are generally discussed in the magazine *Public Garden*, or in such books as Donald Rakow, *Public Garden Management* (Hoboken, NJ, 2011).

3 See 'Living Plant Sculptures at the Montreal Botanical Gardens', 17 July 2013, www.designboom.com.

4 The history of this national garden is set out, illustrated and its future assessed, in Tal Alon-Mozes, 'Landscape as a National Text: The Biblical Landscape Reserve of Neot Kedumim, Israel', *SHGDL*, XXXIII/4 (2013), pp. 305–20.

5 John Prest, *The Garden of Eden: The Botanical Garden and the Re-creation of Paradise* (New Haven, CT, 1981).

6 Catherine Mosbach, *Traversées Crossings* (Paris, 2010), with French and English texts – this has her sketches and designs for this garden.

7 See Udo Weilacher, *In Gardens: Profiles of Contemporary European Landscape Architecture* (Basel, 2005), pp. 158–63. I am also most grateful to my son, Matt Randolph, and his wife Amy Korn, a landscape architect himself, who photographed everything he could find on the site.

8 See entry by Jo Russell-Clarke in *Sunburnt: Landscape Architecture in Australia*, ed. SueAnne Ware and Julian Raxworthy (Amsterdam, 2011). I visited this quite unusual botanical garden in December 2014, and thereafter read both Stephen Forbes's review of the garden opening in *The Adelaide Review* (November 2012) and his essay 'Enquiry into Plants: Nature, Utopia and the Botanic Garden', in *Earth Perfect? Nature, Utopia and the Garden*, ed. A Giesecke and N. Jacobs (London, 2012), pp. 22–241.

9 I am grateful to Ron Henderson for these comments and for his article, 'On Obsolescent Landscapes: The Quarry Garden, Shanghai, China', *int/AR*, II (2011), pp. 98–103.

10 Karl Kullmann makes this point in 'De/framed Visions: Reading Two Collections of Gardens at the Xi'an International Horticultural Exposititon', *SHGDL*, XXXII/3 (2013).

11 With a grant from the Heritage Lottery Fund this landscape is to be restored. The garden's

magazine has an issue on this, with images of the landscape in its heyday: *Yr Ardd*, XXII (Autumn 2014).

12 See Kathryn Gustafson and Jane Amidon, *Moving Horizons: The Landscape Architecture of Kathryn Gustafson and Partners* (Basel, 2005), pp. 128–33.

13 First published in *SHGDL*, XXV/2 (2005) and then in *The Landscape Imagination: Collected Essays of James Corner, 1990–2010* (New York, 2014), pp. 325ff. This botanical item might well have been considered in chap. 13.

10 SCULPTURE GARDENS

1 Robert Smithson, 'A Sedimentation of the Mind: Earth Projects', first published in *Artforum*, and now in *The Collected Writings*, ed. Jack Flam (Berkeley, CA, 1996); see Ian Hamilton Finlay, in one of his 'Unconnected Sentences on Gardening', in *Nature Over Again After Poussin*, with Sue Finlay (1980).

2 Francesca Cigola, *Art Parks: A Tour of America's Sculpture Parks and Gardens* (New York, 2013), pp. 50, 27. I also draw on this below. See also Jane McCarthy and Laurily K. Epstein, *A Guide to the Sculpture Parks and Gardens of America* (New York, 1996).

3 *Landscape Alchemy: The Work of Hargreaves Associates* (San Francisco, CA, 2009); see also Elsa Leviseur, 'Hargreaves' Weaves', *The Architectural Review* (September 1993), pp. 80–84; Kathryn Gustafson, *Sculpting the Land* (Washington, DC, 1998). That Gustafson originally trained in the Fashion Institute of Technology in New York City suggests how potent and fascinating she found the forms of terrain.

4 Robert Smithson, 'A Tour of the Monuments of Passaic, New Jersey', in *Collected Writings*, p. 72. First published in *Artforum* in December 1967.

5 While I only know this from discussions with, and images by, David Leatherbarrow, this seems a wonderful example of the dialogue, not only between architecture and landscape, but of sculpture and their roles in the landscape: see John Pardey, *Beyond Louisiana: The Work of Vilhelm Wohlert* (Hellerup, 2007).

6 A survey of this topic is undertaken by Patrick Eyres and Fiona Russell in their *Sculpture and the Garden* (Aldershot, 2006) and by 'Sculpture in Arcadia', a special issue edited by Sue Malvern and Eckart Marchand, *SHGDL*, XXIX/1–2 (2009).

7 Both are illustrated and discussed in John Dixon Hunt, *A World of Gardens* (London, 2012), fig. 78; and my essay 'Sculpture Gardens and Sculpture in Gardens', in *The Fran and Ray Stark Collection of 20th-Century Sculpture at the J. Paul Getty Museum*, ed. Antonia Boström (Los Angeles, CA, 2008), figs 20 and 22.

8 Sabine Frommel, ed., *Bomarzo, il Sacro Bosco* (Milan, 2009).

9 John Dixon Hunt, *William Kent: Landscape Garden Architect, An Assessment and Catalogue Raisonné* (London, 1987), catalogue nos. 34 and 36.

10 Thomas Whately takes up his remarks on sculptures in *Observations on Modern Gardening* (1770), pp. 150ff; and Horace Walpole, *The History of the Modern Taste in Gardening* [1780] (New York, 1988); p. 41.

11 This maybe explains one of Ian Hamilton Finlay's printed cards that called for 'FEWER SCULPTURES, MORE STATUES', that is, of representative figures.

12 Christopher Tunnard uses this image of Moore's sculpture for the frontispiece of the 1938 edition of *Gardens in the Modern Landscape* and on p. 68 for the 1948 edition. See Alan Powers, 'Henry Moore's *Recumbent Figure*, 1938, at Bentley Wood', in *Sculpture and the Garden*, ed. Eyres and Russell.

13 Martha Schwartz quoted in Tim Richardson, ed., *The Vanguard Landscapes and Gardens of Martha Schwartz* (London, 2004), pp. 192, 197.

14 A remark by the British sculptor Antony Gormley quoted in the *New York Times* (14 August 2014).

15 On the naming of art works, see Ernst Gombrich, 'Image and Word in Twentieth-century Art', *Word & Image*, I/3 (1985), pp. 213–41; and Stephen Bann, 'The Mythical Conception is the Name: Titles and Names in Modern and Postmodern Painting', *Word & Image*, I/2 (1985), pp. 176–90.

16 Storm King is, rightly, much admired and written about: see in particular Rebecca Lee Reynolds, 'The Green Cube: An Arcadian Site for Minimalism at Storm King', *SHGDL*, XXIX/1–2 (2009); and John Beardsley, *A Landscape for Modern Sculpture: Storm King Art Center* (New York, 1985).

17 Rupert Martin, *The Sculpted Forest: Sculptures in the Forest of Dean* (Bristol, 1990), and Bill Grant and Paul Harris, eds, *The Grizedale Experience: Sculpture, Arts & Theatre in a Lakeland Forest* (Edinburgh, 1991).

18 Quoted ibid., p. 69.

19 Rensselaer W. Lee, *Names on Trees: Ariosto into Art* (Princeton, NJ, 1977). For more commentary, see John Dixon Hunt, *Nature Over Again: The Garden Art of Ian Hamilton Finlay* (London, 2008), pp. 129–30.

20 This major museum, dating from 1938, with its public parkland of sculptures started in 1961, is discussed in Rudolf Willem Daan Oxenar, *Kröller-Müller: The First Hundred Years* (Haarlem, 1978).

21 Beyond the examples exhibited here, see Renato Barilli et al., *Art in Arcadia: The Gori Collection, Celle: A Tuscan Patron of Contemporary Art at his Country House* (Turin, 1994).

22 Rosalind E. Krauss, 'Sculpture in the Expanded Field', in *The Originality of the Avant-Garde and Other Modernist Myths* (Cambridge, MA, 1985).

23 As regards Stevens's poem and its invocation by some landscape architects, this Celle 'cube' is so much more exciting than the garden at the Lannan Foundation in Los Angeles. Designed by Siah Armajani, the garden took its cue directly from the same poem and in a courtyard, where we could read books on desks and lines of the poem were inscribed on strange benches, above which were rows and rows of tall purple porcelain jars. It no longer exists.

24 The Getty celebrated the acquisition with Boström, ed., *The Fran and Ray Stark Collection of 20th-Century Sculpture at the J. Paul Getty Museum*, which contains essays on the Stark collection and the history of sculpture gardens and their modern development, followed by a detailed catalogue by Christopher Bedford of the Stark collection; I use here some elements that I wrote in an essay for that volume.

25 This is well known, but the changes of its original layout and presentation of sculptures in 1939 by Alfred H. Barr Jr, its reformulation by Philip Johnson in 1953 and again by César Pelli in 1984 can be traced in Laurie D. Olin, 'The Museum of Modern Art Garden: The Rise and Fall of a Modernist Landscape', *SHGDL*, XVII (1997), pp. 140–62; and in Mirka Benes, 'A Modern Classic', in *Philip Johnson and the Museum of Modern Art*, ed. John Elderfield (New York, 1998).

26 I want to avoid clogging the text with lists, but the range and incidence of these is astonishing, many in the United States: so besides the three discussed, there are the Nelson-Atkins Museum of Art in Kansas City, designed by Dan Kiley; the Museum of Art, in Dallas, also by Dan Kiley; Walter Hood for the Barbro Osher garden at the De Young Museum in San Francisco; Isamu Noguchi's Lillie and Hugh Roy Cullen Sculpture

Garden in Houston; and Marian Cruger Coffin's Nassau County Museum park in Roslyn Harbor, New York. Robert Irwin was involved at the Los Angeles County Museum of Art, and a sequence of designers worked for the Donald M. Kendall Sculpture Gardens in Purchase, New York (the PepsiCo HQ) – Edward D. Stone, Jr, Russell Page, and after the latter's death, François Goffinet. Charles Jencks has invoked his signature form of sculptured mounds for the Jupiter Artland Park, near Edinburgh airport.

27 See Peter Reed, ed., *Groundswell: Constructing the Contemporary Landscape* (New York, 2005), pp. 116–23; and Joan Busquets, ed., *Olympic Sculpture Park for the Seattle Art Museum* (Cambridge, MA, 2008). I am also grateful for a discussion with David Leatherbarrow.

28 Jane Amidon, ed., *Peter Walker and Partners: Nasher Sculpture Center Garden* (New York, 2006), provides a clear and incisive account of how to make a modern sculpture garden.

11 DROSSCAPES

1 Michael Leslie, 'Spenser, Sidney, and the Renaissance Garden', *English Literary Renaissance*, XXII/1 (1992), pp. 3–36.

2 Emily Waugh, ed., *Recycling Spaces: Curating Urban Evolution* (San Francisco, CA, 2011); on 'Power Lines', see pp. 134–49. I have written elsewhere about her Exchange Square in Manchester, a design that, while being unable to 'show' the result of an IRA explosion, makes evident that a new stitching of the urban fabric has taken place and is appreciated: see John Dixon Hunt, *Historical Ground: The Role of History in Contemporary Landscape Architecture* (London, 2014), pp. 76–7. Nor is Schwartz alone, as issues of both *Topos* and *Lotus* in Europe make clear: see the *Topos* issue on 'Culturescapes',

LXXVIII (2012) for the rediscovery of Manchester's 'Lost River', a discussion of a sewage treatment plant in Bottrop, Germany, and an old coal mine at Zollverein, designed by Agence T, now a listed World Heritage Site.

3 I discuss these in 'Reinventing the Parisian Park', in *Tradition and Innovation in French Garden Art*, ed. John Dixon Hunt and Michel Conan (Philadelphia, PA, 2002), pp. 203–20.

4 Pylons were introduced in England during the 1930s, when both Stephen Spender and, here, Stanley Snaith (in 1933) celebrated their pressence in the landscape.

5 The phrase is used by Udo Weilacher in his book on Peter Latz, *Syntax of Landscape* (New York, 2008), to entitle discussions of four 'drosscapes' (though he does not use that word) in Germany, Italy and Israel.

6 Robert Smithson, 'A Tour of the Monuments of Passaic, New Jersey' (1957), in *Robert Smithson: The Collected Writings*, ed. Jack Flam (Berkeley, CA, 1996), p. 70. It is a complex essay that I cannot deal with here, but I am also indebted to Jennifer Roberts, *Mirror-Travels: Robert Smithson and History* (New Haven, CT, 2004), who adduces the term 'lethargic'.

7 Stephen Bann, 'The Landscape Approach of Bernard Lassus', *Journal of Garden History*, III/2 (1983), pp. 79–107, p. 50.

8 There are various ways of explaining this distinction: the poet Edwin Morgan said prose communicated the intelligible on a level which could make it hard or impossible to mistake a writer's meaning (though say that to writings by modern designers!) and that poetry has to do with deep, perhaps irresolvable ambiguities, 'a disturbance and a compensating richness'. Michel de Certeau writes of 'poetic geography on top of the geography of the literal . . . permitted meaning', in *The Practice of Everyday Life* (Berkeley, CA, 1984), p. 105. Udo Weilacher

called small interventions, like pocket parks, 'acupuncture-like interventions' (*In Gardens*, p. 154, Basel, 2005); so poetic moments or spaces do not have to be big disturbances either of a place or person.

9 Jardins d'Eole was designed by Michel and Claire Corajoud and Georges Descombes (2005–6); Parc Clichy-Batignolles by Jacqueline Osty (2013); and Jardin des Etangs Gobert by Michel Desvigne and artist Inessa Hansch (2013). The first of these is discussed by Malcolm Woollen, 'Les Jardins d'Eole: Extending the Picturesque', *SHGDL*, XXXIII/4 (2013), pp. 290–304.

10 Francesco Careri, *Walkscapes: Walking as an Aesthetic Practice* (Barcelona, 2002), text in Spanish and English, p. 166, part of his final meditation on empty city spaces with the character of 'autosimilarity'.

11 See preface by James Corner, *Intermediate Natures: The Landscapes of Michel Desvigne* (Basel, 2009).

12 I owe my insights on this site to Hope Strode; the original plan was proposed by ÖkiCon and Planland, overseen by Grün Berlin.

13 See *Learning from Duisburg* by various authors in honour of Peter Latz (Munich, 2009); also Kerstin Barndt, 'Memory Traces of an Abandoned Set of Futures', in *Ruins of Modernity*, ed. Julia Hell and Andrea Schönle (Durham, NC, 2010); and Niall Kirkwood, ed., *Manufactured Sites* (London, 2001).

14 All three sites are discussed at length in Udo Weilacher, *Syntax of Landscape* (Basel, 2008), pp. 82ff, 134ff and 148ff respectively.

15 Sanda Iliescu, 'The Garden as Collage: Rupture and Continuity in the Landscape Projects of Peter and Anneliese Latz', *SHGDL*, XXVII (2007), pp. 149–82.

16 SueAnne Ware and Julian Raxworthy, eds, *Sunburnt: Landscape Architecture in Australia* (Amsterdam, 2011) has a rather ambiguous description, an uncertain commentary on the site (is it 'magical' or 'twee', 'preservative' or 'mimicking' industrial history'), so I was most grateful to Adrian McGregor for taking us around.

17 See Moerenuma Park, www.sapporo-park.or.jp/moere/english.

12 REINVENTED GARDENS

1 Kathryn Gustafson and Jane Amidon, *Moving Horizons: The Landscape Architecture of Kathryn Gustafson & Partners* (Basel, 2005), pp. 170–75.

2 See *Preserving Modern Landscape Architecture*, papers from a conference at Wave Hill (New York) and the National Park Service (Berkeley, CA, 1999). The Jellicoe work in Exeter was highlighted in the Garden History Society *Micro-news*, 83a (Summer 2008).

3 'The challenge of bringing special places back to life' seems to mean 'adding a new cultural "layer" on well-remembered places', Faye Harwell and Brad Garner, 'Bring Back Olmsted's Planting', *Landscape Architecture*, XCVIII (August 2008), p. 78.

4 David Lowenthal, *The Past is a Foreign Country* (Cambridge, 1985), pp. xvi–xvii.

5 There are other readings of this story: see Howard Giskin, 'Borges' Revisioning of Reading in "Pierre Menard, Author of the Quixote"', *Variaciones Borges*, XIX (2005), pp. 103–23.

6 I am indebted to my colleague, Rebecca Bushnell, for her witty and unsparing analysis in 'Gardens, Memory, and History', *Change Over Time*, III/1 (2013). See also Brian Dix, '". . . With Great Art, Cost and Diligens . . .": The Reconstruction of the Elizabethan Garden at Kenilworth Castle', in *Gardens and Landscapes in Historic Building Conservation*, ed. Marion Harney (London, 2014), pp. 339–44.

7 Allen Samuels and John Dixon Hunt,

'Aberglasney: 'An Enigmatic Cloister Range', *Journal of Garden History*, XI (1991), pp. 131–9; some of the details used there are cited here. A subsequent book that tends to ignore our article and plays down Wilkins's role is Penny David, *A Garden Lost in Time* (London, 1999); the Foreword by Penelope Hobhouse, who designed the new vegetable garden, calls it 'the Cloister Garden (as it is *now* called)' – but it was so named as long ago as 1793.

8 A major survey of 'Japanese' gardens, *Spaces of Translation: Japanese Gardens in the West*, has been written by Christian Tagsold (Philadelphia, PA, 2016). I suspect that Japanese gardens win over China because they are, or seem to be, smaller, more subtle in planting and materials, like standing stones, and rely less on buildings and pavilions. See also Bianca Maria Rinaldi, *The Chinese Garden: Garden Types for Contemporary Landscape Architecture* (Basel, 2011) who considers some neo-historical examples outside China.

9 Kendall H. Brown, *Quiet Beauty: The Japanese Gardens of North America* (North Clarendon, VT, 2013), pp. 48–51; and Yuichi Ozawa, *Story of Shofuso*, published by the Friends of the Japanese House and Garden (2010).

10 In fact, the Pennsylvania State Arboretum some miles away in north Philadelphia contains the remains of stones and plants for a Japanese garden created in 1904 for the Morris estate, also by a Japanese craftsman.

11 Josée Desranleau and Peter Jacobs, 'From Conception to Reception: Transforming the Japanese Garden in the Montreal Botanical Garden', SHGDL, XXIX/3 (2009), pp. 200–216. A wonderfully revealing account of the issues raised in this chapter, from which I draw quotations.

12 The emphatically modern emphasis is spelled out by Kongjian Yu, the lead designer, in his essay 'Complete Water', in *Design in the Terrain of Water*, ed. Anuradha Mathur and Dilip da Cunha (Philadelphia, PA, 2014), pp. 59–5; but he is well known for invoking more traditional Chinese forms and ideas. See also William S. Saunders, *Designed Ecologies: The Landscape Architecture of Kongjian Yu* (Basel, 2012).

13 Marc Treib, *Noguchi in Paris: The UNESCO Garden* (San Francisco, CA, and Paris, 2003).

14 The major source here is *Le Style Duchêne: Henri et Achille Duchêne, Architectes Paysagistes, 1841–1947*, various authors (Paris, 1998); it contains English translations and a large repertoire of images. See also a briefer discussion by Monique Mosser (who also wrote for the previous volume), 'Henri and Achille Duchêne and the Reinvention of Le Nôtre', in *The Architecture of Western Gardens: A Design History from the Renaissance to the Present Day*, ed. Monique Mosser and Georges Teyssot (Cambridge, MA, 1991), pp. 446–50; and Mary Hawthorne, 'The Geometry of Emotion: The Gardens of Henri and Achille Duchêne', *siteLINES*, IX/11 (Spring 2014), pp. 8–11.

15 Ethne Clarke, *An Infinity of Graces: Cecil Ross Pinent, An English Architect in the Italian Landscape* (New York, 2013). Also Benedetta Origo, Morna Livingston, Laurie Olin and John Dixon Hunt, *La Foce: A Garden and Landscape in Tuscany* (Philadelphia, PA, 2001).

16 See Eugenia W. Herbert, *Flora's Empire: British Gardens in India* (Philadelphia, PA, 2011). In Nepal, Kaiser Shumsher Jung Bahadur Rana made a garden, originally called the Nepal Garden of Dreams [sic], rich in planting, wild and with private spaces, designed by the Nepali architect Kishore Narsingh on the basis of the collection of garden treatises on English, Japanese and Mughal gardens in this library (that still exists), with titles like *Green Composting in the Tropics* or *Making a Garden on the Plains of India*; the owner died in the garden in the

1960s, it being inauspicious to die indoors. A garden restoration was carried out between 2000 and 2007 and funded by the Austrian government. I am grateful to Liz Maudslay for this information.

13 GARDENS ON PAPER

1 Slightly un-modern, but an apt note for this chapter: C. F. Bell, ed., *Evelyn's Sculptura with the Unpublished Second Part* (Oxford, 1906), pp. 104–6.

2 Francesco Colonna, *Hypnerotomachia Poliphili* (Venice, 1499), the garden plan on folio t8, and descriptions and other images of details in the garden on the following folios. A modern edition of Bernard Palissy's *Recette véritable* by Frank Lestringant and Christian Barataud was published in Paris (1996); the description of his garden is pp. 67ff. An English translation of the garden segment was published as *A Delectable Garden* by Helen Morgenthau Fox (New York, 1931).

3 Various authors, *Le Jardin des Tuileries de Bernard Lassus* (London, 1991), from which quotations in the text are drawn; also *The Landscape Approach of Bernard Lassus* (Philadelphia, PA, 1998), pp. 74–5 for 'inventive analysis' and the Tuileries project.

4 The Kahn sketch is held by the Philadelphia Museum of Art; for Mendelsohn, see Bruno Zevi, *Erich Mendelsohn* (Basel, 1999), pp. 9–22.

5 The sand model is held at the Isamu Noguchi Foundation, Long Island City, New York.

6 'Idealized or Caricature', *New York Times* (27 August 2013), used two images of the same project to show how its projectors and those who objected to it rendered the insertion of a dozen tall buildings alongside the Hudson River in Brooklyn.

7 See André Rogger, *Landscapes of Taste: The Art of Humphry Repton's Red Books* (London, 2007).

8 I have discussed the park, as built, in my *Nature Over Again: The Garden Art of Ian Hamilton Finlay* (London, 2008), notably pp. 120–28.

9 PROAP, *Concursos Perdidos: Lost Competitions* (Lisbon, 2011), texts in Portuguese and English. The projects discussed here on are pp. 220ff and 168ff and quotations are from those pages.

10 Marianne Barzilay, *L'Invention du Parc: Parc de la Villette, Paris, Concours International Competition, 1982–1983* (Paris, 1984); Tschumi himself wrote *Cinégramme Folie: le Parc de la Villette* (1987). Bernard Lassus who competed unsuccessfully for both Parc de La Villette and for Duisburg-Nord presents some of his ideas for them in *The Landscape Approach of Bernard Lassus*, pp. 116–24, 150–60.

11 Julia Czerniak, *Downsview Park, Toronto* (London, 2001). Quotations in my text are taken from this interesting and provocative book.

12 'The Imaginary Garden of Liu Shilong' is translated with a commentary by Stanislaus Fung in *Terra Nova*, II/4; see also Pierre Ryckmans, 'The Chinese Attitude towards the Past', *China Heritage Quarterly*, XIV (June 2008).

CONCLUSION

1 Małgorzata Szafranska writes essentially of early gardens, but the generality holds: 'Place, Time and Movement: A New Look at Renaissance gardens', SHGDL, XXXVI (2006), pp. 194–208.

2 My version of 'le lieu n'est pas une simple vue de l'esprit, c'est une expérience effective, en vérité c'est le réel même. Comme l'existence l'éprouve, car, celle-ci rencontre le monde du sein d'abord de son lieu et m'accédera à la notion de nature, par exemple, que par un effort second de la pensée', *Le Nuage rouge*, p. 370. Thus a 'lieu' becomes a 'haut lieu', the poetry beyond the

prose of landscape architecture, or in the words of Alasdair Forbes, the creator of the Plaz Metaxu, 'place, needless to say, becomes more, not less, precious within a landscape of infinite disorientation'.

3 Karl Kullmann, 'De/framed Visions: Reading Two Collections of Gardens at the Xi'an International Horticultural Exposition', *SHGDL*, XXXII/3 (2013), p. 182.

4 Anthony Vidler, *The Writing of the Walls: Architectural Theory in the Late Enlightenment* (Princeton, NJ, 1987).

5 Alice Foxley, *Distance and Engagement: Walking, Thinking and Making Landscape* (Zurich, 2010), p. 14. This volume for and on behalf of Vogt landscape architects is, for me, one of the most inspiring guides on how to think about the making of place.

6 I first encountered this site, as so many, in Udo Weilacher, *In Gardens: Profiles of Contemporary European Landscape Architecture* (Basel, 2005), before visiting it in 2013.

FURTHER READING

Amidon, Jane, and Kathryn Gustafson, *Moving Horizons: The Landscape Architecture of Kathryn Gustafson and Partners* (Basel, 2005)

Balmori, Diana, and Margaret Morton, *Transitory Gardens, Uprooted Lives* (New Haven, CT, 1993)

Beardsley, John, *A Landscape for Modern Sculpture: Storm King Art Center* (New York, 1985)

Berger, Alan, *Drosscape: Wasting Land in Urban America* (Cambridge, MA, 2006)

Berrizbeitia, Anita, ed., *Reconstructing Urban Landscapes* (New Haven, CT, 2009)

Brunon, Hervé, and Monique Mosser, *Le Jardin contemporain* (Paris, 2011)

Cooper, Thomas C., *The Roots of My Obsession: Thirty Great Gardeners Reveal Why They Garden* (Beverly, MA, 2012)

Czerniak, Julia, *Downsview Park, Toronto* (Cambridge, MA, 2001)

—, and George Hargreaves, *Large Parks* (New York, 2007)

Doss, Erika, *Memorial Mania: Public Feeling in America* (Chicago, IL, 2010)

Eliovson, Sima, *The Gardens of Roberto Burle Marx* (New York, 1991)

Eyres, Patrick, and Fiona Russell, *Sculpture and the Garden* (Aldershot, 2006)

Foxley, Alice, *Distance and Engagement: Walking, Thinking and Making Landscape* (Zurich, 2010)

Gibson, Trish, *Brenda Colvin: A Career in Landscape* (London, 2011)

Grampp, Christopher, *From Yard to Garden: The Domestication of America's Home Grounds* (Chicago, IL, 2008)

Hoeger, Kerstin, and Kees Christiaanse, eds, *Campus and the City: Urban Design for the Knowledge Society* (Zurich, 2007)

Hunt, John Dixon, *Historical Ground: The Role of History in Contemporary Landscape Architecture* (London, 2014)

Imbert, Dorothée, *The Modernist Garden in France* (New Haven, CT, 1993)

Jencks, Charles, *The Garden of Cosmic Speculation* (London, 2003)

—, *The Universe in the Landscape: Landforms* (London, 2014)

Jones, Louisa, *Reinventing the Garden: Chaumont – Global Inspirations from the Loire* (London, 2003)

Kiley, Dan, and Jane Amidon, *Dan Kiley: The Complete Works of America's Master Landscape Architect* (Boston, MA, 1999)

Krauss, Rosalind A., 'Sculpture in the Expanded Field', in *The Originality of the Avant-garde and Other Modernist Myths* (Cambridge, MA, 1985)

Lassus, Bernard, *The Landscape Approach of Bernard Lassus* (Philadelphia, PA, 1998)

—, *Jardins imaginaires: Les habitants-paysagistes* (Paris, 1977)

Leslie, Michael, and John Dixon Hunt, eds, *A Cultural History of Gardens*, 6 vols (London, 2013), notably vol. VI on the modern period

McKay, George, *Radical Gardening: Politics, Idealism and Rebellion in the Garden* (London, 2011)

Mozingo, Louise A., *Pastoral Capitalism: A History of Suburban Corporate Landscapes* (Cambridge, MA, 2011)

PROAP, *Landscape Architecture* (Lisbon, 2010), with texts in Portuguese and English

—, *Concursos Perdidos: Lost Competitions* (Lisbon, 2011), with texts in Portuguese and English

Richardson, Tim, *Avant-gardeners: 50 Visionaries of the Contemporary Landscape* (London, 2008)

—, *The New English Garden* (London, 2013)

Rocca, Alessandro, ed., *Planetary Gardens: The Landscape Architecture of Gilles Clément* (Basel, 2007)

Saunders, William S., ed., *Designed Ecologies: The Landscape Architecture of Kongjian Yu* (Basel, 2012)

Smith, Ken, *Landscape Architecture* (New York, 2009)

Spens, Michael, *The Complete Landscape Designs and Gardens of Geoffrey Jellicoe* (London, 1994)

Strong, Roy, *Remaking a Garden: The Laskett Transformed* (London, 2014)

Tate, Alan, *Great City Parks* (London, 2001)

Truelove, James Grayson, ed., *Ten Landscapes: Mario Schjetnan* (Gloucester, MA, 2002)

Tunnard, Christopher, *Gardens in the Modern Landscape* [1938 and 1948] (Philadelphia, PA, 2014)

Vogt Landscape Architects, *Günther Vogt: Miniature and Panorama* (Zurich, 2012)

Weilacher, Udo, *In Gardens: Profiles of Contemporary European Landscape Architecture* (Basel, 2005)

—, *Syntax of Landscape: The Landscape Architecture of Peter Latz and Partners* (Basel, 2008)

Waugh, Emily, *Recycling Spaces: Curating Urban Evolution: The Landscape Design of Martha Schwartz Partners* (London, 2011)

Young, James E., *The Texture of Memory: Holocaust Memorials and Meaning* (New Haven, CT, 1993)

ACKNOWLEDGEMENTS

Thanks for help, advice and photographs are due to many friends, colleagues and students: Peter Aeschbacher, Costis Alexakis, Mary Berensfield, Anita Berrizbeitia, Julian Bonder, Paolo Bürgi, Taro Cai, Michael Charlesworth, James Corner, Maria Debije Counts, Jennifer Current, Matthew Dallos, Georges Descombes, Michel Duchêne, Timothy J. Entwisle, Alasdaire Forbes, Stephen Forbes, David Gouverneur, Gert Groening, Kathryn Gustafson, Kenneth Helphand, Ron Henderson, Niall Hobhouse, Charles Jencks, Niall Kirkwood, Karl Kullmann, Bernard Lassus, Peter Latz, David Leatherbarrow, Adrian McGregor, Hal Moggridge, Ellen Neises, Joao Nunes, Laurie Olin, Neil Porter, Witold Rybczynski, Martha Schwartz, Gideon Fink Shapiro, Sir Roy Strong, Nastaran Tebyanian and Sharon Willoughby. Also, as always, thanks and appreciation to colleagues in the Fine Arts Library at the University of Pennsylvania.

For generous help with photographs I am particularly indebted to the designers who provided images, without which the book would be either much poorer, or I would have been sunk in debt in paying professional fees. Particular thanks must be given to Emily T. Cooperman for both her companionship and her skills as a photographer, and to Matt Randolph and Amy Korn, who scoured Spain on my behalf. All other photographs are my own.

Finally, my deep appreciation for the skills and support of my publisher at Reaktion Books, Michael Leaman, and those of Harry Gilonis, Robert Williams and Martha Jay who saw this book through to press.

PHOTO ACKNOWLEDGEMENTS

The author and publishers wish to express their thanks to the below sources of illustrative material and/or permission to reproduce it. Some locations of artworks are also given below, in the interests of brevity. Every effort has been made to contact copyright holders. Any copyright holders we have been unable to reach or to whom inaccurate acknow-ledgements have been made please contact Professor John Dixon Hunt, c/o Reaktion Books, and full adjustments will be made to all subsequent printings.

Courtesy Peter Aeschbacher: 53, 54; © Architectural Research Unit, London: 7; author's collection: 168; photos author: 6, 15, 44, 45, 46, 72, 86, 96, 99, 100, 101, 102, 103, 106, 107, 111, 117, 136, 137, 143, 144, 151, 157, 158, 160, 161; from Pietro Maria Bardi, *The Tropical Gardens of Burle Marx* (London: London Architectural Press, 1964): 27; courtesy Julian Bonder: 97; photo Paolo Burgi: 16; photo Michael Charlesworth: 11; City of Westminster Archives Centre, London (photo Westminster City Archives): 43; photos: Emily T. Cooperman: 1, 4, 12, 13, 14, 17, 18, 19, 20, 21, 22, 24, 56, 57, 58, 59, 60, 61, 62, 68, 69, 70, 71, 73, 74, 81, 82, 83, 87, 88, 89, 90, 91, 113, 114, 115, 116, 120, 121, 122, 123, 124, 125, 126, 128, 131, 132, 133, 134, 135, 148, 153, 154, 155, 162, 171, 172, 173, 174; photography by Maria Debije Counts: 37, 38, 39; photo Eric Crichton photos: 50; photos courtesy Jennifer Currant: 28, 105; photos Matthew Dallos: 10, 140; courtesy of the designer (Paolo Burgi) 149, 150, 167; courtesy of the designer (Georges Descombes): 30; courtesy of the designer (Field Operations): 127; courtesy of the designer (Kathryn Gustafson): 75, 76; courtesy of the designer (Karl Kullmann): 80; courtesy of the designer (Land Collective): 77; photos courtesy of the designer (João Gomes Da Silva) and Emily T. Cooperman: 33, 34; courtesy of the designers (Kathryn Gustafson and Neil Porter): 35, 108; courtesy of the designers (William Lingel & David Hunter), the University of Illinois, and *Studies in the History of Gardens & Designed Landscapes*: 78, 79; courtesy of the designers (David Meyer and Ramsey Silberberg): 36; courtesy of the designers (PROAP): 31, 109, 169; photo Josée Desranteau: 156; reproduced by kind permission of the Domaine de Chaumont-sur-Loire: 32; Dumbarton Oaks Research Library and Collection, Washington, DC: 112; photo courtesy Gideon F Fink: 52; reproduced by courtesy of the Estate of Ian Hamilton Finlay: 168; Fonds Henri et Achille Duchêne: 159; photo Jedidiah Gordon-Moran: 142; photo Glenn Halvorson for Walker Art Center: 139; Harvard University Graduate School of Design, Cambridge, Massachusetts: 170; photo courtesy Charles Jencks: 65; Joe Fletcher Photography – www.joefletcherphoto.com: 8; courtesy Niall Kirkwood: 55; photo Amy Korn: 119; photos Karl Kullmann: 41, 42; courtesy Bernard Lassus: 47, 48, 49, 163, 164, 165, 166; photo Michael Leaman:

INDEX